0050164

‖‖‖‖‖‖‖‖‖‖‖‖‖‖‖‖‖‖‖‖‖
W9-BLM-532

The Logic of Congressional Action

The Logic of Congressional Action

R. Douglas Arnold

Yale University Press   New Haven & London

Set in Melior & Primer types by
The Composing Room of Michigan, Inc.
Printed in the United States of America
by Vail-Ballou Press, Binghamton,
New York.

Library of Congress Cataloging-in-
Publication Data
Arnold, R. Douglas, 1950–
    The logic of congressional action/
R. Douglas Arnold.
        p.   cm.
    Includes bibliographical references.
    ISBN 0–300–04834–3 (alk. paper) :
$29.95
        1. Legislators—United States.
    2. United States. Congress—Voting.
    3. United States. Congress—Leadership.
    4. United States—Economic policy.
    I. Title.
    JK1067.A76   1990
    328.73'073—dc20   90–32834
                          CIP

The paper in this book meets the
guidelines for permanence and durability
of the Committee on Production
Guidelines for Book Longevity of the
Council on Library Resources.

10 9 8 7 6 5 4 3 2 1

To Helen

Contents

Figures and Tables

Acknowledgments

My greatest debt is to four friends, Charles Cameron, Fred Greenstein, Stanley Kelley, and David Mayhew, who offered regular doses of encouragement, advice, and criticism throughout the life of the project. I am also indebted to John DiIulio, Richard Fenno, and Gary Jacobson, who read and commented on the entire manuscript, as well as to David Bradford, John Ellwood, Linda Fowler, Keith Krehbiel, Charles Tidmarch, Peter VanDoren, Craig VanGrasstek, and John Zaller, who commented on portions of it.

For generous financial support, I am indebted to the John Simon Guggenheim Memorial Foundation, the Ford Foundation, and the Everett McKinley Dirksen Congressional Research Center. I have also profited from the regular faculty leave program at Princeton University, from a three-year appointment as Arthur H. Scribner Bicentennial Preceptor, and from the special research funds available at Princeton's Woodrow Wilson School of Public and International Affairs. For assistance in securing these funds, I am grateful for the strong support of Richard Fenno, Fred Greenstein, Stanley Kelley, David Mayhew, and Donald Stokes.

Part One

A Theory of Policy Making

1

Explaining Congressional Action

Why does Congress enact the policies that it does? Why does Congress frequently approve proposals that serve organized interests or that deliver narrowly targeted geographic benefits? Why does Congress sometimes break free of parochial concerns and enact bills that serve more diffuse, general, or unorganized interests? This book attempts to explain both sets of outcomes with a single theory. The theory sets forth both the conditions that encourage legislators to produce particularistic policies and serve organized interests and the conditions that prompt legislators to serve more general interests.

Political scientists can explain with ease why concentrated interests so often triumph. These interests are often organized into groups and easily mobilized for action. Lobbyists and political action committees communicate precise policy messages to legislators, and they lavish special attention on the relevant committee and subcommittee members. Even when these concentrated interests are not well organized, legislators know that the affected publics are both more attentive to Washington action and more likely to show their appreciation at the polls than are those citizens who have less at stake and who are less attentive to what happens in Congress. These simple arguments help to explain why Congress erects trade barriers to protect specific industries, creates an endless stream of special tax provisions, maintains price supports for many agricultural commodities, and refuses to enact restrictions on the ownership of guns.

Explaining why Congress approves so many proposals laden with geographic benefits is also relatively easy. Legislators are elected from geographic districts and they have a natural concern for how specific programs affect their constituents. Legislators have discovered that obtaining benefits for their districts creates opportunities for free publicity and credit claiming, and both are valuable in the quest for reelection. Lawmakers thus enjoy creating and expanding public works programs and intergovernmental grant programs, and each one insists on receiving a share of the benefits. They also have a strong aversion to proposals that impose particular costs on their constituents because they believe that voters might blame them for those costs. This fact helps to explain why Congress has such trouble closing obsolete military bases or choosing sites for the disposal of radioactive waste.

Political scientists have had less success in explaining why Congress enacts proposals that serve more diffuse or general interests. Actually there is no puzzle at all when Congress enacts programs that provide substantial general benefits without generating either group or geographic costs. Legislators enjoy approving programs providing for medical research, for example, because these programs are very popular and because they impose no direct costs on anyone. The puzzle emerges when Congress approves proposals that promise to deliver substantial general benefits while imposing large group or geographic costs. According to the arguments in the two previous paragraphs, legislators should be so interested in protecting the interests of those who are about to bear large and concentrated costs that they would vote to reject such proposals. Quite often they do reject these initiatives, but there are also many occasions in which legislators vote to support the general interest over various group or geographic interests. Examples include most environmental and safety legislation, efforts to reduce the federal deficit, and the deregulation of the airline, trucking, and telecommunications industries.

The greatest puzzle of all is to explain why Congress sometimes reverses itself. Why would Congress first deliver narrowly concentrated benefits to some group in society and then suddenly switch sides, imposing costs on the previously favored group and delivering benefits to those whom it had long neglected? Such reversals are actually quite common. Congress spent several decades happily creating hundreds of special tax provisions, and then it turned around and terminated many of them in 1986. Congress sided with natural-gas producers in the 1940s and 1950s, sided with consumers in the 1960s and early 1970s, and then pursued a middle course on natural gas beginning in 1978. Congress created revenue sharing in 1972, delivering geographic benefits to every state and locality in the nation, and then terminated the entire program in 1986. Explaining these reversals requires a single, unified theory of congressional policy making, one that allows for the triumph of any one of the three competing interests—general, group, or geographic.

In the chapters that follow I set forth a simple theory of congressional policy making. In order to explain why Congress adopts the policies that it does, I first analyze the calculations, actions, and interactions of citizens, coalition leaders, and legislators.[1] Although ordinary legislators make all the final decisions in Congress, their choices are very much constrained by the actions of both coalition leaders and citizens. Coalition leaders design policy proposals and select strategies for enacting them. Citizens have the ability to remove from office legislators with displeasing records. I argue that legislators are partly manipulated by the actions of coalition leaders, they are partly constrained by anticipating the actions of citizens in future elections, and they are partly free agents. Understanding the interactions of citizens, coalition leaders, and legislators thus becomes the key to understanding why Congress acts as it does.

The theory assumes that members of Congress care intensely about reelection. Although they are not single-minded seekers of reelection, reelection is their dominant goal.[2] This means simply that legislators will do nothing to advance their other goals if such activities threaten their principal goal.[3] If reelection is not at risk, they are free to pursue other goals, including enacting their own visions of good public policy or achieving influence within Congress.[4]

The theory does not always predict a unique outcome. My aim is to

1. All terms will be defined shortly.

2. My assumption says nothing about legislators' ultimate goals as individuals, about why they entered politics, originally sought election, or want to be reelected. It is merely a convenient analytic assumption for theorizing about legislative politics and for showing how the quest for reelection leaves an imprint on policy decisions.

3. This is admittedly an artificial assumption. In the real world some legislators make trade-offs among their goals, incurring small electoral costs in the course of achieving some other important goal. Incorporating such realism into my theoretical model would make it vastly more complicated without any obvious gain in explanatory power. Retaining the simpler hierarchy of goals has the added advantage of allowing one to see the extent to which legislators' quest for reelection affects congressional policy making.

4. These three goals are the foundation for Fenno's work on committees. See Richard F. Fenno, Jr., *Congressmen in Committees* (Boston: Little, Brown, 1973), p. 1. Fenno avoids the problem of trade-offs among goals by moving from a single model incorporating three goals to three models with one goal each. He argues that each legislator has a dominant goal and chooses to join a committee in which that goal is also dominant.

show how electoral calculations shape everything from legislators' roll-call decisions to the strategies and tactics of coalition leaders. When electoral calculations yield no specific recommendation, however, legislators are free to pursue other goals. Even when electoral calculations do not produce a single outcome, they often leave a large imprint on policy decisions. For example, they frequently reduce a long list of policy alternatives to a very few that are politically feasible. Eventually it would be nice to explain how Congress selects a single proposal from these few alternatives. For now I am content to show how electoral calculations reduce the many to the few.

My basic argument is that the electoral quest can impel legislators to support policies that serve either particularistic or general interests. The push toward particularism is perhaps easier to recognize, for it frequently places legislators in direct conflict with the president and policy experts. The impulse to serve more diffuse, general, or unorganized interests is less conspicuous, in part because it simply encourages legislators to behave like other policy makers. David Mayhew has already shown how the pursuit of reelection encourages particularism.[5] Here I specify both the conditions under which this is so and the conditions that encourage legislators to support broader interests.

LEGISLATORS AND COALITION LEADERS

This book explains how Congress as a whole makes policy decisions. Why did Congress choose to adopt policy A rather than B? Why did Congress choose to stay with the status quo rather than adopt some other competing alternative? Why did Congress favor oil producers in the 1950s and oil consumers in the 1970s? Why did Congress create tax loopholes for several decades and then decide to eliminate many of them in 1986? Policy is the dependent variable, and the puzzle is to explain why Congress passes or fails to pass the proposals before it.

Explaining congressional decisions requires that I account for the actions of both ordinary legislators and coalition leaders. On any given issue ordinary legislators[6] face either a single dichotomous choice or a

5. David R. Mayhew, *Congress: The Electoral Connection* (New Haven: Yale University Press, 1974), pp. 127–131.
6. Unless the context suggests otherwise, the term *legislator* refers to members of both House and Senate.

series of dichotomous choices. They are asked to pass or defeat a bill, to accept or reject an amendment, to recommit a bill for further work or to allow it to move on to the next stage, to substitute a new bill for a pending bill, to accept or reject a procedural motion, to require or dispense with a recorded vote, to cut off a filibuster or allow it to continue. A series of dichotomous choices can produce a rich array of possible outcomes. Moment by moment, however, legislators simply choose between paired alternatives.

I assume that when legislators have to make a decision they first ask which alternative contributes more to their chances for reelection. If they see a significant difference, they choose the alternative which better serves that cause. If they see no difference, they base their choice on any other criteria they find relevant—perhaps they believe one policy is more effective or desirable than another, or they wish to curry favor with the president or a party leader, or they wish to repay a past favor. My theory is designed to handle only those cases in which legislators expect that the alternatives would yield different electoral consequences. The principal problem is to discover how legislators estimate the electoral consequences of their policy decisions so that they can compare an unending stream of paired alternatives.

Coalition leaders do not live in a dichotomous world. They do not choose among paired alternatives; they define those alternatives. They select problems to attack from the full list of major and minor ailments in society. They shape policy proposals by modifying old remedies, inventing new ones, and combining bits and pieces from here and there. They fashion strategies to enact their proposals from the store of political wisdom about how to build coalitions. Coalition leaders are drawn from both inside and outside Congress. They include rank-and-file legislators, committee and subcommittee leaders, party leaders, congressional staff members, the president, presidential staff members, executive branch officials, bureaucrats, and interest group leaders.

Coalition leaders are free to advance whatever policy alternatives they choose. Successful leaders, however, know that their choices are constrained by the need to attract the support of a majority of legislators. They must learn to anticipate legislators' decisions so that they can structure their proposals and strategies in ways designed to generate support. To complicate matters, legislators' decisions are themselves dependent on how they believe their constituents will react to their roll-call votes, so successful leaders must anticipate citizens' reactions in order to anticipate legislators' decisions.

In this book I seek to explain only one aspect of the work of coalition leaders: How do they anticipate and respond to legislators' electoral needs when they are refining policy proposals and devising strategies to attract legislators' support? I bypass several interesting but thorny questions. I do not examine why individuals choose to become coalition leaders, invest their scarce time and precious resources in mobilizing support for proposals, or choose to attack specific problems or advance specific remedies. The theory regards individuals as volunteering, for reasons of their own, to champion or oppose certain causes.[7] Once they have volunteered, the problem is to explain both why they adopt specific strategies to advance or retard those causes and why one side wins and the other loses.

Legislators choose among the paired alternatives presented to them in part by estimating the electoral consequences of being associated with each option. Coalition leaders design policy proposals and political strategies in part by anticipating legislators' electoral calculations. Both legislators and coalition leaders, therefore, need to estimate the electoral consequences of specific policy decisions. In effect, both need a model about how citizens incorporate policy positions and policy effects into their choices among candidates in congressional elections.

CITIZENS AND POLICY JUDGMENTS

Prevailing scholarly wisdom suggests that policy issues play a small role in congressional elections. Most voters appear to know little

7. I should say for the record that I believe that deciding to become a coalition leader has to do more with voluntaristic and altruistic behavior than with electoral calculation. Consider the case of legislators. Although it is easy to see how working to build a coalition could yield *some* electoral dividends, it is generally true that investing time and energy in other activities (casework, newsletters, trips home, personal appearances, fund raising, and the like) produces larger and more secure dividends than building policy coalitions. Many legislators choose to become coalition leaders because they have a strong interest in policy. For many that is why they first entered politics and why they struggle to stay in office. Not surprisingly, they champion causes about which they care deeply. Electoral calculations can explain only two minor details: (1) legislators do not champion causes that might hinder their reelection chances, and (2) most legislators devote only their "spare" time to building policy coalitions—spare time being that which is left over once they have created relatively secure electoral coalitions. For a discussion of how members of the House first establish relatively secure electoral bases before becoming active in Washington, see Richard F. Fenno, Jr., *Home Style: House Members in Their Districts* (Boston: Little, Brown, 1978), pp. 171–189, 214–224.

about candidates' policy positions, and few elections appear to hinge on them.[8] Given these findings, some people have concluded that legislators need not worry about which policy positions to take.[9] Scholars who have interviewed legislators, however, find that legislators worry constantly about the electoral consequences of their decisions.[10] In fact, the most persuasive explanation for why policy issues do not play a larger role in congressional elections is that legislators constantly adjust their decisions in Washington to satisfy their constituents back home.

Those who have studied the link between constituency opinion and legislative decisions have found little evidence to support such a strong claim about legislators responding to opinion in their home districts. In their classic study of representation, Warren Miller and Donald Stokes asked whether legislators' attitudes, positions, and roll-call votes were closely related to their constituents' policy positions.[11] Their answer— as yet unrefuted—was that such links were weak.[12] The question really needs to be recast, however, as John Kingdon has demonstrated most forcefully. Kingdon, who interviewed congressmen just after they had made specific roll-call decisions, showed that legislators regularly attempt to *anticipate* how specific roll-call votes might be used against them and regularly adjust their votes in ways designed to forestall electoral problems.[13] Moreover, they do so on ordinary issues as well as the

8. For evidence on these matters, see Gary C. Jacobson, *The Politics of Congressional Elections*, 2d ed. (Boston: Little, Brown, 1987), pp. 125–139.

9. After surveying the evidence on the impact of constituency opinion on roll-call decisions, Bernstein concludes: "Constituencies do not control the policies adopted by their representatives; they have some influence over what these policies are, but members are by and large free to adopt what they think is best." See Robert A. Bernstein, *Elections, Representation, and Congressional Voting Behavior: The Myth of Constituency Control* (Englewood Cliffs, N.J.: Prentice Hall, 1989), p. 104.

10. Fenno, *Home Style*, pp. 10–18; and John W. Kingdon, *Congressmen's Voting Decisions*, 2d ed. (New York: Harper and Row, 1981), pp. 60–67.

11. Warren E. Miller and Donald E. Stokes, "Constituency Influence in Congress," *American Political Science Review* 57 (1963): 45–56.

12. A host of conceptual, methodological, and measurement problems have interfered with any straightforward tests of the hypotheses, the result being that we still know very little about the true relation between citizens' preferences and legislators' actions. See Christopher H. Achen, "Measuring Representation," and Robert S. Erikson, "Constituency Opinion and Congressional Behavior: A Reexamination of the Miller-Stokes Representation Data," both in the *American Journal of Political Science* 22 (1978): 475–510, 511–535. For citations to the complete literature see, Malcolm E. Jewell, "Legislator-Constituency Relations and the Representative Process," *Legislative Studies Quarterly* 8 (1983): 303–337.

13. Kingdon, *Congressmen's Voting Decisions*, pp. 60–68.

major issues of the day. Kingdon recounted how one congressman agonized over an amendment against college disruptions (in 1969) and
then, when he was asked if anybody in the district would actually notice
his vote, replied:

> No. I know that nobody will notice it right now. People never do. But
> it may be used against you in the next campaign. I learned that
> lesson in my first campaign for reelection. About five days before the
> election day, they hauled out the charge that I was prohomosexual
> because I cast a vote against some ridiculous District [of Columbia]
> bill. You see, most people don't notice it. But your opponent will
> comb down through every aspect of your record, every vote you've
> ever cast, looking for dirt and using it.[14]

Legislators' anticipation of future opinion can be a powerful constraint
on their voting decisions. Unfortunately, the effects of these electoral
calculations will never show up in a study of representation that
searches for correlations between measures of constituency opinion and
legislators' actual decisions.

In this book I offer a reinterpretation of the link between citizens'
policy preferences and legislators' actions. Rather than assuming that
policy preferences are fixed and asking what impact established preferences have on legislators' decisions, I introduce the notion of "potential
preferences" and ask how legislators adjust their decisions in anticipation of them.[15] The notion of potential preferences provides little explanatory leverage if one defines it to include all imaginable preferences. Its
value depends on limiting it to those preferences which legislators believe might easily be created either by interested parties dissatisfied
with legislators' decisions or by future challengers searching for good

---

14. Ibid., p. 60.

15. The notion of potential preferences is similar to Key's notion of latent opinion. Key
warns that analyzing latent opinion is a difficult task that is nevertheless crucial for
understanding government. He writes: "If public opinion has a quality of latency, discussion of such opinion would appear to present a singularly slippery problem. Until the
opinion moves by activation from its state of hibernation, one can know neither its form nor
its direction. So long as it remains latent, it cannot well be inspected. By the time it reaches
a state of activation, it has ceased to be latent. Yet in the practice of politics and government
latent opinion is really about the only type of opinion that generates much anxiety. What
opinion will develop about this prospective candidate? What opinions will be stirred by this
legislative proposal? What opinions, anxieties, and moods will be generated by this event
or by that action?" See V. O. Key, Jr., *Public Opinion and American Democracy* (New York:
Knopf, 1961), p. 263.

campaign issues. The task for theory is to show how legislators estimate the shape of these potential preferences.

This reinterpretation of the link between citizens' policy preferences and legislators' actions is intended to capture in theory what Kingdon observed in reality. It is also designed to enable one to address the question of why Congress sometimes enacts bills that serve diffuse or general interests rather than always choosing proposals that benefit concentrated interests. According to the traditional view of representation, citizens who have no opinions about a policy at the time it is being considered cannot possibly have any impact on legislators' decisions. Influence is, almost by definition, reserved for citizens with established opinions, who, for most questions of policy, are but a small segment of society. Under my view of representation, citizens who have no opinions about a policy at the time it is being considered can still have a large impact on legislators' decisions as long as legislators anticipate and respond to these citizens' potential preferences as if they already existed.

Citizens influence legislators' actions to the extent that legislators' decisions reflect in some way citizens' preferences or potential preferences about policy issues. Jack Nagel has defined influence as "the causation of outcomes by preferences."[16] I have simply extended his definition to encompass the notion of potential preferences. This extension introduces no conceptual difficulties. No fundamental difference exists between legislators estimating the exact contours of citizens' current preferences and estimating how those preferences might evolve in future months. There is also no fundamental difference between legislators responding to their own estimates of current preferences and responding to their own estimates of future preferences.

Estimating current and potential policy preferences is more art than science. Although experts in public opinion can show how to use scientific methods to measure current preferences, legislators rarely employ such methods outside of electoral campaigns. These methods are not only expensive and cumbersome, they do not allow one to estimate potential preferences. Instead legislators use a form of political intuition

---

16. More formally, influence is "a causal relation between the preferences of an actor regarding an outcome and the outcome itself." See Jack H. Nagel, *The Descriptive Analysis of Power* (New Haven: Yale University Press, 1975), pp. 24, 29. For an extension of Nagel's argument, see my chapter on "Measuring Influence," in R. Douglas Arnold, *Congress and the Bureaucracy: A Theory of Influence* (New Haven: Yale University Press, 1979), pp. 72–91.

that comes with experience. They talk with and listen to their constituents, they read their mail, they watch how past issues develop over time, they look for clues about salience and intensity, they consider who might have an incentive to arouse public opinion, they learn from one another and from others' mistakes.

What initially looks like a daunting task is eased somewhat by the fact that legislators themselves choose among paired alternatives. Legislators do not require a complete map of citizens' potential preferences for each alternative put before them. They do quite nicely by focusing on the differences between paired alternatives. They ask whether two alternatives differ significantly in their propensities to create negative opinions and consider whether one or the other is more likely to give a challenger an easy issue with which to arouse a voter backlash. They inquire whether citizens are more likely to notice the costs associated with one alternative or another. The analytic task is also eased by the fact that individual legislators need not estimate potential preferences all by themselves. Congress is an extraordinary institution for creating, analyzing, and sharing politically relevant information; legislators need only combine estimates from various sources in order to estimate their own constituents' potential preferences.

Estimating citizens' preferences provides legislators with half the information they need for prudent action. Estimating the likelihood that citizens might incorporate these policy preferences into their evaluations of congressional candidates is the other half. What legislators fear is not merely that citizens might disagree with their positions and actions, but that their disagreements might affect voters' choices in congressional elections. The recent notion of a "Teflon president" reminds us that even the most visible elected politician may escape electoral retribution for actions that do not conform with citizens' preferences. The possibilities for escape are even greater for legislators, in part because their actions are less visible and in part because each legislator is but a small cog in a large machine.

There are several paths by which judgments about policy can affect citizens' choices in congressional elections. Voters may base their judgments either on policy positions or on policy effects, and they may connect their policy evaluations either to the candidate directly or to the party first and then, indirectly, to the candidate. Each route offers a plausible interpretation of how citizens incorporate policy judgments into their choices among candidates. Each is supported by some empirical evidence. Each also provides a sensible mechanism by which citizens can hold their representatives accountable. Unfortunately, each offers legislators somewhat different advice about how they should adjust their voting decisions in order to maximize their chances of reelection.

POLICY ATTRIBUTES AND POLICY PREFERENCES

How can one estimate citizens' potential policy preferences? On what do such preferences depend? Here I shall argue that these preferences relate directly to two attributes of policies: the incidence of costs and benefits and the nature of the causal chain that links a policy instrument with policy effects. These two attributes define the distribution of interests in society, and this distribution of interests provides the foundation on which citizens' current preferences rest and from which their future policy preferences may arise.

The incidence of costs and benefits determines who will profit and who will pay under a proposed policy. Those who profit are potential supporters, those who suffer are potential opponents. To simplify the analysis, I focus on three types of costs and benefits—general, group, and geographic—and discuss the degree to which they are either concentrated narrowly or dispersed widely.

The causal chain that links a policy instrument with policy effects is the mechanism that connects a congressional decision with actual changes in the incidence of costs and benefits. Debates about the causal chain emerge in two forms, one prospective and the other retrospective. People may debate what consequences will follow from a proposed policy. People may also notice various agreeable or disagreeable conditions in society and then search for governmental decisions that may have produced those conditions. As I shall soon demonstrate, both the shape of policy preferences and their political consequences can differ, depending on whether people are reasoning about the effects of proposed policies or the causes of known effects.

Although these policy attributes are not the only things in the real world that affect citizens' preferences, they are the only elements that I have incorporated into my theoretical world. The simple reason is that these policy attributes influence the evaluations of all the participants in the policy process—citizens, legislators, and coalition leaders—and serve to link their separate evaluations. Moreover, they are the very items that coalition leaders adjust as they modify their proposals in search of larger coalitions. The more we understand what impact such policy attributes have on citizens' preferences, the more we can learn about both how coalition leaders design their strategies and why Congress passes the proposals it does.[17]

THE LOGIC OF CONGRESSIONAL ACTION

By now I have assumed away many of the complexities of the real world in order to reveal some of the principal factors that affect congressional policy making. What remains are three groups of actors— citizens, legislators, and coalition leaders—who make four separate decisions:

1. Citizens establish policy preferences by evaluating both policy proposals and policy effects.
2. Citizens choose among congressional candidates by evaluating both the candidates' policy positions and their connections with policy effects.
3. Legislators choose among policy proposals by estimating citizens' potential policy preferences and by estimating the likeli-

17. The notion that the attributes of policies affect the nature of governmental decision making is not new. Schattschneider first suggested it in the 1930s, and Lowi later developed a three-fold classification of the world into distributive, regulatory, and redistributive arenas. Lowi's typology has had little impact on the development of theory, however, because it was largely a bundle of generalizations about interest groups, legislators, bureaucrats, and the executive, and these generalizations were linked neither to basic concepts nor to explicit theories about the behavior of individuals. Wilson offered a major modification of Lowi's scheme by focusing on the degree to which both costs and benefits are narrowly concentrated or widely distributed. The advantage of Wilson's approach is that costs and benefits are variables, and one can inquire about how various quantities of these costs and benefits affect congressional action. Although Wilson has shown how the incidence of costs and benefits affects the organization and activities of interest groups, no one has yet specified exactly how these variables affect the calculations and choices of individual citizens, legislators, and coalition leaders. See E. E. Schattschneider, *Politics, Pressures, and the Tariff* (New York: Prentice-Hall, 1935), p. 288; Theodore J. Lowi, "American Business, Public Policy, Case Studies, and Political Theory," *World Politics* 16 (1964): 677–715; Lowi, "Four Systems of Policy, Politics, and Choice," *Public Administration Review* 32 (1972): 298–310; James Q. Wilson, *Political Organizations* (New York: Basic Books, 1973), pp. 330–337; and Wilson, *American Government*, 4th ed. (Lexington, Mass.: D. C. Heath, 1989), pp. 422–447, 590–604.

hood that citizens might incorporate these policy preferences into their choices among candidates in subsequent congressional elections.

4. Coalition leaders adopt strategies for enacting their policy proposals by anticipating legislators' electoral calculations, which in turn requires that they estimate both citizens' potential policy preferences and the likelihood that citizens might incorporate these policy preferences into their choices among congressional candidates.

These four decisions are the subjects of the next four chapters. After analyzing these decisions, I return to the central question: Why does Congress enact the policies that it does? I discuss the conditions that encourage Congress to produce particularistic policies and to serve organized interests. I also set forth the conditions that prompt Congress to serve more diffuse, general, or unorganized interests.[18]

In the second half of the book I analyze congressional decision making in the fields of economic, tax, and energy policy. Each of these chapters examines the evolution of policy over several decades. My aim is to show that the theory is a useful device for explaining the dynamics of policy decisions and that it is capable of explaining shift points in congressional decisions. It is an important test of the theory to explain not only why Congress pursues one course of action, but why it sometimes switches directions and enacts programs that serve formerly disadvantaged interests. In the chapter on energy, for example, I attempt to show why Congress first regulated the prices of petroleum and natural gas, allowed those regulations to remain in effect for several decades, refused to deregulate prices for nearly a decade despite repeated presidential requests, and eventually deregulated both petroleum and gas prices just when everybody agreed it was impossible.

In a concluding chapter I discuss the ability of citizens to control their government. After first showing that political parties no longer provide an adequate mechanism for citizens' control, I examine the potential for control when citizens base their voting choices on candidates rather

18. The theory is designed to fit a Congress where most members seek to be reelected, where parties are relatively weak, and where members face repeated demands to stand up and be counted on roll-call votes. It thus fits the Congress of the 1970s and 1980s quite well. It also provides a reasonable approximation to the Congress of the 1950s and 1960s, but the lack of frequent roll-call votes and the existence of stronger parties makes the fit less perfect. Before that time, I would guess that the fit is relatively poor.

than parties. I show that under the proper conditions it is possible for citizens to hold legislators accountable for the effects they produce and not just for the positions they take. I also explain how reformers can foster those conditions and how past reform efforts have been misguided.

2

Policy Attributes and Policy Preferences

Legislators and coalition leaders must estimate citizens' preferences and potential preferences for the various policy proposals put forth in Congress. Legislators need to know whether enacting a new proposal might generate a storm of protest that might endanger their political careers, to anticipate whether some small part of a complex bill might eventually offend some of their constituents and diminish their political support, and to recognize which proposals might become popular among their constituents so that they can position themselves accordingly. For each issue before Congress, legislators need to estimate which of their constituents might someday acquire policy preferences, how those constituents might divide on the issue, and how deeply they might feel about it.

Legislators and coalition leaders need a simple, reliable model for estimating citizens' potential policy preferences. Because they must choose among competing policy alternatives, they need a model that focuses on the relevant differences between policy alternatives and that shows how these differences might generate distinct patterns of policy preferences. In this chapter I show how citizens' potential policy preferences relate to the incidence of costs and benefits and the nature of the causal chain that links policy instruments with policy effects. After first discussing these two attributes of policies, I use them to explain the existence, direction, and intensity of citizens' preferences and potential preferences. Throughout the book I assume that citizens have *outcome* preferences (for clean air, safe streets, and a sound economy), even though they may not have well-defined *policy* preferences. They often lack policy preferences simply because they don't understand the precise relationship between policies and outcomes.[1]

BELIEFS ABOUT CAUSE AND EFFECT

Citizens' policy preferences depend, in part, on how they believe the world works. Those who believe that welfare payments encourage poor mothers to have more children take a dim view of increasing those payments. Those who believe that a policy of free trade contributes to American unemployment are less likely to support free trade legislation than are those who believe that free trade produces a net gain in employment. Those who believe that the quality of American secondary education is declining because salaries are too low to attract talented teachers are more likely to support increased aid to education than are those who believe that the problem stems from poor management, changes in the curriculum, or too much federal control.

A large part of any policy discussion is a debate about cause and effect, and it is so whether the debate occurs on the evening news, in living rooms across America, in the halls of academe, or in the halls of Congress. One cannot attack a problem without some sense of what caused it or choose among alternative solutions without considering how each would manage to produce the intended effects. One cannot ignore the

---

1. Specialists in public opinion may find this chapter less than satisfying. Not only do I cite few of their studies, I make no effort to show that citizens do, in fact, reason as I assume they do. I offer two defenses for my apparent neglect. First, although I have read widely in the public opinion literature and have explored relevant literatures in cognitive and social psychology, I have discovered very little that helps me to understand how policy attributes affect citizens' preferences and potential preferences. Second, my principal concern is to show how legislators *anticipate* citizens' acquisition of policy preferences. Unless it can be shown that legislators regularly search the scholarly literature on public opinion for hints about how to do this (they do not, any more than they notice what congressional scholars write), my neglect should not interfere with my analysis. The aim is to show how legislators *think* citizens might react, not to establish how accurate legislators are in their predictions. My approach has been to pretend to be a legislator for a while, steep myself in congressional hearings and debate, reacquaint myself with the legislators brought to life by Fenno, Kingdon, Asbell, and Drew, and do everything I could (short of throwing my own hat into the ring) to see the problem through legislators' eyes. Then, I have simply transformed myself back into a scholar and attempted to generalize about the process. The test of whether I have captured the way legislators analyze potential policy preferences is the degree to which I can explain the logic of congressional action. The test of whether citizens *actually* reason like this is a question best left for specialists in public opinion.

possibility that the best solution to one problem may exacerbate several others.

Debates about cause and effect are of two types. *Prospective evaluation* involves estimating what consequences would follow if the government adopted and implemented a specific program. How would the behavior of individuals, firms, and agencies change? How likely is it that a policy would achieve its intended purpose? What unintended conse quences might occur? How much would it cost to implement the program fully? *Retrospective evaluation* reverses the direction of analysis; here the goal is to find the causes of known problems, conditions, or events. How has governmental policy contributed to recent increases in inflation? What could the government have done to forestall those increases? To what extent are these increases beyond the control of government?[2]

Prospective evaluation is done as a matter of course whenever Congress considers a new program. Proponents are expected to show how the chosen policy instrument (the means) will produce the intended effects (the ends), and how they can be accomplished at a reasonable cost and with few undesirable side effects. At a minimum, proponents need a good story about how a program would transform certain inputs into more desirable outputs. Opponents may attack on several fronts. They may try to discredit the proposed causal chain by showing that the policy instrument could not possibly produce the intended effects, by arguing that the probability of success is very low, or by advocating a competing program that promises to achieve the same results by some other route. Alternatively, they may concede that the proposed program would produce the intended effects, but then object that it would also generate a series of undesirable side effects or that it would cost more than the benefits it could ever yield.

Policy proposals differ in the number of intermediate steps that must occur in order for a policy instrument to produce the intended effects. Some policies have no intermediate steps between adoption of the policy and production of the effects. These I shall call *single-stage policies*. A proposal to provide pensions for presidents' widows is an example. Once Congress passes a law that provides the pensions, the problem of des-

---

2. The distinction between prospective and retrospective evaluation will prove useful for my analysis, even though in practice the two are often intertwined. For example, prospective evaluation of a proposed antipoverty program may be informed by retrospective evaluations of both poverty and poverty programs.

titute presidential widows disappears. Similarly, if one believes married couples bear too heavy a tax burden, one need only convince Congress to amend the tax code. There are no intermediate stages between adopting the instrument and achieving the end.[3]

Most policies incorporate a series of intermediate steps that must occur before the intended effects can be achieved. These I shall call *multi-stage policies*. For example, some people believe that sluggish economic growth and low productivity can be traced to the state of American education and that increased federal aid is the solution. The argument envisions a series of stages: that federal aid to local districts would increase total expenditures on education, that these increases would help to raise teachers' salaries, that better pay would attract better teachers, that better teachers would produce better students, that these students would grow up and become more creative and productive workers, and that this increased productivity would yield more rapid economic growth.

I shall also speak of the *order* of the effects in a multi-stage policy, referring to the stage in which an effect should occur. In the example just mentioned, the increase in educational budgets is a first-order effect, higher teachers' salaries a second-order effect, and greater economic growth a sixth-order effect. More generally I shall speak of *early-order effects* and *later-order effects*, meaning those near the beginning and those near the end of a proposed causal chain. Most programs produce early-order effects with far greater certainty than they do later-order effects. Early-order effects also emerge much closer to the present, whereas many later-order effects may be delayed until far into the future. Pumping more money into local school budgets produces higher teachers' salaries with near certainty, however problematic the eventual connection to better education, increased productivity, or long-term economic growth. More distant effects are less likely because there is so much that can go wrong in a long causal chain. Imagine, for example, that the probability of one stage producing the next is a robust 0.80, for all adjacent stages in a six-stage policy. The probability of the policy

3. Strictly speaking, there are always intermediate stages and administration is never automatic. In this case the Internal Revenue Service must revise its tax forms, the new regulations must be publicized, and affected taxpayers must read and take advantage of them. These intermediate steps are relatively automatic, however, which means that one introduces little distortion by ignoring them and considering this a single-stage policy. From here on I shall refer to a policy as single-stage whenever there are no uncertain or problematic stages between the policy instrument and the policy effects.

instrument producing the intended sixth-order effect, therefore, is only 0.26.

For short causal chains, retrospective evaluation is not fundamentally different from prospective evaluation. It is just as easy to project how a 10 percent surtax would affect people's take-home pay as it is to notice that one's pay has declined and then figure out that the cause was a 10 percent surtax approved by Congress. When causal chains are very long, however, retrospective evaluation becomes virtually impossible. Imagine for a moment that the ultimate cause of the explosion of the space shuttle *Challenger* was congressional stinginess with NASA's budget, which had led the agency gradually to reduce funds for quality control. It is hard to imagine anyone other than a dedicated expert with full access to internal proceedings establishing this single factor as the cause, for there were too many intermediate steps and too many other contributing causes.

People differ widely in their knowledge of how the world works and in their ability to forecast the consequences of specific policy interventions.[4] Here I differentiate between three participants in the policy process: experts, generalists, and ordinary citizens. Experts are those professionals who investigate causal chains as part of their jobs (for example, natural scientists and social scientists). Most experts specialize in small slices of the policy world: investigating the causes of inflation, exploring the connection between fluorocarbons and the depletion of the ozone, analyzing the link between segregated schools and educational attainment, investigating the impact of airline regulation on the cost of travel, or exploring the link between smoking and health. As a result, most come to believe that the world (or at least *their* slice of it) is a complicated system and that only the most carefully crafted interventions can change it in the intended direction. They tend to argue that poorly designed policies are as likely to make a problem worse as they are to improve it.

Ordinary citizens acquire their views of cause and effect more haphazardly, and with little attempt at specialization. Sometimes their views reflect the findings of experts—for example, citizens' current views on the link between smoking and health seem to be informed by the pronouncements of experts. More frequently citizens' views reflect

4. For further discussion on the differences between ordinary and expert knowledge, see Charles E. Lindblom and David K. Cohen, *Usable Knowledge: Social Science and Social Problem Solving* (New Haven: Yale University Press, 1979).

their own life experiences, their own intuitions, or arguments they have picked up from friends or from the mass media.[5] We don't know exactly why most citizens believe that capital punishment is a strong deterrent to crime or that balanced budgets make good economic policy, we only know that they do *and* that their beliefs on these subjects are relatively stable and unrelated to changing fads among experts in criminal justice or macroeconomics.[6]

Generalists are legislators, presidents, bureaucrats, staff members, editorial writers, columnists, and others who specialize in policy making and policy evaluation but who are not professionals trained in isolating cause and effect. Generalists often take a middle position between experts and ordinary citizens. They consult frequently with experts, invite them to formal hearings, and canvass their writings. Occasionally they establish commissions and fill them with experts to investigate especially difficult problems. Generalists' own views on cause and effect, however, tend to reflect both the findings of experts and their own intuitions and observations about how the world works.[7]

The differences distinguishing citizens, experts, and generalists are easiest to see in the world of macroeconomic policy. Prior to the 1930s economists, legislators, and citizens agreed that balanced budgets were essential for economic health—at least no one was arguing in favor of intentional deficits. Beginning in the 1930s some economists began to advocate the virtues of Keynesian deficits as a spur to economic growth, and by the 1960s economists were relatively united in the belief that balancing the budget every year might actually be detrimental to economic health. Their views reflected new theories about cause and effect. Citizens were apparently unmoved by the experts' arguments and con-

5. This is an observation, not the conclusion of any research. I am unaware of any literature that investigates the origins of citizens' beliefs about cause and effect in the policy world. For a recent article that makes some progress in this direction, see Paul M. Sniderman, Michael G. Hagen, Philip E. Tetlock, and Henry E. Brady, "Reasoning Chains: Causal Models of Policy Reasoning in Mass Publics," *British Journal of Political Science* 16 (1986): 405–430.

6. Although there are problems with changes in question wording, see the polls related to balanced budgets that are cited in George H. Gallup, *The Gallup Poll: Public Opinion, 1935–1971* (New York: Random House, 1972), p. 2354. See also Arthur L. Stinchcombe, *Crime and Punishment: Changing Attitudes in America* (San Francisco: Jossey-Bass, 1980), p. 28.

7. This is also an observation, not the conclusion of any research. Although I would welcome studies about how legislators reason about cause and effect in the policy world and about how their beliefs affect their actions, I know of no such studies.

tinued to believe that the rules of prudence in household finance made equal sense for the nation's finances. Opinion surveys have long shown that most citizens believe strongly in balanced budgets and view deficits as the root cause of countless economic problems.[8] Most legislators apparently agreed with citizens, not economists. There is little evidence that the legislators who supported the Keynesian tax cut of 1964 (or the supply-side tax cut of 1981) actually believed in the arguments that promised dramatic improvements in the economy as a consequence of those cuts.[9]

We know a great deal about how economists see cause and effect because they write for a living. We know far less about citizens' views, both because citizens are less inclined to put pen to paper and because specialists in public opinion have largely ignored these kinds of questions.[10] From the work of Donald Kinder and Walter Mebane we do know that most citizens can construct plausible explanations for inflation and that many can offer remedies for the problem.[11] Their solutions, however, tend to diverge from those of economists. Most citizens believe that wage and price controls are the best remedy for high inflation, while most economists believe such controls are the worst solution.[12] In general, citizens conceive of the economic world as a less complicated place than economists do, and they are far more comfortable with single-stage policies that attack problems directly. Economists see a more complicated world full of interconnections and feedback loops. They are far

8. Gallup, *Gallup Poll*, p. 2354.

9. On the attempt to sell Keynesianism to a reluctant Congress, see James L. Sundquist, *Politics and Policy* (Washington, D.C.: Brookings Institution, 1968), pp. 13–56. For further discussion of both the 1964 and 1981 tax cuts, see Chapters 7 and 8.

10. There is an emerging literature in cognitive and social psychology that explores the tacit theories (called schemas) that people use to understand the world. Although this approach offers some promise for the future, it is still very basic and has yet to be applied to the kind of policy questions that drive my own research. See Hazel Markus and R. B. Zajonc, "The Cognitive Perspective in Social Psychology," in Gardner Lindzey and Elliot Aronson (eds.), *Handbook of Social Psychology*, 3d ed., vol. 1 (New York: Random House, 1985), pp. 137–230; James A. Galambos, Robert P. Abelson, and John B. Black (eds.), *Knowledge Structures* (Hillsdale, N.J.: Erlbaum, 1986); and Donald R. Kinder, "Diversity and Complexity in American Public Opinion," in Ada W. Finifter (ed.), *Political Science: The State of the Discipline* (Washington, D.C.: American Political Science Association, 1983), pp. 414–415.

11. Donald R. Kinder and Walter R. Mebane, Jr., "Politics and Economics in Everyday Life," in Kristen R. Monroe (ed.), *The Political Process and Economic Change* (New York: Agathon Press, 1983), pp. 141–180.

12. Ibid., p. 153.

more likely to recommend multi-stage policies, such as Keynesian surpluses, monetarist targets, or supply-side solutions, which attack problems by more indirect means.

Perhaps nowhere is there a greater gulf between economists' notions
of a good solution and legislators' and citizens' sense of what would work
best than in the field of environmental, health, and safety policy. Most
people who are not economists prefer regulatory programs: prohibiting
firms from discharging specific pollutants, inspecting dangerous industrial facilities, setting standards for the removal of asbestos, and regulating the use of pesticides. These interventions attack the problems directly, contain either a single stage or a very few stages, and are
relatively easy to understand. Such programs are also very popular,
judging by public opinion polls and by the overwhelming majorities
they garner in Congress. Most economists deplore regulatory programs
and offer sophisticated incentive programs in their place: effluent
charges to control air or water pollution, injury taxes to make employers
more safety-conscious, or congestion fees to reduce rush-hour traffic.[13]
Economists have made few converts in the policy world. Few people
understand the complicated and often counterintuitive causal logic of
incentive programs, and few can recall why an indirect approach is
supposed to be superior to a direct prohibition of evil.[14]

These differences in how citizens, legislators, and experts reason
about cause and effect would be of no consequence if citizens and legislators concentrated on choosing what ends to pursue and then delegated to policy experts the task of devising and implementing the most
appropriate means. This is not the American way. When legislators
choose among competing programs they are choosing among alternative packages of both ends and means. When citizens evaluate legislators' choices they may base their evaluations on either the ends, the
means, or both. Even if legislators suddenly became converts to the
notion that effluent charges were superior to environmental regula-

13. On the economic advantages of these programs, see Allen V. Kneese and Charles L.
Schultze, *Pollution, Prices, and Public Policy* (Washington, D.C.: Brookings Institution,
1975); and Charles L. Schultze, *The Public Use of Private Interest* (Washington, D.C.:
Brookings Institution, 1977).

14. This conclusion is true even for those with a great deal at stake who have been
exposed to economists' arguments. For the results of interviews with environmental and
industrial lobbyists on their attitudes toward effluent charges, see Steven J. Kelman, *What
Price Incentives? Economists and the Environment* (Boston: Auburn House, 1981), pp.
93–123.

tions, they would still be reluctant to support such charges if they believed that future challengers might convince their constituents that they intended to sell "licenses to pollute." Even if legislators believed the argument that laws raising the minimum wage actually hurt the poor, they might still be reluctant to oppose a raise if their constituents believed that it would help the poor. Citizens may have an imperfect understanding of cause and effect in the policy world. Nevertheless, their beliefs about cause and effect are important, for beliefs may affect both their preferences about policy issues and their choices among congressional candidates.

THE INCIDENCE OF COSTS AND BENEFITS

Citizens' policy preferences depend on the incidence of costs and benefits as well as on their beliefs about cause and effect. The incidence of costs and benefits refers to (1) who would profit and who would pay under a proposed policy, (2) how much the beneficiaries would reap and the contributors would suffer, and (3) when the various beneficiaries would receive their benefits and the various contributors would suffer their losses. The incidence of costs and benefits affects whether citizens might someday acquire preferences about a policy, how they might divide on the issue, and how deeply they might feel about it.

Specific costs and benefits may be narrowly concentrated or widely distributed.[15] The ultimate in concentration is for benefits (or costs) to be centered on a single individual. Such cases are not unusual; special tax provisions, for example, tend to be drafted as if they applied to a class of individuals when, in fact, each affects a class of one.[16] The ultimate in dispersion is for benefits (or costs) to be distributed uniformly across all members of society. National security is an example: we are all equally protected (and threatened) by the nuclear umbrella.

---

15. This distinction is introduced by James Q. Wilson in *Political Organizations* (New York: Basic Books, 1973), pp. 330–337. For his most recent analysis of American politics based on the distribution of costs and benefits, see James Q. Wilson, *American Government*, 4th ed. (Lexington, Mass.: D. C. Heath, 1989), pp. 422–447, 590–604.

16. See Stanley S. Surrey, "The Congress and the Tax Lobbyist: How Special Tax Provisions Get Enacted," *Harvard Law Review* 70 (1957): 1145–1182. The same is true when Congress decides to reform the tax law and then inserts transition rules to insulate specific individuals or firms from the new and tougher provisions. See Chapter 8.

When policy effects fall uniformly on members of society I shall refer to them as *general benefits* or *general costs*. General benefits include economic growth, stable prices, improved public health, and other collective goods that people value because they believe everyone profits, including themselves. General costs include across-the-board tax increases, economic decline, inflation, health epidemics, and those losses of liberty associated with a bureaucratic state and a regulated economy. When policy effects do not fall uniformly on members of society I shall refer to them as either *group costs and benefits* or *geographic costs and benefits*.

Group costs and benefits include policy effects that accrue to particular segments of society. Often these are economic groups, such as specific occupations, industries, professions, or income classes. They may also include noneconomic segments of society, whether defined along demographic lines, such as race, gender, age, or ethnicity; by common interests, such as hunting, bird watching, opera, or sky diving; or by common condition, such as suffering from blindness, alcoholism, or cancer. These segments may or may not be organized into formal interest groups. All the definition requires is that some nonrandom collection of individuals receives disproportionate benefits or bears disproportionate costs.

Geographic costs and benefits refer to policy effects that accrue disproportionately to particular geographic areas, whether regions, states, or localities. Geographic effects are actually a special type of group effect, one in which locality is the common element. The distinction is nevertheless useful, both because geographic areas enjoy direct representation in Congress whereas other groups do not and because the recipients of geographic benefits (and the payers of geographic costs) are necessarily in close proximity to one another whereas their counterparts who receive group benefits (or pay group costs) may have absolutely no contact.

Group and geographic effects are not necessarily mutually exclusive. Although some policy effects have a group impact without any differential geographic impact (benefits for cancer victims or regulations imposed on used car dealers), and others have a geographic impact without a differential group impact (federal loan guarantees for New York City), many policy effects have concurrent impacts on both groups and geographic areas. Price supports for milk provide group benefits to dairy farmers and geographic benefits to agricultural areas. Import quotas on automobiles provide group benefits to auto makers and geographic benefits to the Detroit metropolitan area. Ceilings on the price of natural gas impose group costs on gas producers and geographic costs on the states of Texas, Louisiana, and Oklahoma. Even though it is generally considered bad form to establish categories that are not mutually exclusive, in this case the advantages outweigh the disadvantages.

Most policies embrace all six types of costs and benefits. The Stealth bomber, for example, promises enhanced national security as a general benefit, an increased tax burden as a general cost, substantial group benefits to those who manufacture the bomber, unknown but real group costs to the manufacturers of competing weapons, considerable geographic benefits to the areas where the bomber is manufactured, and possible geographic costs to areas where it is deployed. Similarly, a proposal that would require utilities in the Midwest to cut their emissions from coal-fired plants in order to reduce acid rain in the Northeast and Canada promises improved relations with Canada as a general benefit, somewhat diminished economic growth as a general cost, group benefits for those coal producers who mine clean coal, group costs for those who mine dirty coal, geographic costs in the form of larger utility bills throughout the Midwest, and geographic benefits in the Northeast where less acid rain would fall. Although most policies include all six types of costs and benefits, the relative proportions vary widely. One common complaint about Congress is that it frequently endorses programs that offer substantial group and geographic benefits but that promise relatively few general benefits.

The perceived incidence of costs and benefits is partly a function of the length of the causal chain that links the policy instrument with the policy effects. When a causal chain is very short—perhaps a few simple stages—the incidence of costs and benefits is often easy to predict. There can be little question of who would suffer if Congress enacts a $100,000-per-farmer limit on dairy price supports. When a causal chain is long, the incidence of later-order effects may be totally unknown (even though the incidence of early-order effects continues to be quite predictable). This is not simply because later-order effects occur with far less certainty than early-order effects. Even if one expects that a long causal chain will work perfectly and that the later-order effects are certain to emerge, the precise incidence of those later-order effects may be unknowable simply because the final incidence depends on a host of unpredictable decisions by individuals, firms, and agencies. Consider, for example, a proposal to cut corporate tax rates in order to stimulate investment and spur economic growth. At the first stage, corporate taxes decline, and here the incidence is certain. These reductions are supposed to stimulate investment, which they may, but where will all those corporations or their shareholders choose to invest? Investment is supposed to increase employment, but who will be hired? Eventually the nation may experience economic growth, but which regions, states, and localities will share in that growth? The longer the causal chain, the more difficult it is to predict anything about the incidence of costs and benefits at the final stage.

POLICY PREFERENCES

How do citizens' policy preferences depend on the incidence of costs and benefits? Let us begin with an admittedly naive model of how citizens might acquire their preferences. Let us assume that each citizen performs a miniature cost-benefit analysis for a policy proposal, incorporating all costs and benefits that might affect his or her own personal welfare. The task requires the citizen to measure and sum all costs, measure and sum all benefits, discount each for time, and then support any proposal for which the discounted benefits exceed the discounted costs. The model is naive only because most citizens do not notice most costs and benefits, even those that we arm-chair analysts know will affect them. The question then becomes, What determines whether or not someone will detect a particular cost or benefit? Here I argue that the probability that a citizen will notice a particular effect depends on its magnitude, its timing, the proximity of other people who are similarly affected, and the availability of an instigator to help reveal the citizen's stake in the matter.

The *magnitude* of a specific cost or benefit directly affects the probability that a citizen will perceive it. Few citizens will notice if the price of milk increases a penny per gallon, and even if they do happen to notice, it is unlikely to make a lasting impression. In contrast, most citizens will notice a 10 percent surcharge on their income taxes, and many of them will acquire strong and intense preferences on the matter. The relative magnitude of a specific cost or benefit appears to be more important than its absolute magnitude. House members refused to be associated with a surcharge on local telephone bills of six dollars per month because they feared that citizens would notice such an increase and they would care—especially those from low-cost areas where monthly bills would double.[17] Yet legislators regularly demand safety equipment or

17. Richard Whittle, "House Votes to Block FCC Phone Rate Plan," *Congressional Quarterly Weekly Report* 41 (November 12, 1983): 2396.

emissions controls that add several hundred dollars to the price of an automobile, knowing that such charges will remain imperceptible to most car buyers, who already face sticker prices in five figures.

The *timing* of a specific cost or benefit also affects the probability that a citizen will notice it. Citizens are far more likely to detect early-order effects than later-order effects, in part because they are more likely to understand the first few stages of a multi-stage policy than they are to appreciate fully the entire causal chain, and in part because of the more certain incidence of early-order effects. For both reasons we expect doctors and hospital administrators to be more likely to anticipate the early-order costs of a proposal to control health care expenses than are patients to anticipate the later-order benefits of such a proposal (and this conclusion holds true even for those who regularly pay high medical bills). Similarly, workers in industries that are suffering from import competition tend to anticipate the early-order benefits of restrictive trade legislation more than workers in export industries anticipate the later-order costs (even though the magnitude of the group costs may exceed the magnitude of the group benefits).

The *proximity* of a citizen to others who are similarly affected by a specific cost or benefit may also affect the probability that he or she will notice it. People who live together, work together, or play together discover their common interests more easily than do those who never interact with others who have similar interests. The victims and potential victims of both black lung disease and AIDS became aware of policy proposals relating to their ailments far more quickly than have the victims of most other diseases, simply because these two diseases first struck relatively small, close-knit communities.

Proximity is itself a function of the degree to which group or geographic effects are narrowly concentrated. Geographic concentration has the more obvious impact. Those who share in benefits (or costs) that are concentrated geographically are quite literally neighbors, if not friends. Important information travels quickly within most local communities, whether from neighbor to neighbor or with the help of the local media. Notice how quickly everyone learns when their county is being considered as the site for a new prison, a nuclear waste dump, a military installation, or a particle accelerator.

The impact of concentrated group effects is similar, but only if the lines of concentration coincide with existing communications networks. Information is readily exchanged within the national communities of doctors, city managers, environmental engineers, bird watchers, and stamp collectors because members of these communities are linked together in various ways: they read the same specialized publications, they regularly gather together in conventions, they seek each other out for friendship and company, and they keep in touch by telephone. Imagine how quickly most serious stamp collectors would hear about a proposal to issue all postage stamps with a fixed design (like coins) rather than with designs that change with the seasons. When the lines of concentration fail to coincide with an existing communications network, individuals who have common interests are in a poor position to discover those common interests. The victims of auto accidents, the purchasers of defective automobiles, and asthmatics who suffer from severe air pollution all bear large and concentrated costs, but they do so alone.

Many of the specialized communications networks that link together citizens who have common interests are maintained by organized interest groups. Many other networks exist independently of organized groups. Thousands of small magazines, journals, and newsletters, for example, cater to individuals' extraordinarily specialized tastes. As a sideline, they help disseminate information about the impact of federal policy on their readers' special interests. Stamp collectors need not be members of an interest group to learn about upcoming federal decisions. They need only subscribe to a philatelic magazine or read the weekly stamp column in their local paper.

The availability of an *instigator* to help reveal citizens' stakes in an outcome also affects the probability that an individual will notice a specific cost or benefit. Ralph Nader helps to identify the effects of proposed bills and regulations on consumers' interests. Common Cause does the same for those who care about clean and open government. Both rely on the mass media to disseminate their messages for free. Before Ralph Nader and Common Cause set up shop in Washington, it was much more difficult for individuals to acquire information about how specific policies would affect their interests as consumers or as concerned citizens. Business organizations also act as instigators, attempting to mobilize their customers or shareholders to help achieve their own ends. Banks bombarded their customers with announcements of how Congress had just enacted a tax-withholding system for bank accounts, and then watched their customers bombard Congress with letters of protest.[18] TIAA-CREF, the pension fund for college teachers, sent letters to its

18. "Interest Withholding Requirement Repealed," *Congressional Quarterly Almanac, 1983* 39 (1984): 261–264.

1.1 million members in 1986 showing how an obscure provision in the proposed tax reform bill would end the fund's tax exemption and thereby reduce teachers' pensions. Many instigators are also leaders of interest groups, but they need not be. Ralph Nader became a powerful instigator first and later decided to build several organizations. Most presidents also attempt to become opinion leaders and to educate citizens about their stakes in specific matters before Congress.

Together these four factors—magnitude, timing, proximity, and the availability of an instigator—affect the likelihood that a citizen will perceive a specific cost or benefit. Large, early-order effects that are concentrated by both group and geographic area practically guarantee that an attentive audience will emerge. Most dairy farmers would quickly hear about a proposal to end dairy subsidies, and most would have no trouble establishing a preference on the matter. Small, later-order effects that are widely distributed are unlikely to cross the threshold of perception. Most consumers of dairy products don't have the foggiest idea that they collectively pay between $1 and $4 billion annually in subsidies to dairy farmers, because they pay these costs a few pennies at a time. Occasionally an instigator can raise citizens' consciousness on matters such as this, but it is not easy. In the early 1970s instigators used several scandals involving campaign contributions from the dairy industry to educate some citizens about their interests as dairy consumers, but as the scandals faded so too did citizens' attention.[19]

Once we restrict our attention to *perceived* costs and benefits, the notion of a citizen performing a miniature cost-benefit analysis for each policy proposal makes more sense. For many proposals a citizen will notice neither costs nor benefits, and thus he will have no policy preference at all. For others he may detect only a single effect. If he notices a program's benefits, he will favor it; if he notices its costs, he will oppose it. Only if he sees both costs and benefits does he weigh them to determine which side is larger.

One of the best places to observe citizens actually weighing complicated streams of costs and benefits is in small communities where voters must approve school budgets. In some communities it is quite common for voters to reject the first few budgets proposed by school boards, until

19. For accounts of the recent politics of dairy programs, see Martha Derthick and Paul J. Quirk, *The Politics of Deregulation* (Washington, D.C.: Brookings Institution, 1985), pp. 224–233; and R. Kent Weaver, *Automatic Government: The Politics of Indexation* (Washington, D.C.: Brookings Institution, 1988), pp. 146–172. See also Chapter 6.

the boards pare back both school expenditures and school taxes to a point where a majority of voters believe that the benefits will equal or exceed the costs. School referenda are unusual only because some of the same citizens perceive both large, direct, and early-order costs (their own property taxes) and large, direct, and early-order benefits (educational opportunities for their children). Although we should expect few such unambiguous examples in federal programs (because few federal programs impose on the same individuals both large, early-order costs and large early-order benefits), the example assures us that citizens are quite capable of weighing complicated streams of costs and benefits and that modest adjustments in the magnitude of either the costs or the benefits can change their preferences.

By identifying and comparing a program's perceived costs and benefits, we can establish the existence and the direction of citizens' potential policy preferences. We can also estimate the intensity of their preferences by reasoning from these same two elements. Intensity is a function of the magnitude of the difference between a program's perceived costs and its perceived benefits. The larger the difference, the more intense are citizens' preferences. Intensity is not, however, a symmetrical function. Intensity is greater for a given measure of costs than it is for the same measure of benefits.[20] Depriving someone of one thousand dollars produces a reaction far more intense (and politically dangerous) than delivering one thousand dollars in the first place.[21]

Exactly why citizens feel more intensely about a given measure of costs than they do about the same measure of benefits is not clear. It may simply be that citizens grow accustomed to a particular flow of benefits, assume that it will continue, and structure their lifestyles and consumption accordingly. Decreasing that flow imposes very serious costs on citizens, for they must change their expectations, habits, and lifestyles. They must forfeit what they have come to regard as the necessities of life. As a consequence they have very intense preferences about any proposal to reduce those benefits. When the flow of benefits happens to

20. Psychologists refer to this property as *loss aversion*, which implies that "a loss of $X is more aversive than a gain of $X is attractive." See Amos Tversky and Daniel Kahneman, "The Framing of Decisions and the Psychology of Choice," *Science* 211 (1981): 453–458; and Daniel Kahneman and Amos Tversky, "Choices, Values, and Frames," *American Psychologist* 39 (1984): 341–350.

21. See John D. Steinbruner, *The Cybernetic Theory of Decision* (Princeton: Princeton University Press, 1974), p. 33.

increase, however, citizens regard those new benefits as luxuries. At least in the short term, they do not alter their expectations about the future or their patterns of consumption. Although citizens find luxuries desirable, the "extras" do not elicit the same intensity of feelings associated with the necessities of life. Of course, after citizens have received luxuries for a while, they begin to regard them as necessities. At that point they begin to feel intensely about the continuance of those benefits.[22]

The only other adjustment we need make to this simple model of how citizens acquire their preferences is to note that people value many things that do not directly contribute to their own material welfare. Anyone who attempts to anticipate citizens' preferences by assuming that all they care about is whether some proposal makes them richer or poorer will miss a great deal. Some of the same citizens who voluntarily contribute $70 billion to charity each year also support federal programs that serve charitable ends. Programs that assist the blind, the physically handicapped, and the mentally ill are, in fact, quite popular among the sighted, the able-bodied, and the sane.[23] Many citizens also support governmental programs that are designed to save whales they will never see, preserve Arctic wilderness they will never visit, and protect endangered species they never knew existed.

These complications arise because many people believe that government has a duty to assist and protect less fortunate groups in society and to provide general benefits for both present and future generations. Although many citizens agree on these basic ends, they disagree about which groups merit attention and which general benefits are most desirable. This simple fact makes politics vastly more complicated than economics. Economists have learned a great deal about market behavior by assuming that consumers always seek to improve their material welfare. Political scientists would learn much less about electoral and legislative behavior if they assumed that citizens would support only those proposals that appeared to improve their own material welfare. Politics is simultaneously a struggle among individuals attempting to advance

22. For a more formal and detailed discussion of this asymmetrical attitude toward change, see R. Douglas Arnold, *Congress and the Bureaucracy: A Theory of Influence* (New Haven: Yale University Press, 1979), pp. 24–25.

23. For example, 95 percent of citizens interviewed in 1977 supported the existing special tax exemption for blind people. See John F. Witte, *The Politics and Development of the Federal Income Tax* (Madison: University of Wisconsin Press, 1985), p. 350.

their own private interests and a competition among citizens who have different conceptions of the public interest.

This complication is not particularly troublesome so long as a citizen is comparing alternatives that differ on only one of the two dimensions. If alternatives differ only in their impact on a citizen's private interest, she would clearly prefer the one that leaves her better off. If they differ only in their impact on the public interest, she would clearly prefer the one that better advances what she believes the public interest to be. Only if two alternatives differ on both dimensions must she calculate trade-offs among disparate ends. Here I ignore the problem of trade-offs among public and private ends because the problem does not severely affect my analysis of legislative action. Most of the time Congress considers paired alternatives that differ from each other in small ways and that, for any given individual, differ significantly on only one of the two dimensions.

It is relatively easy to analyze from afar how a given program will affect a citizen's private interests. Knowing whether someone is a dairy farmer or a dairy consumer is ordinarily sufficient for estimating an individual's potential preferences about a proposal that would triple the price of milk. It is considerably tougher to anticipate how citizens might evaluate alternative packages of general benefits. No single piece of data allows one to predict whether a citizen might support opening up more Alaskan wilderness for oil exploration—a proposal that risks some environmental degradation for a possible increase in the supply of petroleum. As usual, legislators have an advantage over distant analysts. The more they know about their constituents' fundamental beliefs and values, the more they can anticipate how their constituents might evaluate alternative packages of general benefits.

Citizens can easily misperceive how a specific program will affect them. Since citizens are more likely to notice early-order effects than later-order effects, it follows that citizens' preferences are powerfully influenced by those early-order effects. People who are worried about accelerating inflation may end up favoring wage and price controls because they promise to restrain prices quickly, without ever appreciating the later-order effects on the flexibility and efficiency of the economy. People who are delayed by congested highways may support road-building programs without ever considering that better highways may stimulate new development and thereby produce even greater congestion. Many citizens oppose foreign aid programs because the later-order benefits are difficult to detect while the early-order costs are easy to see (higher taxes or foregone expenditures on domestic programs).

THE DYNAMICS OF POLICY PREFERENCES

Citizens' policy preferences are not fixed. They may change either while Congress is considering a proposal, after Congress has approved or rejected it, or during a subsequent electoral campaign. Some people have absolutely no preferences about a proposal when it is first introduced, but they later acquire such preferences. Other people have preferences from the very beginning, but they modify them over time. Their preferences may change in intensity, in direction, or they may fade away completely. Still others begin with no preferences and persist happily in that condition, yet they might well have acquired preferences if legislators had not anticipated their needs and removed any stimuli that might have generated the acquisition of preferences.

This chapter argues that citizens change their preferences in predictable and understandable ways. The stimulus for change may simply be that citizens notice something new about a policy or that they begin to see a new cost or benefit. The predictability of change is derived from the fact that the probability of citizens noticing a particular effect is related to its magnitude, its timing, the proximity of other people who are similarly affected, and the availability of an instigator. All four factors are known or knowable (at least in a probabilistic sense) when a policy is first adopted. The acquisition of preferences is also affected by a host of exogenous events that are inherently unpredictable in a model like this one.

Sometimes a single event can provide the stimulus for change. Many residents of Tennessee who favored the Endangered Species Act when it was first passed in 1973 modified their views in 1978 when the Supreme Court prohibited the opening of the $131 million Tellico Dam on the Little Tennessee River because it would threaten the habitat of the snail darter.[24] Suddenly, the group and geographic costs seemed enormous, while the general benefits appeared insignificant. Certainly no one would have predicted in 1973 that Tennesseeans would lead the opposition to the Endangered Species Act five years later. The tiny snail darter was still an unknown species at the time. Yet is was perfectly predictable that opposition to the act would involve those who found themselves bearing substantial group or geographic costs, not by those who were concerned about the act's general costs. Large, concentrated early-order

24. "Endangered Species Curbs," *Congressional Quarterly Almanac, 1978* 34 (1979): 707–708.

effects offer some of the finest stimuli for changing people's minds. The initial opposition to the antiballistic missile system in 1969 was unrelated to issues of nuclear strategy. Opponents emerged first in Libertyville, Illinois, where the missiles were scheduled for deployment.[25] A decade later Utah became the center of opposition to the MX missile system for the same reason.

The availability of an instigator does not guarantee that citizens' preferences will change. An instigator needs opportunity as well as motive. For many years most citizens had no opinions at all about American sugar policy (which imposed restrictive quotas on low-cost foreign sugar), and it would be hard to imagine how any instigator could make ordinary citizens interested in the subject. Sugar was cheap, and sugar policy was one of the great nonissues. When the retail price of sugar suddenly tripled in 1974 and the existence of quotas was front-page news, many people did acquire preferences about quotas. It was relatively easy for the opponents of quotas to use these events to stimulate policy preferences against quotas because the effects were relatively large: American prices were higher than world prices and quotas were the likely culprit. When prices went down again, people's preferences faded; today few citizens know anything about American sugar policy.[26]

These simple precepts about how policy attributes affect policy preferences may or may not help to explain the dynamics of public opinion in the United States. My sense is that they do, but I leave it to specialists in public opinion to establish whether my sense corresponds with reality. My argument is that legislators employ these precepts (at least intuitively) to estimate citizens' preferences and potential preferences for a host of new and emerging policy issues. The proper test of whether I have captured the way legislators estimate the dynamics of public opinion is the degree to which these simple rules help to explain legislators' actions in Washington.

25. Roger W. Cobb and Charles D. Elder, *Participation in American Politics: The Dynamics of Agenda-Building* (Baltimore: Johns Hopkins University Press, 1972), pp. 71–77.

26. See Chapter 6 for a discussion of the politics of sugar.

3

Policy Preferences and Congressional Elections

Legislators need more than a map of citizens' preferences and potential preferences for the various policy proposals put forth in Congress. They need to know the conditions under which citizens might incorporate policy preferences into their decisions in subsequent congressional elections. What legislators fear is not merely that citizens might disagree with their positions and actions but that such disagreements might affect voters' choices. To assess accurately the likelihood of electoral retribution, legislators need to understand the ways in which policy preferences can affect citizens' electoral decisions.

If legislators consulted the scholarly literature on congressional elections, they might conclude that they need not worry much about either the positions that they take or the effects that they produce because these are not the major determinants of electoral outcomes. This would be a dangerous conclusion. It would be equivalent to concluding that one need not file a tax return because the Internal Revenue Service prosecutes only a few thousand individuals each year for tax evasion. The problem is that legislators as a group have not offered congressional scholars much variance to analyze. No legislators have offered to take positions directly opposite to their electoral interests so that we may measure the full impact of positions on electoral margins. None have acknowledged selecting their positions by flipping a coin. Legislators as a group have been quite uncooperative in providing scholars with the kind of evidence we would need to assess the potential importance of issues in congressional elections.

The case for believing that issues are potentially important is nevertheless strong. The strongest evidence is that legislators believe that issues matter and that they act in accordance with this belief. They devote two of their scarcest resources—their own time and that of their staffs—to gathering and analyzing information that helps them avoid positions and actions that are politically risky. Since legislators are not a frivolous lot given to squandering their scarce resources, it seems reasonable to believe that they know what they are doing when they work diligently to identify safe positions.

The acknowledged importance of issues in presidential elections provides additional support for their potential importance in congressional elections.[1] After all, most of the voters in presidential and congressional elections are the very same citizens.[2] The skills and cognitive abilities required for analyzing issues in presidential contests are essentially the same as those required for lesser contests. The more one finds evidence that issues matter in presidential elections, the more one must accept the possibility that, under the proper conditions, issues could become equally important in congressional elections.

This conclusion might be unwarranted if voters in congressional elections knew little about the candidates and simply voted blindly on the basis of party. Although this was once a reasonable view of congressional elections, it no longer fits the facts.[3] In some recent years nearly a quarter of all voters who identified with one of the major parties voted for the opposite party's candidates in elections to the House.[4] Moreover, defections in congressional elections are not simply a consequence of partisan defections in presidential elections. Presidential and congressional elections are increasingly independent of each other. In 1972 and 1984, for example, 44 percent of all House districts delivered split verdicts—supporting the presidential candidate of one party and the

1. V. O. Key, Jr., *The Responsible Electorate* (Cambridge: Harvard University Press, 1966); Benjamin I. Page, *Choices and Echoes in Presidential Elections* (Chicago: University of Chicago Press, 1978); Morris P. Fiorina, *Retrospective Voting in American National Elections* (New Haven: Yale University Press, 1981); and Stanley Kelley, Jr., *Interpreting Elections* (Princeton: Princeton University Press, 1983).

2. Raymond E. Wolfinger, Steven J. Rosenstone, and Richard A. McIntosh, "Presidential and Congressional Voters Compared," *American Politics Quarterly* 9 (1981): 245–255.

3. On the importance of party in congressional elections during the 1950s, see Donald E. Stokes and Warren E. Miller, "Party Government and the Saliency of Congress," in Angus Campbell et al., *Elections and the Political Order* (New York: Wiley, 1966), pp. 194–211.

4. Gary C. Jacobson, *The Politics of Congressional Elections*, 2d ed. (Boston: Little, Brown, 1987), p. 107.

House candidate of the other.[5] The notion that congressional elections are dominated by either party or presidential coattails is no longer supportable.[6]

It is similarly untrue that congressional elections are low-information events in which voters have little contact with the candidates and little basis for independent judgment. Consider, for example, the results of a survey of citizens who voted in House elections in 1984. Ninety-one percent recognized the name of their incumbent representative, 74 percent recalled receiving mail from him, 69 percent remembered reading about him in the newspaper, 55 percent recalled seeing him on television, 18 percent claimed to have seen him at a meeting, and 20 percent claimed that they had met their representative personally.[7] This is an extraordinary amount of contact. To be sure, much of the information derived from these contacts is devoid of issue content. Yet it is easy to imagine how the issue content could increase dramatically. If legislators were careless in how they voted, they might find that journalists would cover their actions more extensively than before and that the increased coverage would focus on the issues. They might also discover that their constituents were showing up at their district meetings in greater numbers than ever before and that they, too, wanted to talk about the issues.

Knowing that issues are potentially important in congressional elections does not tell legislators how to adjust their behavior in Washington in order to minimize the electoral risks at home. If they wish to accomplish this feat, they need to understand the ways in which issues can affect congressional elections. Do citizens care more about the positions legislators take or about the effects that Congress produces? Are legislators judged as individuals or as members of party teams? Should legislators respond to the known preferences of a small minority or to the

5. These are the two peak years for split verdicts. Over the last six presidential elections (1964 to 1984), an average of 36 percent of all House districts delivered split verdicts. Ibid., pp. 150–151.

6. On the decline of presidential coattails, see Randall L. Calvert and John A. Ferejohn, "Coattail Voting in Recent Presidential Elections," *American Political Science Review* 77 (1983): 407–419.

7. Voters have far less contact with challengers than they do with incumbents. In 1984 only 54 percent recognized the name of the challenger, 25 percent recalled receiving mail, 38 percent remembered something in the newspaper, 29 percent recalled something on television, 3 percent saw him at a meeting, and 5 percent claimed they had met the challenger personally. Ibid., pp. 111, 116.

potential preferences of a large majority? Under what conditions will citizens notice a legislator's positions and actions? Under what conditions will citizens alter their opinions of an incumbent legislator?

There are at least four separate paths by which judgments about policy can influence citizens' choices in congressional elections. Voters may decide how to vote on the basis of either policy positions or policy effects, and they may connect their policy evaluations either to the candidate directly or to the party first and only indirectly to the candidate. *Policy positions* refer to opinions about the desirability of specific policy instruments, whether proposed, under consideration, or already passed and implemented. They arise as a consequence of prospective evaluation of the desirability of the consequences that would follow from that policy. *Policy effects* refer to conditions in society that are somehow attributable to governmental action or inaction. Here one begins with actual policy outcomes, effects, or conditions and searches retrospectively for someone to reward or punish.[8]

Table 3.1 summarizes the four basic decision rules available to citizens. The first two are prospective rules; the other two are retrospective. The *party position rule* states that a citizen first chooses a favorite party on the basis of the parties' positions and then selects the candidate who wears the label of the favored party. The *candidate position rule* states that a citizen chooses between the candidates by comparing their positions on the issues. The *party performance rule* states that a citizen first decides whether the party in power deserves to be rewarded or punished for the effects that it has produced and then selects the legislative candidate of the favored party. Finally, the *incumbent performance rule* states that a citizen chooses between the candidates by deciding whether the incumbent legislator deserves to be rewarded or punished for his connection with various pleasing or displeasing effects.[9]

---

8. On the distinction between retrospective and prospective evaluation, see Chapter 2. For a discussion of retrospective and prospective voting, see Fiorina, *Retrospective Voting in American National Elections*, pp. 3–19.

9. Citizens in the real world can also combine elements from these four decision rules (for example, they may use some information for past policy effects to form expectations about future policies). Although it might make sense to create a single decision rule that simply incorporates the information processing implicit in the four separate rules, that approach would not further my own theoretical ends. The principal difference between citizens basing their choices on policy effects rather than policy positions is that the former are much more tangible. For example, legislators saw a significant political difference between taking a position in favor of deregulating natural gas in principle and actually deregulating natural gas and watching their constituents' heating bills triple (see Chapter 9).

Table 3.1. Alternative decision rules for citizens in congressional elections

Object of choice	Basis of choice	
	Policy positions	Policy effects
Parties	Party position rule	Party performance rule
Candidates	Candidate position rule	Incumbent performance rule

THE PARTY PERFORMANCE RULE

The two retrospective voting rules—the party performance rule and the incumbent performance rule—allow citizens to monitor the performance of government and to reward or punish those responsible for its performance. The simplest of the two is the party performance rule. This rule requires that a citizen first evaluate current conditions in society, decide how acceptable those conditions are, and then either reward or punish the governing party by supporting or opposing its legislative candidates.

To use the party performance rule a citizen needs to know only two pieces of information: (1) whether conditions in society are improving or deteriorating and (2) which party controls the government. The first piece of information is readily available, especially given that citizens are free to monitor whatever conditions they choose. Those who care about the general course of the economy, foreign affairs, or ethical standards in government find that television, newspapers, and magazines are full of clues about the status of each. Those who care about narrower matters, such as the price of tobacco or the general health of the auto industry, acquire the appropriate information effortlessly if they happen to be tobacco farmers or auto workers.

Knowing which party controls the government is more problematic, especially when no single party does control the House, Senate, and White House. Split control has actually been more common than unified control for several decades now, so the problem is a recurrent one. Between 1953 and 1989 the three institutions were controlled by the same party for only 14 out of 36 years. During six of these years (1981–1987) the Congress itself was split, with the Democrats organizing the House and the Republicans organizing the Senate. So which party should citizens reward or punish? If the question is posed in normative terms, there is no clear answer.[10] If the question is posed in empirical terms—Which party *do* citizens reward or punish?—the answer is clear. When citizens use the party performance rule, whether in presidential or congressional elections, they reward and punish the party that controls the presidency.[11] Perhaps this decision reflects ignorance about the existence of split control.[12] Perhaps it reflects a greater appreciation of the ability of presidents to effect change. Such distinctions are not critical to the general point: most citizens who believe in rewarding and punishing the governing party act as if the governing party were the president's party.

V. O. Key was the first to show that citizens employ something like the party performance rule.[13] He also defended the rule on normative grounds, arguing that it was an excellent mechanism by which citizens could hold government accountable for its actions.[14] Of all four decision rules for incorporating issues into congressional elections, the party performance rule requires the least information and analysis on the part

10. Perhaps the most defensible answer is that citizens should reward and punish the president's party in presidential elections, the party that controls the Senate in senate elections, and the party that controls the House in elections to that body. Such a decision rule might help to ensure that each institution acted responsibly, although it would still do little to command coordination among the three institutions. Alternatively, citizens might vote in ways designed to bring all three institutions under the same party's control, so that in the future split control would not thwart the incentives for accountable government that are inherent in the party performance model.

11. See any of the following works that concern the impact of economic conditions on electoral outcomes.

12. This was certainly the case in 1958, when Republicans controlled the White House and Democrats controlled the Congress. About a fifth of all voters confessed they did not know which party controlled Congress and another fifth thought that the Republicans were in control. See Stokes and Miller, "Party Government and the Saliency of Congress," pp. 199–200. In 1982, when Republicans controlled both the White House and the Senate while Democrats controlled the House, voters were even more confused. Of those who were asked which party controlled the House, 40 percent admitted they did not know, 32 percent thought the Democrats did, and 28 percent thought the Republicans did. Of those asked about the Senate, 50 percent did not know, 39 percent thought the Republicans were in control, and 11 percent thought the Democrats were. See NES/CPS, *American National Election Study, 1982* (Ann Arbor, Mich.: Center for Political Studies, 1983).

13. V. O. Key, Jr., *Public Opinion and American Democracy* (New York: Knopf, 1961), pp. 472–480; and Key, *Responsible Electorate.*

14. Key, *Public Opinion and American Democracy*; and Key, *Responsible Electorate.* See also Page, *Choices and Echoes in Presidential Elections*, pp. 220–223, and Fiorina, *Retrospective Voting in American National Elections*, pp. 193–211.

of citizens and demands the most in performance on the part of legislators. Citizens need never evaluate policy instruments to determine
which is the best at producing pleasing outcomes. They need know
nothing about what the in-party has been doing in office, what it proposes to do in the future, or whether it is in any way responsible for
current conditions. They need never learn anything about the legislative candidates. Citizens can relax between elections, take care of their
own affairs, and leave the details of government to elected officials. Then
on election day they need only decide whether they are happy with
conditions in society and whether they believe the governing party deserves to stay in office. Elected officials, on the other hand, have every
incentive to anticipate citizens' needs, to devise and enact efficient and
effective programs for fulfilling those needs and to produce pleasing
outcomes by election day. Their very jobs depend on it.

The evidence is fairly strong that at least some citizens use something
like the party performance rule in congressional elections. At first scholars thought they had found compelling evidence in support of this rule.
The earliest studies of the impact of economic conditions on congressional elections demonstrated that congressional candidates of the president's party suffered during times of inflation, stagnation, or recession
and profited when the economy was healthy.[15] These aggregate results
are now known to be partly the consequence of strategic behavior by
politicians. The party that is favored by economic conditions has an
easier time recruiting experienced and talented candidates and obtaining adequate campaign funds, while the opposite party finds that
both talented candidates and financial contributors prefer to wait for a
more favorable season.[16] Even so, evidence from survey research still
shows that some citizens incorporate their own assessments of the performance of the economy into their decisions in congressional elections.[17] Whether they also incorporate assessments of other types of
conditions is not presently known.[18]

15. See Gerald H. Kramer, "Short-Term Fluctuations in U.S. Voting Behavior, 1896–
1964," *American Political Science Review* 65 (1971): 131–143; and Edward R. Tufte,
Political Control of the Economy (Princeton: Princeton University Press, 1978).

16. Gary C. Jacobson and Samuel Kernell, *Strategy and Choice in Congressional Elections* (New Haven: Yale University Press, 1981), pp. 19–59.

17. D. Roderick Kiewiet, *Macroeconomics and Micropolitics* (Chicago: University of
Chicago Press, 1983), pp. 127–129; and Fiorina, *Retrospective Voting in American National Elections*, pp. 165, 173, 206.

18. The problem is that survey researchers have not asked the appropriate questions.

THE INCUMBENT PERFORMANCE RULE

The incumbent performance rule provides citizens with an alternative approach for monitoring the performance of government and for rewarding or punishing those responsible for its performance. The incumbent performance rule requires that voters first evaluate current conditions in society, decide how acceptable those conditions are, and then either reward or punish incumbent legislators for actions that they think contributed to the current state of affairs. In structure this rule is very similar to the party performance model. The only difference is that citizens hold legislators accountable for their own individual actions rather than for their affiliation with the governing party.

But what a difference this shift in focus makes! It is perfectly reasonable for citizens to hold the in-party accountable for conditions without knowing exactly how it contributed to those conditions. Parties are supposed to act as teams, so if the results are displeasing it makes sense to send in a new team. Without parties, however, this form of accountability makes little sense. Few citizens are likely to punish their own representative without knowing something about how he or she contributed to the current state of affairs.[19] After all, the incumbent might be the one bright and shining knight who is battling against a horde of incompetent and irresponsible legislators.[20] Even if that is not the case, each legislator is only one of 535 elected representatives who together share the responsibility for policy outcomes.

When the objects are individual legislators, then, citizens must know something about the policy-making process. The question for each voter is whether the representative up for reelection is somehow responsible for the current state of affairs. An appraisal could occur something like this. A citizen notices that some condition that matters to him is either deteriorating or improving. He searches for governmental responsibility, asking how the federal government contributed to the changed conditions. He then searches for the contribution of his own representative to that governmental action. Finally he rewards or punishes his representative. The accountability here is for specific actions or inactions by

19. Certainly there is no evidence that incumbents as a group suffer when economic conditions deteriorate. Such suffering is reserved for incumbents of the president's party.

20. This is certainly the image that most House members peddle. See Richard F. Fenno, Jr., *Home Style: House Members in Their Districts* (Boston: Little, Brown, 1978), pp. 162–168.

one's representative, rather than for mere association with the party in power.

Although the informational needs are considerably greater for the incumbent performance rule than they are for the party performance rule, they are still within the capacity of many citizens. Under the proper conditions it is easy to imagine almost any citizen acquiring the necessary information and reacting appropriately. Consider, for example, how a struggling single mother might respond when she discovers that her three children no longer qualify for subsidized school lunches. Knowing that her own financial circumstances have not changed much, she will probably be prepared to blame others for the increased burden placed upon her. School officials will quickly deflect criticism by noting that it was Congress that voted to tighten eligibility standards. Someone— perhaps an enterprising journalist, a PTA leader, or a potential challenger—will scrutinize the local representative's voting record to see if he supported the change. If he did, others will help disseminate the message until our struggling mother and others like her know whom to blame. In the short term, she feels less kindly to the incumbent, and perhaps quite hostile. Over time she may forget the reason for her negative opinion, but the opinion may persist independently of the reason. Alternatively, the issue may be raised in the campaign itself and, thus, enter her voting calculus more directly.

How frequently citizens employ something like the incumbent performance rule is not known. To my knowledge, there are no studies that systematically explore the connection between policy outcomes and legislators' electoral margins. There is circumstantial evidence, however, that several leaders in Congress have been punished for effects that were traceable to their own actions. Senator Warren Magnuson (D., Wash.) met his match in 1980 when his opponent, Slade Gorton, charged that he was personally responsible for inflation because of the bloated spending bills he had championed as chairman of the Senate Appropriations Committee. Gorton defeated Magnuson, 54 percent to 46 percent.[21] Representative Al Ullman (D., Ore.) met a similar fate after he had championed a value-added tax as the solution to the federal deficit. Perhaps if Ullman had just been an ordinary congrooomen his constituents would have forgiven him for this lapse; but, as chairman of the House Ways and Means Committee, he was thought to be in an

21. "The 1980 Elections: Washington," *Congressional Quarterly Weekly Report* 38 (October 11, 1980): 3080.

especially good position to enact such a tax. A fellow Democrat nearly defeated him in the 1980 primary on the basis of this one issue; a Republican then delivered the fatal blow in the general election.[22] Representative Timothy Wirth (D., Colo.) watched his winning margin slip from 62 percent in 1982 to 53 percent in 1984, after his challenger exploited consumer frustration with the breakup of AT&T. As chairman of the Telecommunications Subcommittee of the Energy and Commerce Committee, Wirth had been one of the leading advocates of competition in the telephone industry. Apparently many of his constituents were less than pleased with the consequences of deregulation.[23]

Even though it is easy to show instances in which citizens seemed to employ something like the incumbent performance rule, the exact frequency of its use is not the issue. My intent is to show how legislators' fear of this form of retrospective voting affects their behavior in Washington, not to establish how frequently they miscalculate citizens' preferences or potential preferences, nor how frequently their miscalculations lead to diminished electoral margins.[24] What is relevant is how frequently legislators stop to calculate whether their actions in Congress might stimulate citizens to reward or punish them at the polls. For that task we first need a fuller understanding of the conditions under which the incumbent performance rule operates.

The incumbent performance rule requires that citizens have some knowledge of the causal chains that link policy instruments with policy effects and some knowledge of the policy-making process itself. A citizen

22. Christopher Buchanan, "VAT Plan Weakens Ullman," *Congressional Quarterly Weekly Report* 38 (May 24, 1980): 1440; and Christopher Buchanan, "Republicans Make Substantial House Gains," *Congressional Quarterly Weekly Report* 38 (November 8, 1980): 3320.

23. Deregulation itself was the consequence of an agreement between the Department of Justice and AT&T; Wirth's bill played no direct role. This distinction did not seem to make much difference in Colorado, for Wirth's bill would have had very similar effects. See "Congressional Outlook: Colorado," *Congressional Quarterly Weekly Report* 44 (February 22, 1986): 353; and Alan Ehrenhalt (ed.), *Politics in America, 1986* (Washington, D.C.: Congressional Quarterly, 1985), pp. 242–243.

24. I should state for the record that I do not expect that citizens employ the incumbent performance rule with much frequency. Those who specialize in congressional elections can probably continue to explain such elections by ignoring its existence. I do maintain that many citizens are perfectly capable of employing such a rule if a legislator becomes careless. That citizens do not resort to its frequent use is partly a tribute to legislators' talent for keeping away from serious electoral danger and partly a consequence of the special conditions that must hold for this form of retrospective voting to occur.

Figure 3.1. Simple model of policy making for the incumbent performance rule

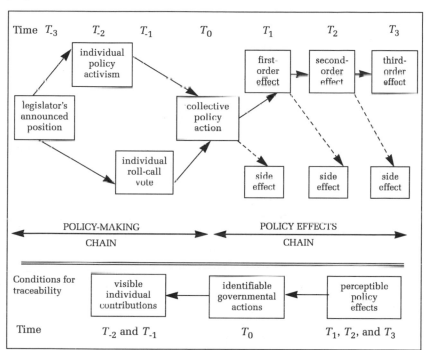

begins by noticing that some condition is either deteriorating or improving. Knowledge of the causal chains that link policy instruments with policy effects allows her to search for a governmental action that may have produced or influenced this condition. Having identified the alleged governmental cause, she then searches through the policy-making record to determine whether her own representative contributed to the governmental action.

I shall call an effect *traceable* if a citizen can plausibly trace an observed effect first back to a governmental action and then back to a representative's individual contribution (see Figure 3.1). I shall argue that traceability requires the existence of three conditions: a perceptible effect, an identifiable governmental action, and a legislator's visible contribution. If all three conditions hold, the prospects for citizens using the incumbent performance rule are good. Lacking even one of the conditions for traceability, this form of retrospective voting becomes virtually impossible.

Perceptible effects are conditions that a citizen notices on his own and that either stimulate a search for explanations or create an interest in explanations offered by others. Perceptible effects include 10 percent inflation, losing one's job, paying a new tax, or having one's student loan terminated. Imperceptible effects include paying a penny more for milk, marginal changes in air quality, or a small increase in auto prices to pay for a new safety feature. Many imperceptible effects may add up to equal one very large effect, but as long as these effects are delivered in small packages they usually remain imperceptible. Governmental regulation of agriculture, for example, is said to increase slightly the cost of everything we eat; yet we pay these costs a few pennies at a time and, thus, never notice them. Perceptible effects are the stimuli for this form of retrospective voting, for they activate the entire search process.

Identifiable governmental actions are the specific deeds that citizens believe caused the perceptible effects. Such actions include both laws enacted by Congress and presidential, bureaucratic, or judicial decisions. The causal connections between governmental actions and policy effects must be plausible, not necessarily established as fact. Traceability depends on what people believe caused the effects, not on what forces actually produced them.[25] Identifiable governmental actions must be specific decisions—passing or rejecting a law, adding or deleting an amendment, funding or terminating a program. Items that never made the congressional agenda and items that are never explicitly rejected (nondecisions) do not meet this test. Effects that are the result of multiple governmental decisions also fail this test. General economic conditions, for example, cannot ordinarily be traced to any single governmental action, because things like inflation and unemployment are the products of many different actions.

Visible individual contributions are the specific deeds that a representative performed to promote or impede some identifiable governmental action. Roll-call votes are the most common, visible, and unambiguous type of contribution. All forms of policy activism also belong in this class, although no straightforward indicators of activism exist as they do for roll-call votes. The search is for what a single representative

25. Traceability is a subjective process, depending as it does on what citizens believe about cause and effect. This subjective process is also related, though imperfectly, to the objective relationships between cause and effect. Although I have not attempted to identify all the conditions that affect citizens' beliefs, the correlation between these beliefs and objective reality is surely higher for short and simple causal chains than for long and complex chains.

has done, not merely what Congress has accomplished. If Congress passes an amendment by voice vote, the individual contributions are invisible. If Congress delegates broad authority to the bureaucracy, the president, or the courts, the decisions may be identifiable but legislators' individual contributions remain invisible.

The incumbent performance rule depends on the existence of all three conditions. Without perceptible effects there is nothing to activate the search process. Lacking an identifiable governmental action, there is nothing to suggest whether or not government is at fault, and if so whether Congress contributed to the effects or worked to forestall them. In the absence of visible individual contributions, one cannot know whether a particular representative should be praised or blamed.

We need not imagine each citizen spending hours in the local library attempting to construct traceability chains for various policy effects. Surely that view is contrary to everything we know about the incentives for citizens to acquire information about public affairs.[26] Fortunately, no elaborate search procedures are required, for many others are eager to do the research and share their findings with citizens.

Challengers are perhaps the most diligent players in this game. Few challengers fail to sift through incumbents' records in search of the smoking gun. They then employ their newly discovered evidence to persuade citizens how poorly their current representatives have served their interests. Citizens who are upset about the closing of the local steel mill learn that their representative opposed legislation specifying domestic auto content that might have saved it. Retirees who must pay taxes on part of their Social Security earnings discover that their congressman was the leading advocate of the proposal. Farmers who watch grain prices plummet are reminded that their representative was the first to urge President Carter to impose an embargo on grain exports after the Soviet Union invaded Afghanistan.

Others play the game too. Groups that suffer major costs under a particular governmental policy help to spread the word about how the incumbent contributed to their plight. Similarly, those who reap substantial group or geographic benefits may work to guarantee that all beneficiaries know whom to reward. More disinterested parties such as the media often help citizens to see the connections between legislators' deeds, governmental actions, and policy effects. They may do so either at

26. Anthony Downs, *An Economic Theory of Democracy* (New York: Harper and Row, 1957), pp. 207–276.

the time a policy is adopted or in the midst of electoral campaigns. Many newspapers, for example, like to give reasons for their political endorsements, so they list all the wonderful or dreadful conditions for which the incumbent should be held responsible.

Incumbents do not stand by idly, waiting for the axe to fall. They try to take credit for positive outcomes[27] and to explain away alleged connections between their actions in Washington and adverse conditions at home.[28]

Traceability is not equally likely for all types of policy effects. In general, citizens can trace early-order effects to their initial governmental causes more easily than they can trace later-order effects. Consider how readily American farmers connect their own financial condition to governmental actions on price supports, grain embargoes, and disaster assistance. The connection is clear, direct, and simple. The government acts, and farmers either prosper or suffer in a perfectly predictable way.[29] Contrast this case with the plight of home builders. Their fate is equally affected by governmental policy, but through a longer and more indirect causal chain. The chain runs from the myriad governmental actions that shape monetary and fiscal policy, to the general rate of inflation, to interest rates, to the ability of families to buy homes, to the fate of home builders across the land. Home builders know that governmental actions affect their well-being, but few can trace their fate back to any identifiable governmental action.

The problem is not just one of later-order effects. Traceability is nearly impossible for any effects that stem from a multitude of complex governmental actions. General rates of inflation, unemployment, crime, and the like are the consequences of thousands of governmental (and nongovernmental) actions. No matter how much citizens may wish to punish their representatives for deterioration in these conditions, the lack of any single, identifiable cause is an obstacle to doing so. One may attempt to overcome this obstacle by focusing on a string of votes on related actions. Those who believe that excessive governmental spend-

27. On credit claiming, see David R. Mayhew, *Congress: The Electoral Connection* (New Haven: Yale University Press, 1974), pp. 52–61.

28. On explaining, see John W. Kingdon, *Congressmen's Voting Decisions*, 2d ed. (New York: Harper and Row, 1981), pp. 47–54; and Fenno, *Home Style*, pp. 141–146.

29. The evidence is also clear that a larger proportion of farmers vote than do any other occupational group, presumably because their financial health depends so directly on government. See Raymond E. Wolfinger and Steven J. Rosenstone, *Who Votes?* (New Haven: Yale University Press, 1980), pp. 30–34.

ing is the root cause of economic stagnation, for example, simply count how frequently a legislator voted to increase spending. Or they may focus on a single action that could have had relatively large effects—for example, a president's economic recovery program.

Citizens are far more likely to pursue traceability chains when they incur perceptible costs than when they reap an equal measure of benefits. Part of the reason is that costs produce more intense preferences than do benefits (see Chapter 2). In addition, costs inspire people to search for someone to blame, whereas benefits are usually enjoyed without a corresponding effort to discover whom to reward.[30] Large and perceptible costs, then, are the principal stimuli for voting by the incumbent performance rule.

Finally, retrospective voting works well for effects that are traceable to governmental action, but only rarely for those that stem from inaction. Isolating the individual contributions to congressional action is relatively straightforward, especially now that recorded votes are the norm throughout the congressional process. Inaction, on the other hand, leaves few footprints. Who, for example, might one blame for the lack of national health insurance? No proposal has ever emerged from subcommittee, so no legislator has ever voted for or against it. Inaction is traceable only if Congress explicitly decides to do nothing, by rejecting a bill, a program, or an amendment. The one exception involves congressional leaders who, much like presidents, are in a better position than ordinary legislators to produce action. The chairman of the Ways and Means Committee cannot pretend to be blameless if Congress never acts on tax reform, national health insurance, or import quotas, unless the record is clear that he has battled fiercely against very long odds.

THE PARTY POSITION RULE

The two prospective voting rules—the party position rule and the candidate position rule—require that citizens acquire and process substantially more information than does the party performance

---

30. Politicians apparently calculate in a similar fashion. Kingdon discovered that winning candidates in Wisconsin tended to believe that their own efforts were the decisive elements in victory, while losers settled on factors beyond their control, such as party identification, to explain their defeats. See John W. Kingdon, *Candidates for Office: Beliefs and Strategies* (New York: Random House, 1968), pp. 22–34.

rule. Citizens need to know both where the parties (or candidates) stand on the issues and what the consequences would be if particular policies were enacted. The two prospective voting rules are similar to the incumbent performance rule in that they all require citizens to have some understanding of the causes of policy effects. They differ in that citizens need not know anything about the policy-making process, as they must for the incumbent performance rule.

The party position rule requires that a citizen first identify the party that offers the most pleasing package of policy positions and then support the legislative candidate wearing that label.[31] Parties establish and display their positions in various ways. Every four years the national parties draft elaborate party platforms that set forth their positions on broad national issues as well as on issues of concern to various groups in society.[32] Parties also display their alternative plans for the future by the collective actions of their members when they are in office. One would hardly have to consult party platforms to conclude in the 1960s that the Democrats were more likely to push for civil rights laws or to predict in the early 1980s that the Republicans were more likely to cut taxes. One could simply observe both the rhetoric and the actions of the Democrats and Republicans who were already in office.[33]

Most citizens do not know the details of the parties' platforms, so the notion that citizens are choosing among detailed blueprints for the future is clearly false. Yet many citizens do see clear and persistent policy-related differences between the parties. Observing such differences is relatively easy because the parties do not change their spots overnight.

31. The normative version of this model, which passes under the name of the doctrine of responsible party government, requires that parties offer detailed and specific platforms, both so that voters may choose on the basis of these platforms and so that the winning party will have a detailed agenda for action—an agenda approved by the voters themselves. See Austin Ranney, *The Doctrine of Responsible Party Government* (Urbana: University of Illinois Press, 1954); and Stokes and Miller, "Party Government and the Saliency of Congress."

32. On party platforms, see Gerald M. Pomper and Susan S. Lederman, *Elections in America*, 2d ed. (New York: Longman, 1980), pp. 128–178.

33. These examples also show how elements of one decision rule (party performance rule) can affect choices made with the other (party position rule). My insistence on analyzing these four decision rules separately has more to do with my attempt to isolate how legislators' own calculations differ depending on whether they are dealing with positions alone or positions that can be connected to real effects than it does with any belief that citizens actually choose by using a single decision rule, uncontaminated by knowledge from another.

For more than half a century many people have viewed the Democrats as champions of labor, farmers, minorities, city dwellers, and the poor while seeing Republicans as creatures of big business and the rich. Although these people may not know from year to year exactly what each party proposes to do, they can be reasonably certain that the Democrats are more sympathetic to providing direct assistance for these five groups than are the Republicans. The parties can (and do) change their positions over time, and citizens' perceptions change too. The Republican party, which had the more secure reputation for favoring civil rights from the time of Reconstruction to the 1930s, lost that reputation when Democrats began to do something about the treatment of black citizens. Blacks noticed the difference and gradually switched their party allegiance.[34]

Do citizens employ something like the party position rule in congressional elections? At least on the surface it appears that they do. Most voters (over 90 percent) either identify with or lean toward one of the parties, and most of these voters (over 75 percent) support the congressional candidates of the party that they favor.[35] Whether this provides support for the party position rule depends on how one interprets the notion of party identification.[36] If one interprets party identification as some sort of fundamental belief, inherited from one's parents and completely unrelated to the issues of the day, then it clearly does not. Under this interpretation party preference is not a considered choice but rather an inherited trait. If party identification is a considered choice, one that changes in response to the emergence of new issues or that changes when the parties switch positions, then the correlation between party preference and voting in congressional elections provides powerful support for the party position rule. The truth is somewhere in between. For

34. Blacks identifying with the Democratic party increased from perhaps 10 or 20 percent in 1930, to 44 percent in 1937, 61 percent in 1952, and 85 percent in 1976. See Everett C. Ladd, Jr., *Transformations of the American Party System*, 2d ed. (New York: Norton, 1978), pp. 57–60; and Warren E. Miller, Arthur H. Miller, and Edward J. Schneider, *American National Election Studies Data Sourcebook, 1952–1978* (Cambridge: Harvard University Press, 1980), p. 89.

35. In the ten elections to the House of Representatives from 1966 to 1984, 92 percent of all voters identified with or leaned toward one of the major parties. Of these partisan voters, 82 percent supported their own party's candidates in the first five elections, and 78 percent did so in the last five elections. Data recomputed from Jacobson, *Politics of Congressional Elections*, p. 107.

36. For a discussion of alternative views of party identification, see Fiorina, *Retrospective Voting in American National Elections*, pp. 84–102.

some citizens, party identification is probably close to being an inherited trait. For many others, party affiliation more closely resembles a current assessment of the parties, an assessment that is not only subject to change but that does change.[37]

THE CANDIDATE POSITION RULE

The candidate position rule requires that a citizen decide which candidate to support by comparing the candidates' positions on the issues and then choosing the candidate with the most pleasing package of positions. Perhaps in an ideal world citizens would know and compare the candidates' positions on a long list of issues facing the country. The rule itself requires no such knowledge. A citizen can actually make informed choices with a minimum of knowledge.

Most scholars seem to assume, implicitly or explicitly, that a citizen must know the positions of both (or all) candidates in order to select the one with the most compatible package of positions.[38] In fact, citizens can make satisfactory issue-based choices even if they know only one of the candidates' positions. A citizen who finds that one candidate's positions are basically compatible with his own can "satisfice" by supporting that candidate.[39] Searching further in hopes that the other candidate is even closer to his most preferred positions may be a waste of effort, especially given the small stakes. Similarly, a citizen who disagrees with most of the policy positions of one candidate might choose to support the other candidate without any additional search—the assumption being that the second candidate's positions cannot possibly be much worse and are probably far more agreeable. One can hardly fault a liberal from North Carolina for opposing Senator Jesse Helms (R., N.C.), whose conservative credentials are well known, simply because the citizen has not carefully investigated his opponent's positions. Citizens can minimize information costs and still make satisfactory (though perhaps not optimal) voting decisions.

---

37. Ibid.; and Page, *Choices and Echoes in Presidential Elections*, pp. 62–107.

38. Angus Campbell, Philip E. Converse, Warren E. Miller, and Donald E. Stokes, *The American Voter* (New York: Wiley, 1960), p. 170; and Michael Margolis, "From Confusion to Confusion: Issues and the American Voter (1956–1972)," *American Political Science Review* 71 (1977): 31–43.

39. The concept of satisficing (as opposed to maximizing) was introduced by Herbert A. Simon, "A Behavioral Model of Rational Choice," *Quarterly Journal of Economics* 69 (1955): 99–118.

Few citizens know the whole range of positions even for a single candidate. But why should they? Sampling is a highly effective oversight mechanism in any control relationship, and the case is particularly compelling for voters who individually have so little influence over outcomes.[40] A citizen who happens to know a candidate's positions on four or five issues and who finds them disagreeable may well conclude that the candidate is too. A citizen who knows both candidates' positions on two important issues and who finds the first candidate more agreeable on both counts has little reason to search for information on even more issues. Citizens do not sample candidates' positions in any scientific sense, but they probably do treat the fragments they see as representative of the whole.

Candidates display their policy positions to citizens in two ways: by their records in office and by the statements they choose to make in campaigns. Incumbents have no choice but to establish firm positions on issues that require roll-call votes. House members face between 400 and 600 roll-call votes each year, and even after discounting for procedural and other minor motions, they quickly establish a long list of recorded positions.[41] Challengers may or may not have previous records to defend, depending on what previous offices they may have held. Both incumbents and challengers can take additional positions in the course of campaigns. The ability to do so is particularly useful for challengers who seek to show how they are different from the incumbents they are trying to unseat.

Information on candidates' positions is readily available. Some incumbents work hard to publicize their own policy positions, or at least those that they think will help generate support.[42] Challengers work even harder to identify and expose any of an incumbent's past policy positions that might prove controversial. During the actual campaigns both incumbents and challengers may highlight the differences between their positions if they believe that doing so helps them either to persuade voters of their virtues or to mobilize those who are already committed. Interested parties and the media also unearth and publicize some of the candidates' stands.

Do citizens employ something like the candidate position rule when

40. On sampling as a method of control, see Robert A. Dahl and Charles E. Lindblom, *Politics, Economics, and Welfare* (New York: Harper and Row, 1953), pp. 69–71.

41. Norman J. Ornstein, Thomas E. Mann, and Michael J. Malbin, *Vital Statistics on Congress, 1987–1988* (Washington, D.C.: Congressional Quarterly, 1987), p. 168.

42. Others avoid issues as much as they can. See Fenno, *Home Style*, pp. 54–135.

they decide how to vote in congressional elections? Once again the evidence is difficult to interpret, although it is generally supportive. Consider first of all whether citizens possess the minimum information that is required for using the candidate position rule—some knowledge of at least one of the candidates' policy positions. According to the National Election Studies survey for the 1982 House elections, 57 percent of all voters were able to express general agreement or disagreement with their representative's votes in Congress, and 15 percent were able to express agreement or disagreement with his or her vote on a specific bill.[43] When voters were asked to mention the things they liked and disliked about the incumbent or the challenger in their district, they mentioned either ideology or policy positions about 18 percent of the time. References to ideology and policy made up 14 percent of the positive comments and 31 percent of the negative ones.[44] To be sure, voters know a great deal more about incumbents than they know about challengers, but the disparity is far less for references to ideology and policy. References related to the incumbent's ideology or policy outnumbered references to the challenger's ideology or policy by only 1.6 to 1, whereas references related to all other matters favored the incumbent by 3.2 to 1.[45] All of this evidence suggests that some voters do have the minimum information required for using the candidate position rule.

How much citizens' policy preferences actually affect their choices in congressional elections is more difficult to assess, in part because most voters are relatively satisfied with their representatives.[46] More variance would be helpful. One gains some perspective by examining the behavior of the small minority who are dissatisfied. Only 5 percent of all voters interviewed in 1982 expressed general disagreement with their representative's voting record, but of these, 96 percent voted against the incumbent. Only 7 percent of all voters disagreed with the incumbent's position on a specific bill, but of these, 61 percent voted against him or

43. Jacobson, *Politics of Congressional Elections*, p. 130.

44. These data are from the 1984 NES survey and are recomputed from ibid., p. 133.

45. Ibid.

46. The effects are easiest to see when legislators make serious miscalculations. For example, the Republican members of the House Judiciary Committee who supported the impeachment of President Nixon were rewarded at the polls in 1974, while those who supported the president suffered significant declines (some were even defeated). See Gerald C. Wright, "Constituency Response to Congressional Behavior: The Impact of the House Judiciary Committee Impeachment Vote," *Western Political Quarterly* 30 (1977): 401–410.

her.[47] The numbers may not be impressive, but the relationship between policy positions and electoral support is clear. A second vantage
point for observing this relationship is to look at what was distinctive
about those (admittedly few) elections where challengers defeated incumbents. Gary Jacobson shows that the voters in these districts were
far more likely to believe that the challenger would be better at handling
what they believed were the most important problems in society than
would be the incumbent, and voters were also more likely to feel closer
to the challenger in an ideological sense (both such comparisons ordinarily favor the incumbent).[48] It is clear that one of the reasons that
incumbents sometimes lose is that some challengers are able to make
campaign issues out of the incumbents' policy records.[49]

MAKING CHOICES

These four decision rules suggest the different ways in which
judgments about policy can affect citizens' choices in congressional
elections. In addition to these policy-related matters, a host of other
factors affect citizens' choices, including how well they know the candidates, how much they trust them, how satisfied they have been when
they have seen or communicated with one of the candidates, how accessible their representative seems to be, and how successful their representative appears to be in providing district services.[50] In fact for many
citizens, these latter factors may be far more important than the policy-
related factors.

How do citizens combine information from these various sources to
reach a decision? We know that most citizens do not follow congressional elections very closely, and they do not spend much time making
their electoral decisions. So how do inattentive citizens handle what
looks like an enormous analytic task? A simple model for processing

47. Data recomputed from Jacobson, *Politics of Congressional Elections*, p. 130.

48. Ibid., p. 135. See also the first edition (1983), pp. 116–117.

49. Evidence from Senate elections suggests that citizens are far more likely to vote on
the basis of issues when the candidates themselves differ significantly on the issues. Large
differences are easier to perceive and therefore are more likely to enter voters' calculations.
See Gerald C. Wright, Jr., and Michael B. Berkman, "Candidates and Policy in United
States Senate Elections," *American Political Science Review* 80 (1986): 567–588.

50. Bruce Cain, John Ferejohn, and Morris Fiorina, *The Personal Vote: Constituency
Service and Electoral Independence* (Cambridge: Harvard University Press, 1987).

information shows how citizens can handle the task with little effort. The key is to realize that citizens receive and process political information regularly, not merely in the campaign season. Once processed, citizens may forget most of the information. What remains, however, is a changed attitude toward either the parties or the candidates. Near election day they need only combine their separate attitudes toward each of the parties and each of the candidates in order to make their choices.

Imagine that a citizen maintains four accounts in some accessible portion of his brain, in which he stores one integer apiece to represent his current attitudes toward the two parties, the incumbent, and the challenger (if any). The two accounts for the parties receive their initial values sometime during childhood, when our future voter first learns to feel distinctively about each. Throughout life he is bombarded by information about the parties' positions and their accomplishments in office. Some of this information may persuade him to alter the value he assigns to each party, in a manner described by the party position and party performance rules. Whenever he first becomes aware of his incumbent representative, he opens a third account with an initial value that captures his assessment of her. New information about issues may alter this value in ways described by the candidate position and incumbent performance rules. Non-policy-related factors may also nudge the value one way or another. Finally, if he happens to learn anything about the challenger, he opens yet a fourth account. This value varies in accordance with the candidate position rule and with various other rules that describe the impact of non-policy-related factors. Whenever an election occurs a citizen merely retrieves the four values, combines them into a single net present value, and votes according to its sign.

How well this simple model captures the way citizens process information is unknown and perhaps unknowable, given that forgetting one's reasons is an integral part of it.[51] Yet it is consistent with the way people make scores of evaluations in daily life. Ask any regular moviegoer whether Bette Davis or Katharine Hepburn is the better

---

51. Recent experimental evidence supports this model of information processing. Using data from an ingenious experiment, Lodge, McGraw, and Stroh demonstrated that an impression-driven model, in which people evaluate information as they encounter it without ever storing the information, fits the evidence better than a memory-based model, in which voters store information as they encounter it and later retrieve and combine the information to reach a decision. See Milton Lodge, Kathleen M. McGraw, and Patrick Stroh, "An Impression-Driven Model of Candidate Evaluation," *American Political Science Review* 83 (1989): 399–419.

actress and you may well hear some strong opinions. Do we then expect our moviegoer to be able to recount all the reasons that contributed to this conclusion? Surely not. Such evaluations are derived from viewing dozens of movies, thousands of scenes, and millions of frames. We should be lucky if our moviegoer can name even half the movies that she has seen featuring these actresses.

The model of information processing is also consistent with recent work on parties and elections. Morris Fiorina conceives of party identification as a running tally of citizens' evaluations of issues, events, and conditions, and he shows how citizens incorporate new information by adjusting this tally.[52] Stanley Kelley offers a decision rule for presidential elections in which a voter first canvasses his likes and dislikes for candidates and parties and then combines these attitudes by simple addition to reach a decision. His evidence from eight recent presidential elections is entirely consistent with the notion that voters actually operate in this fashion.[53]

52. Fiorina, *Retrospective Voting in American National Elections*, pp. 84–105.

53. Kelley, *Interpreting Elections*, pp. 225–238. Kelley tests his decision rule for presidential elections by relying on what voters say they like and dislike about both the parties and candidates. My sense is that voters are less likely to recall a fair sample of their likes and dislikes about congressional candidates than they are for presidential candidates. For presidential elections the media help voters to review the reasons they like or dislike particular candidates and help to guarantee that those interviewed will recall some of their reasons. Most congressional elections are much less visible. Citizens' views of incumbents are often shaped over a span of years and get little reinforcement at all during the campaign season.

4

Electoral Calculations and Legislators' Decisions

How do legislators decide which side to support when a policy proposal comes before Congress? How do they estimate the impact that their decisions in Washington might have on their electoral margins at home? How do they adjust their decisions in Washington in order to maximize their electoral advantages? Now that we have some sense of how legislators estimate citizens' preferences and potential preferences, and now that we have several models that show how citizens' policy preferences can affect their choices in congressional elections, we can answer these questions directly.[1]

This chapter rests on the assumption that the quest for reelection is legislators' dominant goal (see Chapter 1). This assumption asserts that whenever legislators are asked to choose between two alternative policies they first ask which alternative would contribute more to their chances for reelection. If they see a significant difference, they choose the alternative that contributes more to their electoral margins. If they see no difference, they may base their choice on any other criteria they find relevant, including their intent to make good public policy and their need to trade favors with congressional leaders, other legislators, and the president.[2]

---

1. This entire chapter relies extensively on John W. Kingdon, *Congressmen's Voting Decisions*, 2d ed. (New York: Harper and Row, 1981). This is the best single work on roll-call voting; it shows how legislators think, whom they consult, and how they balance competing interests. Kingdon is especially interested in showing how various actors affect legislators' decisions, including constituents, colleagues, party leaders, and staff, whereas my framework focuses more on attributes of the policies themselves. I intend for the two approaches to be complementary, not competitive.

2. Legislators often face a string of votes on a complicated bill, including votes on

The question facing a legislator is seldom whether a specific roll-call vote might cost him the next election. Most legislators win elections by at least five to ten percentage points,[3] and few single issues could possibly diminish their winning margins by that much. Yet legislators are a cautious lot. Even though a legislator may have won his most recent election by a comfortable margin, most of them have had at least one close election,[4] and all of them can recall stories of "safe" congressmen who are no longer congressmen.[5] Cautious legislators take advantage of

procedural matters, substantive amendments, and final passage. Although legislators are asked at each stage to choose among paired alternatives, they can incorporate calculations about subsequent stages into their decisions about how to vote at earlier stages. For example, they might decide to vote strategically, choosing the less-preferred alternative at one stage because it would be more likely to lead to a better outcome at the final stage. In this book I make little allowance for strategic voting on substantive issues, because I am interested in showing how legislators adjust their individual roll-call decisions in anticipation of citizens' future actions. As long as citizens evaluate legislators by their individual votes, it makes sense for legislators to worry about their individual positions. Only when citizens are sophisticated enough to appreciate legislators' strategic votes do legislators have an electoral incentive to vote strategically. Although such cases do exist (especially for organized and attentive publics), I have chosen to keep the model as simple as possible by avoiding the problem of strategic voting on substantive issues. I do allow for strategic voting on procedural matters because the electoral constraints tend to be much smaller at this stage (though for an exception consider the procedural vote on President Reagan's 1981 budget package, discussed in Chapter 7). On strategic voting, see Robin Farquharson, *Theory of Voting* (New Haven: Yale University Press, 1969). On the tension between electoral calculation and strategic voting, see Arthur Denzau, William Riker, and Kenneth Shepsle, "Farquharson and Fenno: Sophisticated Voting and Home Style," *American Political Science Review* 79 (1985): 1117–1134. For other arguments about why legislators infrequently engage in sophisticated voting, see Keith Krehbiel and Douglas Rivers, "Sophisticated Voting in Congress: A Reconsideration," Working Paper in Political Science (Palo Alto, Calif.: Hoover Institution, Stanford University, 1988), pp. 1–7.

3. In four recent elections (1980 to 1986), 76 percent of House members and 53 percent of senators were reelected with at least sixty percent of the major party vote. See Norman J. Ornstein, Thomas E. Mann, and Michael J. Malbin, *Vital Statistics on Congress, 1987–1988* (Washington, D.C.: Congressional Quarterly, 1987), pp. 59–60.

4. Consider the members of the 100th Congress (1987–1988). Of the House members, 73 percent had won at least one congressional election by sixty percent or less, and 54 percent had won at least one election by fifty-five percent or less. The corresponding statistics for senators were 87 and 76 percent. Ibid., p. 60.

5. On both of these issues, see David R. Mayhew, *Congress: The Electoral Connection* (New Haven: Yale University Press, 1974), pp. 33–38. House members today are simultaneously less vulnerable to national partisan swings and more vulnerable when talented, well-funded candidates emerge to challenge them. This provides legislators with an even more powerful incentive to vote very carefully, lest they give challengers easy issues to use

whatever opportunities come their way to protect or expand their electoral coalitions, and many issues provide excellent opportunities to do
just that. One roll-call vote may help to attract a few new friends to one's
electoral coalition, another may increase the attachment of some habitual supporters, another may keep one from alienating some occasional
supporters, another may help one to raise campaign funds, and yet
another may keep some disillusioned constituents from actively searching for a replacement. Each issue may have only a slight impact on a
legislator's electoral margin; yet small effects can quickly add up to
become large effects when summed over the many issues that Congress
considers each year.[6]

Strictly speaking, legislators always face three options: supporting a
policy, opposing it, or abstaining. In fact, abstention rarely makes political sense. The problem with abstaining is that it counts against one in
the annual scores for voting participation, and challengers love to use
below-average voting scores as evidence that incumbents are not diligently doing their jobs.[7] Given that most legislators end up missing
some votes for good reasons—illness, traveling abroad, or trips to their
districts—they can hardly afford to miss even more votes because they
prefer not to take sides.[8] Abstention also makes legislators look like
cowards, and few legislators care to provide challengers with solid evidence that they are anything less than fearless representatives battling
for their constituents' interests. Abstention makes even less sense for
those controversial votes that legislators would most like to miss—votes
on issues such as abortion that pit polarized, single-issue groups against
each other. Single-issue groups tend to believe that those who are not

against them. See Gary C. Jacobson, "The Marginals Never Vanished: Incumbency and
Competition in Elections to the U.S. House of Representatives, 1952–82," *American
Journal of Political Science* 31 (1987): 126–141; and Stephen Ansolabehere, David Brady,
and Morris Fiorina, "The Marginals Never Vanished?," Working Paper in Political Science
(Palo Alto, Calif.: Hoover Institution, Stanford University, 1988).

   6. House members face 400 to 600 roll-call votes each year, and senators face 300 to 600
votes. Ornstein et al., *Vital Statistics*, p. 168.

   7. Challengers use these voting participation scores so frequently that Congressional
Quarterly, the nonpartisan organization that compiles them, now publishes a disclaimer
along with the scores. The essence of the disclaimer is that voting participation is only one
of many elements needed to assess a member's performance and that responsible legislators often miss roll-call votes for very good reasons. See "A Note of Caution to Readers,"
Congressional Quarterly Weekly Report 46 (January 16, 1988): 118.

   8. The average member of Congress votes on about 93 percent of all roll calls. Ibid., pp.
118–121.

with them are against them, so abstention compounds the usual problem by alienating both sides.

How much should legislators worry about their own policy positions and their own connections with policy effects, and how much should they worry about their party's positions and their party's performance in office?[9] If the question is which of these four factors has the greatest impact on congressional elections, then the award may well go to the parties' general stands on the issues. Most voters support the legislative candidates of their favorite party, and for some of them, this choice reflects the differences between the parties. Unfortunately, a legislator can do virtually nothing to affect her party's general stance. Although the parties do change their positions over time, the impact of a single legislator on that change is necessarily small. A Republican incumbent from a Democratic district just has to live with the fact that many of her constituents prefer Democrats, for she can do little to make Republicans as a class more appealing.

Fortunately, a legislator can do a great deal to differentiate herself from her party (if that is to her advantage). A legislator may have little control over her party's positions, but she has complete control over her own policy positions. A Republican from a Democratic district can vote like a Democrat. She can fine-tune her policy positions to fit even the most complicated district. Her strategies may not persuade the most steadfast partisan voters to support her, but they may convince more amenable citizens to focus on her own, not her party's, positions.

When it comes to being rewarded or punished for policy effects, legislators can profit or suffer both from their own direct connections with those effects and from the actual performance of their party when it is in office. Once again legislators find it far easier to do something about their own personal actions. To avoid direct electoral retribution for producing displeasing effects, legislators can simply refuse to join in any actions that might produce large and traceable costs. To avoid electoral retribution for their *party's* actions in office, however, they must actually join together to produce pleasing effects. Not only is there a collective action problem in bringing legislators together to do anything,[10] but legislators must actually agree on how best to produce pleasing effects before they can enact appropriate policies. In some fields, such as economic policy, that in itself is a major undertaking.

9. On this entire subject, see Mayhew, *Congress: The Electoral Connection*, pp. 17–38.
10. Ibid., pp. 32–33.

Wherever they turn, legislators see opportunities to make themselves look good or to make their parties look good. If there is a conflict between the two they invariably choose the former, not because the parties are irrelevant to their electoral fortunes but because as individuals they can do so little to influence where their parties stand or what their parties do. When they can make both themselves and their parties look good, partisanship does provide an added incentive to come together. Senate Republicans have seldom been as united as they were in 1981, when they gained control of the Senate for the first time in twenty-eight years. They wanted to make the Republican party look good so that they could retain control of the Senate, and to that end they stood together on most major issues, especially on those related to the economy.[11] In the following three years, as the deficit grew out of control, Senate Republicans took the lead in devising schemes to raise taxes and control spending— both actions designed to deflect criticism that Republicans could not govern (see Chapter 7).

ATTENTIVE PUBLICS

Legislators know that all citizens are not equally interested in the resolution of specific policy conflicts. Some citizens have strong preferences about a given policy problem, know what Congress is doing on the subject, and are not bashful about communicating their preferences to their representatives. Others may have no preferences at all about an issue and may be completely unaware that Congress is considering a change in national policy in that field. In between these two extremes are yet others who may have preferences about an issue but remain ignorant of Washington activity. Legislators may differentiate among citizens according to their interest in an issue, their knowledge of what is happening, and whether or not they already have policy preferences on the subject.

Here I differentiate between two classes of citizens: attentive and inattentive publics.[12] *Attentive publics* are those citizens who are aware

11. In 1981 the average Republican senator voted the party line 81 percent of the time; Republicans were completely united on 39 occasions. See Richard Cowan, "Partisan Voting Averages Increased in 97th Congress," *Congressional Quarterly Weekly Report* 40 (January 9, 1982): 61–62.

12. The distinction is from V. O. Key, Jr., *Public Opinion and American Democracy* (New York: Knopf, 1961), pp. 265, 282–285.

that a specific issue is on the congressional agenda, know what alternatives are under consideration, and have relatively firm preferences about what Congress should do. *Inattentive publics* are those who have neither firm policy preferences about an issue nor knowledge of what Congress is considering. The question for legislators is how much they should consider the known policy preferences of attentive publics as opposed to the potential policy preferences of inattentive publics when they are deciding which side to support in a policy dispute.

At least if this question is approached as an analytic task, legislators have an easier time dealing with the known preferences of attentive publics than with the unstable or potential preferences of the inattentive. Attentive publics may feel very strongly about issues, and they may watch their representatives very closely, which can be a bother; but at least legislators know where they stand. With inattentive publics, however, legislators must imagine what preferences might arise in the future and estimate how those preferences might affect citizens' electoral decisions.

What produces attentive publics? Why do some citizens acquire firm policy preferences and notice what is on the congressional agenda while others do not? A general answer would emphasize the ways education, occupation, and political experience affect citizens' interest in politics and their acquisition of politically relevant information.[13] These factors help to explain why better-educated citizens and those employed in professional and managerial occupations are more likely to be attentive than are poorly educated citizens, but they do little to explain the enormous variance across policy areas. For that task, we need to recall the ways in which policy attributes affect policy preferences.

Policy attributes affect the likelihood that citizens will have policy preferences in several ways. Citizens are more likely to have preferences about an issue when they see relatively large costs or benefits for themselves, when these costs or benefits are early-order effects, and when citizens interact regularly with others who have similar interests (see Chapter 2). They are especially likely to have intense policy preferences when they already receive benefits (or pay costs) under a governmental program. When Congress is considering the initiation of a new benefit program, the intended beneficiaries may hardly notice, but when Congress considers terminating a similar program, thus imposing costs on

13. Sidney Verba and Norman H. Nie, *Participation in America* (New York: Harper and Row, 1972), pp. 95–101.

the current beneficiaries, the affected group tends to have very intense preferences.

When one thinks of attentive publics, one usually thinks of organized interest groups, and indeed the two are closely related. The Washington representatives of organized groups certainly keep informed of what Congress is doing. When important interests are at stake, they communicate with their members in an attempt to create and mobilize larger attentive publics. Attentive publics can also arise where there are no organized groups at all. When the House held hearings to consider impeaching President Nixon on nationwide television and during prime time, most of the nation constituted an attentive public, though a completely unorganized one. Some Social Security recipients are organized in various senior-citizens' groups, but many of the others are equally attentive when Congress is voting on Social Security benefits or extending the Medicare program. Appropriate publicity, whether a natural product of the media covering the news or generated by some of the participants in policy making, can produce attentive publics even among the unorganized and unorganizable.

A simple example shows how a talented activist can create an attentive public where one would not ordinarily arise and how the mere existence of an attentive public can then pressure a legislator to switch his position on an otherwise obscure policy issue. In early 1988 the Senate added an amendment to a House-passed bill that would have required random drug testing for all rail workers, but House conferees refused to accept the amendment. Proponents identified Representative Thomas Luken (D., Ohio), chairman of the Transportation Subcommittee of the Energy and Commerce Committee, as the chief obstacle to their goal. Then in late April, Roger Horn, a professor of mathematics at Johns Hopkins University, visited Luken's Cincinnati district. Horn's only interest in the matter was that his daughter was one of sixteen victims killed a year earlier when a freight train, under the control of an engineer who later admitted to having smoked marijuana on the job, collided with an Amtrak train in Maryland. Horn made several appearances during his brief visit: at a press conference with Luken's opponent in the fall election, at five local radio stations, and with the editorial boards of two major papers in Cincinnati. Both papers promptly published strong editorials in favor of random drug testing and urged Luken to join the effort. Visibly upset by all the fuss in his constituency over an issue that had previously generated little interest, Luken reversed course. Within three weeks he had drafted a bill that was much tougher than the Senate's version, requiring random tests for alcohol as well as drugs and requiring both preemployment and postaccident tests. As Horn said with some satisfaction, "Saint Paul had a miraculous conversion on the road to Damascus, and this sounds like another one."[14]

This example also reminds us that not all attentive publics arise as a consequence of large, concentrated effects of the group or geographic variety (see Chapter 2). People who have strong preferences about general costs and benefits can be equally attentive to Washington action. Those who feel intensely about capital punishment, abortion, nuclear proliferation, or the fate of whales provide excellent examples.

Ordinarily legislators do not have much trouble discerning the shape of opinion within the various attentive publics that might affect their political support. Those that are organized into groups use their hired lobbyists to reveal their policy preferences in hearings, position papers, and private meetings. The rest communicate their views to legislators both in letters and during personal meetings. Opinion regarding recurring issues is particularly easy to decipher, for attentive publics have well-established positions, and little communication is necessary. New issues require that attentive publics first identify their interests and then transmit their preferences to appropriate legislators. Again this task is relatively easy for the organized. Legislators and coalition leaders deal with unorganized attentive publics by launching various trial balloons in speeches and the like, to see which survive and which are shot down.

Similarly, few legislators have much trouble estimating how the relevant attentive publics will react if they vote contrary to their expressed preferences. Most attentive publics communicate not only where they stand but how intensely they feel about a specific vote. Surely no legislator can doubt that the various single-issue groups, ranging from the National Rifle Association to the antiabortion groups, make their support absolutely contingent upon legislators' decisions in these areas. Most attentive publics, however, are interested in several issues. Here legislators deal at the margin, gaining some increment of support for correct votes and risking some contraction for wrong votes, but not worrying about massive shifts on the basis of a single vote. Yet electoral coalitions are built and maintained at the margin, so legislators cannot

14. The entire story is recounted in Paul Starobin, "Tide Turns on Drug Testing of Rail and Other Workers," *Congressional Quarterly Weekly Report* 46 (May 28, 1988): 1452–1453.

ignore multi-issue attentive publics simply because their support is not wholly contingent upon a single vote.

INATTENTIVE PUBLICS

Dealing with inattentive publics is inherently more difficult. By definition these citizens do not have firm positions about the policies under consideration. They may have "opinions" that register in public surveys when they are asked fixed-choice questions, but there can be no assurance that their answers reflect politically relevant attitudes.[15] Such opinions are notoriously unstable, fluctuating with even slight changes in question wording or with the ebb and flow of events.[16] Surely they don't provide secure anchors for legislators worried about troubled waters ahead. Legislators ignore inattentive publics at their peril. Latent or unfocused opinions can quickly be transformed into intense and very real opinions with enormous political repercussions. Inattentiveness and lack of information today should not be confused with indifference tomorrow. The cautious legislator, therefore, must attempt to estimate three things: the probability that an opinion might be aroused, the shape of that opinion, and its potential for electoral consequences.

How do legislators estimate the likelihood that inattentive publics might be transformed into attentive publics, either while Congress is still considering a program or between the time of enactment and the next election? Such transformations require both an instigator who can communicate with relevant publics and the appropriate policy attributes that the instigator can then use to generate policy preferences. Of course, challengers are always ready to play the role of instigator, though they are not always the most effective choice. It would be hard to imagine that any challenger to Representative Luken could have been as effective as Professor Horn was in generating or activating opinions in favor of random drug testing, because people can easily ignore or discount the actions of challengers as politically motivated, whereas the actions of victims look both purer and more newsworthy.

15. Philip E. Converse, "The Nature of Belief Systems in Mass Publics," in David Apter (ed.), *Ideology and Discontent* (New York: Free Press, 1964), pp. 206–261.

16. Howard Schuman and Stanley Presser, *Questions and Answers in Attitude Surveys: Experiments on Question Form, Wording, and Context* (New York: Academic Press, 1981).

When talented instigators are waiting in the wings, legislators must exercise far more caution than if none are present. Consider how the rise of Ralph Nader changed legislators' voting calculus when consumer interests are at stake.[17] Before Nader, legislators could ignore the consumers' point of view, confident that no one would ever be able to rally the unorganized masses against them. Nader's contribution was not to organize consumers—a nearly impossible task—but rather to label legislative votes as pro- or anticonsumer. The media then disseminated these messages, challengers helped citizens reach the proper political conclusions, and suddenly a formerly inattentive public was alive. Once Nader had demonstrated his ability to mobilize an otherwise inattentive public several times, he no longer had to do so regularly; simply labeling legislative votes as anticonsumer provided ammunition that others could use, and the mere existence of this ammunition was threatening enough to some legislators. The environmental movement adopted a similar approach. Here one of the finest tactical maneuvers was to label legislators who had the worst environmental records as "The Dirty Dozen," in order to generate media attention and make it easier for inattentive citizens to identify the obstacles to clean water and fresh air.[18] According to one of the originators of the Dirty Dozen campaign, the tactic "was very effective at making congressmen think twice about certain votes. There were numerous examples of members or their staff calling and saying 'Is the congressman close to being on the list?' or 'Is this vote going to be used to determine the list?'"[19]

Instigators need good material to activate inattentive publics. Not even President Reagan—the great communicator—was able to convince many people that a bill that would require industry to provide workers with sixty days' notice of plant closings would make American industry less competitive. The causal connection was too remote. It is far easier to activate an inattentive public when the connection between

17. Mark V. Nadel, *The Politics of Consumer Protection* (New York: Bobbs-Merrill, 1971).

18. Instigators not only chose those with poor environmental records, but also intentionally chose those with shaky electoral coalitions. As expected, many of these legislators lost, instigators claimed credit, and other legislators became even more careful of their environmental records. Nearly half of the fifty-two who made the list during the 1970s were defeated. See Bill Keller, "The Trail of the 'Dirty Dozen,'" *Congressional Quarterly Weekly Report* 39 (March 21, 1981): 510; and Gary C. Jacobson, *The Politics of Congressional Elections*, 2d ed. (Boston: Little, Brown, 1987), p. 194.

19. Keller, "The Trail of the 'Dirty Dozen,'" p. 510.

policy instrument and policy effect is clear. When legislators voted on whether the FCC should be allowed to impose a six-dollar-per-month access fee on all residential telephone bills, they knew that a talented instigator could easily make an issue of their votes once the fees began to appear on consumers' bills.[20] When legislators deal with complex and arcane provisions of the tax code that define how capital goods may be depreciated, they can be equally certain that no instigator will be able to mobilize inattentive publics on this issue.

It is also far easier to activate inattentive publics when those publics bear large and direct costs. The banking industry by itself was unable to block the federal government from withholding for taxes a portion of each depositor's interest earnings until the banks began to mobilize their depositors. Depositors turned out to be a very receptive audience, since it was their money that would be withheld.[21] Once the political liabilities became clear, legislators scrambled to repeal the law.[22] Consider also the difference between dairy subsidies and sugar quotas. Ordinarily instigators have a tough time mobilizing dairy consumers because the cost of dairy subsidies is hidden in the federal budget. By comparison, they had an easy time mobilizing sugar consumers in 1974 because the cost of America's restrictive sugar policy was displayed at supermarkets in the rapidly multiplying retail price of sugar.[23]

How, then, do legislators anticipate the possibility that inattentive publics might rise and give them trouble? A talented legislator need ask himself only two simple questions: First, if I were on the other side, could I figure out how to incite inattentive publics against legislators like me who voted on the wrong side? Second, are there, in fact, potential instigators who might mobilize inattentive publics against me? Only if both questions yield positive answers must he consider adjusting his decision to reflect the potential preferences of these inattentive publics.

Legislators need to respond to attentive publics and anticipate the preferences of inattentive publics, yet the advantage surely belongs to the attentive. Activists transmit precise requests for action, leaving little

20. The story is recounted later in this chapter.

21. The banks implied that it was a new tax, rather than a measure designed to reduce cheating on the income tax, and they also failed to mention that senior citizens and others who paid little tax were exempt. The perceived incidence of costs, therefore, differed considerably from the true incidence.

22. "Interest Withholding Requirement Repealed," *Congressional Quarterly Almanac, 1983* 39 (1984): 261–264.

23. On the politics of the dairy and sugar programs, see Chapter 6.

doubt where they stand or what they expect legislators to do. Inattentive publics have a considerably less precise form of control, for theirs is based solely on the rule of anticipated reactions. Their potential policy preferences set the outer boundaries for what policies legislators may support, but they cannot dictate exactly what legislators should advocate. As long as legislators stay within these boundaries, no instigator can transform latent preferences into politically relevant attitudes, and these citizens remain unaware of what Congress has done. In fact, for many policies the probability of ever activating inattentive publics is near zero. In such cases, legislators may ignore these citizens completely and respond only to the preferences of attentive publics.

How do legislators decide which side to support when the known preferences of attentive publics are in direct conflict with the potential preferences of inattentive publics? At least in principle, the calculations are quite simple, for they all reduce to how many votes are gained or lost from each group. Whether a legislator sides with an attentive or inattentive public therefore depends on the size of each public, as well as the intensity of each public's preferences or potential preferences. It also depends on whether legislators are dealing with policy effects that are directly traceable to their own individual actions or whether the electoral connection involves only policy positions.

POLICY EFFECTS

How much do legislators have to be concerned about the effects that they produce? David Mayhew seems to imply that, particularistic policies aside, congressmen need not worry much about policy effects. He argues that "in a large class of legislative undertakings the electoral payment is for positions rather than for effects."[24] The argument is perfectly sound as long as it concerns benefits rather than costs and involves electoral payment rather than electoral retribution. When legislators are dealing with costs that are directly traceable to their own actions, however, they must consider the possibility that those costs might be used to activate otherwise inattentive publics.

How can we be sure that policy effects alter the electoral equation from what it would be if citizens considered only legislators' policy positions? The case of Representative Timothy Wirth (D., Colo.) and the

24. Mayhew, *Congress: The Electoral Connection*, p. 132.

deregulation of telecommunications helps to make the case (see Chapter 3). Wirth began to stake out a position against AT&T and in favor of telephone deregulation as early as 1976.[25] Several years later he became chairman of the Telecommunications Subcommittee of the Energy and Commerce Committee and the most visible proponent of deregulation in the House. To the best of my knowledge, his position was never an issue in his reelection campaigns of 1978, 1980, or 1982.[26] Perhaps his good fortune reflects nothing more than an oversight on the part of his three opponents, but it is hard to imagine how anyone could have made a good campaign issue out of a complicated proposal like deregulation. Once deregulation was implemented, however, the short-term effects were apparent, and many of them were displeasing to consumers (cumbersome procedures to establish service, difficulties in arranging for repairs, rapidly escalating local rates). Suddenly, it was easy to make a campaign issue out of deregulation. Wirth's challenger exploited consumer frustration with these negative effects, and Wirth's winning margin slipped from 62 percent in 1982 to 53 percent in 1984.[27] Although this example does not show a legislator anticipating the impact of policy effects, it does illustrate the consequences of failing to do so. It also suggests that the electoral impact of policy effects can be quite different from the impact of policy positions alone.

How do legislators know whether citizens will hold them accountable for the effects they produce rather than simply for the positions they take? We know from Chapter 3 that citizens employ the incumbent performance rule only if they can trace specific effects back to their own legislators' contributions. Traceability requires perceptible effects, identifiable governmental actions, and visible individual contributions. Roll-call votes are themselves visible contributions, so one of the conditions is already satisfied. The probability of this form of retrospective voting, then, depends directly on the nature of the effects and on whether they can be connected to a single governmental action (rather than to many unrelated actions).

Legislators' fear of retrospective voting[28] impels them to avoid a class

25. Martha Derthick and Paul J. Quirk, *The Politics of Deregulation* (Washington, D.C.: Brookings Institution, 1985), p. 107.

26. This was also the opinion of one of Wirth's principal assistants. Ibid., p. 140.

27. "Congressional Outlook: Colorado," *Congressional Quarterly Weekly Report* 44 (February 22, 1986): 353; and Alan Ehrenhalt (ed.), *Politics in America, 1986* (Washington, D.C.: Congressional Quarterly, 1985), pp. 242–243.

28. Unless the context suggests otherwise, I shall henceforth use the term *retrospective*

of policy alternatives that I shall call *politically infeasible policies*. Specifically, legislators shun policies that would impose large and direct early-order costs on their constituents, for these effects are easily traced to their roll-call votes. Whether or not there happen to be attentive publics opposed to these policies is irrelevant. Legislators vote against them in anticipation of future punishment, not in response to current pressures.

Consider the proposal advanced in the early 1970s to impose a national tax on gasoline to encourage conservation, with the proceeds to be redistributed to taxpayers generally. The economic case for the tax was strong, since domestic prices were well below the replacement cost of imported oil. Unfortunately, the political logic was wholly untenable. All the benefits were general, indirect, and later-order, with most occurring far in the future. No legislator would ever profit from any connection to such benefits. The costs, on the other hand, were large, direct, and early-order, and thus fully traceable to legislators' roll-call votes. Furthermore, taxation requires an act of Congress, which meant that Congress could not even delegate vague authority to the executive in an attempt to break the traceability chain. The result was perfectly predictable. Presidents repeatedly proposed such a tax, while legislators avoided like the plague any contact with it (see Chapter 9). The case was completely different some years later when a nickel-per-gallon rise in the gasoline tax was tied to increased expenditures on highway construction and maintenance.[29] Such expenditures offered very large, early-order benefits to construction firms and workers, plus considerable benefits down the line to drivers. With roads and bridges deteriorating and the economy in deep recession, this tax passed easily. The point is not that legislators cannot vote for taxes, for surely if that were true we could never have acquired the current tax burden. But taxes need to be connected to something more than a vague promise of energy conservation and better times in the future.

The reluctance of legislators to be associated with direct, early-order costs is also clear in the case of the telephone access fee.[30] Here the

---

voting to refer to the habits of citizens employing the incumbent performance rule (and not the party performance rule).

29. "Taxes Hiked to Finance Roads, Mass Transit," *Congressional Quarterly Almanac, 1982* 38 (1983): 317–330.

30. The House voted overwhelmingly to bar the FCC from imposing an access fee. The Senate was about to do the same when the FCC retreated and announced that it would impose no fee for at least two years. See Richard Whittle, "House Votes to Block FCC Phone

Federal Communications Commission, as part of the deregulation of the phone industry and the divestiture of AT&T, had agreed to impose a six-dollar-per-month access fee on all residential telephone bills, thus shifting costs from long-distance users to local callers. The decision was completely within the jurisdiction of the FCC (established in 1934), and therefore legislators were immune from any blame for the action. Once a small group of legislators introduced a bill to stop the access fee, however, the political logic shifted. Now legislators who failed to oppose the fee could be blamed once the fee appeared on their constituents' bills. Coalition leaders stopped the fee by creating an identifiable congressional action on which legislators were forced to take a position. The nature of the costs then guaranteed that legislators would oppose the fee.[31]

How do we know that these two examples show legislators anticipating the effects of retrospective voting rather than responding to the pressures of attentive publics? In both cases, although there was little lobbying against the fees, legislators quickly established firm positions in opposition—just as one would expect if they were, on their own, estimating the political stakes. All this happened while lobbyists worked feverishly to promote the fees. Successive administrations advocated the gasoline tax as a central element in a national energy policy. And the usually powerful coalition of telephone executives, workers, and shareholders argued that the access fee was an essential part of the complicated divestiture agreement. In both cases, legislators' fear of retrospective voting was the more powerful force. They responded to the potential policy preferences of inattentive publics rather than to the strong preferences of organized groups.

So, one consequence of retrospective voting is the creation of a class of politically infeasible policies. A second is the instigation of a search for alternative policies that could achieve the same ends with fewer political risks. Typically these alternative policies spread the costs more widely, impose them as later-order effects, or push them further into the future. Each response either makes the effects less visible or conceals the con-

Rate Plan," *Congressional Quarterly Weekly Report* 41 (November 12, 1983): 2396; and Robert Rothman, "Senate Buries Telephone Bill after FCC Delays Access Fees," *Congressional Quarterly Weekly Report* 42 (January 28, 1984): 129.

31. The FCC has since taken a more gradual approach, first instituting a $1.00 fee, then $2.00, $2.60, $3.20, and $3.50—with the increases phased in annually. These slow increases have not generated much congressional reaction. See Martin Tolchin, "FCC Board Urges $1.50-a-Month Rise in Telephone Charge," *New York Times* (March 13, 1987): A1.

nection between these effects and governmental action, so that traceability is less likely. If a gasoline tax is politically infeasible, how can one raise the price of gasoline anyway? One response is to deregulate the oil industry and then allow domestic prices to rise naturally to world levels. As long as deregulation is phased in slowly, no abrupt increase in prices will stimulate a search for governmental causes. Blame for higher prices will fall on the oil companies, for they are the ones who control prices. As Chapter 9 shows, gradual deregulation was essentially how coalition leaders made energy policy more palatable, with a windfall-profits tax thrown in for good measure.

Finally, retrospective voting creates a class of policies that are *politically attractive* to legislators. These are policies that are not just feasible but genuinely profitable for legislators seeking to maintain or expand their political support. They differ from the infeasible policies by delivering perceptible benefits (not costs) for which legislators can then claim credit. On their own, citizens seldom trace benefits back to their governmental causes, as they do costs (see Chapter 3). Legislators, therefore, must work to establish connections between their own individual actions and these pleasing effects. This task is easiest for policies that provide explicit geographic benefits for a legislator's own constituency. Bills that provide particularistic benefits, in the form of specific dams, highways, or buildings, create superb opportunities for what Mayhew calls credit claiming, in part because there are no competitors.[32] Each legislator claims responsibility only for the geographic benefits in his own district, leaving the rest for his colleagues to claim as their own handiwork. Bills that provide geographic benefits universally and automatically, either in equal parts or according to some formula, are far less useful. Legislators could no more claim credit for the regular disbursement of checks for highway assistance, Medicaid, or revenue sharing than they could for Social Security checks. Legislators can be punished for opposing such formula programs, especially if they are terminated, but there is very little net profit in supporting them.[33]

32. This is Mayhew's argument about the circumstances under which legislators do care about the effects they produce. See Mayhew, *Congress: The Electoral Connection*, pp. 127–130. See also Morris P. Fiorina, *Congress: Keystone of the Washington Establishment* (New Haven: Yale University Press, 1977); and R. Douglas Arnold, *Congress and the Bureaucracy: A Theory of Influence* (New Haven: Yale University Press, 1979).

33. R. Douglas Arnold, "The Local Roots of Domestic Policy," in Thomas E. Mann and Norman J. Ornstein (eds.), *The New Congress* (Washington, D.C.: American Enterprise Institute, 1981), pp. 250–287.

Legislators may also profit by supporting policies that deliver large group benefits to their constituents, but credit is far from automatic; when beneficiaries are unorganized, there may be none at all. It is doubtful that college students and their parents, who together benefit from the various student loan programs, reward their representatives for repeated support of these programs.[34] Yet legislators who oppose these same programs may discover that those who benefit from these programs do practice electoral retribution. Among the unorganized, blame is easier to express than gratitude. On the other hand, when beneficiaries are organized, they can use their organizational resources to reward legislators who repeatedly support their programs. The dairy and maritime industries, for example, have demonstrated that magnificent campaign contributions make splendid rewards for legislators who support their causes, both for those with dairy farms or ports in their districts and for those without any constituents who benefit from governmental assistance. Labor unions also keep track of who their supporters are on a wide range of issues and then reward them with money or campaign workers.

For each legislator, retrospective voting immediately divides policy options into politically infeasible and politically attractive policies. These divisions arise not because citizens have firm positions on the policies, but rather because legislators believe that citizens may like or dislike specific effects, and because legislators seek to become either associated with or disassociated from the production of those effects.

POLICY POSITIONS

The potential for retrospective voting keeps legislators worried about the effects they produce, or at least about those that citizens might trace back to legislators' actions. At the same time, the potential for policy voting forces them to consider how their positions on various issues will sound to citizens. The logic of policy voting leaves its own distinctive imprint on legislators' decisions and, in fact, it may force legislators in directions contrary to those suggested by retrospective voting.

34. Senator Claiborne Pell (D., R.I.) may be an exception to the rule because each year two million students collect "Pell grants" through their colleges in the largest assistance program for higher education.

How can the two different decision rules for citizens—the incumbent performance rule and the candidate position rule—supply contrary advice to legislators who are deciding which of two alternatives to support? First, citizens may prefer policy A because they believe (rightly) that it will produce the desired effects; but unfortunately it will also produce various unanticipated consequences for which legislators can be blamed. Such is the case of the standby gasoline rationing plan, where popular support for the concept of rationing suggested easy congressional passage under the logic of the candidate position rule, while legislators feared that citizens would eventually blame them for the actual allocations if a specific plan were ever implemented (see Chapter 9). Second, citizens may prefer policy A today, believing that it will solve some important problem. Unfortunately, some other problem will emerge near election day, and for that problem policy A is the cause, not the solution. This predicament is one in which some representatives found themselves in 1982, after supporting President Reagan's 1981 budget package (see Chapter 7). At the time, many citizens seemed to support the notion of cutting the federal budget as a solution to various economic problems. By election day, however, some citizens traced cuts in specific programs back to the very same votes on budget reconciliation and found their representatives wanting.[35] Third, some attentive publics may strongly favor policy A, while other citizens appear indifferent; yet policy A imposes substantial costs on these indifferent citizens. Legislators can be fairly certain that if policy A is passed and implemented, these inattentive publics will not remain indifferent when the next election comes around. This outcome might have occurred with the telephone access fee, if legislators had responded to the pressures from AT&T rather than anticipating the wrath of residential customers.

One consequence of policy voting is that legislators feel compelled to support certain policy options because the intended effects are popular, irrespective of whether the proposed means will really achieve those

35. Consider the 1982 campaign literature of the challenger, Adam Levin, pointing out the deficiencies of the incumbent, Matthew Rinaldo (R., N.J.). Six separate paragraphs argued that Rinaldo had voted to cut Social Security, Medicare, elementary and secondary education, higher education, consumer protection, and environmental protection, yet all six votes were actually a single vote in favor of the 1981 Budget Reconciliation Act. Democrats used this strategy widely, attempting to blame moderate and liberal Republicans for cuts in specific programs. See Martin Tolchin, "G.O.P. Cries 'Foul' on News Releases," *New York Times* (October 19, 1981): A18.

ends. These alternatives I shall call *politically compelling policies*. They are compelling because legislators must vote for a policy proposal as a package, not in sequence, first for the ends and then for the proposed policy instrument. Thus, legislators who oppose a policy because they disagree with the proposed means risk having their opposition misconstrued as lack of sympathy for the ends themselves.

Consider, for example, the bill passed in 1971 to change the organization and emphasis in federal efforts to discover a cure for cancer.[36] Essentially the bill tilted away from scientists and basic research and toward doctors and applied research, with the argument that a cure was "just around the corner." In retrospect, of course, it was a poorly conceived bill, which was just what many scientists argued at the time.[37] For legislators, however, the political arguments were compelling once the bill reached the floor. Since this bill was the only alternative put before them, legislators were practically forced to support it so that they would appear to be battling this dread disease. Doing nothing was probably the superior policy, but it was poor politics once the bill was on the floor.

This case is generalizable to the whole field of federal funding of medical research. The strategic breakthrough that facilitated massive growth in federal expenditures for medical research was the naming of specific institutes to combat specific diseases. Any amendment to increase funding for research on cancer, stroke, heart disease, or arthritis was then practically guaranteed success, because legislators were eager to establish that they too were dedicated to wiping out these scourges.[38] The same was true when the federal government considered subsidizing the treatment of specific diseases. Once someone proposed that the government underwrite the cost of long-term dialysis for those suffering from kidney failure, it was perfectly predictable that legislators would support the plan. No one inquired about costs or whether this policy was the best investment of scarce health funds.[39]

36. Richard A. Rettig, *Cancer Crusade: The Story of the National Cancer Act of 1971* (Princeton: Princeton University Press, 1977); Jeffrey Toder, "The National Cancer Program and the Scientific Mystique" (senior thesis, Princeton University, 1979).

37. Unfortunately, these scientists never recruited coalition leaders in Congress to draft a superior policy instrument that could have defeated the winning proposal.

38. See Aaron Wildavsky, *The Politics of the Budgetary Process* (Boston: Little, Brown, 1964), p. 70; David Price, *Who Makes the Laws?* (Cambridge: Schenkman, 1972), pp. 216–219; and Stephen P. Strickland, *Politics, Science, and Dread Disease* (Cambridge: Harvard University Press, 1972).

39. The program was launched on the Senate floor with an amendment to a 1972 Social

These are politically compelling policies because the ends are so popular that legislators must support whatever alternatives are put before them in order to demonstrate their own commitment to those ends. Legislators may also feel compelled to support certain policy options because the policy instruments are popular, regardless of whether these instruments would produce the intended effects. Many citizens, for example, believe that balancing the federal budget is the ticket to better macroeconomic outcomes. As a consequence, some legislators support the notion of a balanced budget whenever the opportunity presents itself. Unfortunately, legislators seldom have a chance to vote on how large the deficit shall be, for the deficit is actually the product of many separate decisions on taxing, spending, and entitlements. As a result, other decisions have become surrogates, allowing legislators to show their abhorrence of deficits without actually affecting them. For two decades one of the favorite vehicles for protest has been the bill that authorizes the Treasury to borrow money to pay governmental obligations. The recurring dilemma for congressional leaders is how to pass such legislation, which is absolutely crucial if the government is to pay its bills, when most legislators wish to be counted against deficit financing.

A second consequence of policy voting is the reluctance of legislators to support certain policy options simply because citizens don't see any connection between the proposed policy instruments and the intended effects. These alternatives I shall call *politically repellent options*. Economists, for example, argue that market-like incentives are superior to command-and-control techniques for changing social behavior, yet their proposals seldom advance very far in Congress.[40] The political problem is that effluent charges (to take the example of pollution control) make the government appear to sell rich corporations licenses to pollute, whereas prohibitions against emissions allow legislators to de-

---

Security bill, proposed by Senator Vance Hartke (D., Ind.) and approved by a margin of 52 to 3. By 1977 the program treated 36,000 patients, at a cost of $1 billion a year, with costs projected to reach $6 billion a year by 1992. In 1978 Congress changed the reimbursement scheme, emphasizing home dialysis over hospital treatment, and costs have leveled off at about $2 billion annually. See "Senate Floor Action," *Congressional Quarterly Almanac, 1972* 28 (1973): 911; "Kidney Dialysis Program," *Congressional Quarterly Almanac, 1977* 33 (1978): 517–518; "Kidney Dialysis Program," *Congressional Quarterly Almanac, 1978* 34 (1979): 581–582.

40. Charles L. Schultze, *The Public Use of Private Interest* (Washington, D.C.: Brookings Institution, 1977).

clare unequivocally that they are opposed to pollution.[41] Similarly, injury taxes sound like an attempt to legitimate unsafe workplaces, whereas prohibitions and government inspections leave no doubt about where legislators stand.[42] With policy voting, it is the causal logic of citizens that is important, not that of experts.

Politically repellent options may also include programs for which citizens have little sympathy for the affected groups. Those who doubt the power of the electoral connection should watch legislators squirm whenever they must vote on a bill or amendment that mentions homosexuality. Most legislators adopt a safe strategy and avoid giving future opponents any evidence that they condone homosexual activity, even if the real issue is discrimination in housing, employment, immigration, or legal assistance.[43] Issues related to welfare also raise problems for many legislators, given the popular image of those who accept such assistance. Compare the reluctance that legislators display whenever welfare programs are on the agenda with the exuberance they show when they vote to expand school lunch programs. The image of hungry school children who need one square meal daily so that they can concentrate on their studies is a powerful one, and it easily overcomes the image of welfare recipients who are thought to be too lazy to work and who, according to legend, produce even more children to increase their government stipends. In fact, most welfare recipients are truly needy, whereas many of the beneficiaries of the school lunch program are comfortably middle class, but image counts in politics.

Some individual roll-call votes seem to have no electoral consequences. Even careful legislators cannot imagine how their support of one side or the other could possibly affect their electoral margins. Collections of otherwise inconsequential votes, however, can have electoral consequences, and thus legislators need to watch the general patterns they create as well as the individual positions they take. Interest groups in Washington compile and publish ratings of legislators to show how friendly or unfriendly individual legislators are to the causes they promote. Some of these groups incorporate the major issues of the day, and

41. Steven Kelman, *What Price Incentives? Economists and the Environment* (Boston: Auburn House, 1981), pp. 44–49.

42. John Mendeloff, *Regulating Safety: An Economic and Political Analysis of Occupational Safety and Health Policy* (Cambridge: MIT Press, 1979), pp. 6–35.

43. Steven Pressman, "The Gay Community Struggles to Fashion an Effective Lobby," *Congressional Quarterly Weekly Report* 41 (December 3, 1983): 2543–2547.

their ratings amount to broad ideological rankings of legislators. The Americans for Democratic Action (ADA) and the American Conservative Union are leading examples. Others pursue more specialized agendas, including the American Civil Liberties Union, the League of Conservation Voters, the National Taxpayers Union, and the Chamber of Commerce. Still others attempt to capture legislators' records toward even narrower special interests, policies that affect publics ranging from senior citizens and farmers to realtors and small businesses.

Groups do not compile and publish these ratings as a public service. They do so to give their members a chance to reward their friends and punish their enemies. Ratings can affect not only how citizens see particular legislators but how campaign contributors and political action committees (PACs) allocate their campaign funds.[44] Some groups announce their positions in advance, in an attempt to influence legislators who might be eager to increase their ratings.

I know of no better example of how an interest group can combine legislative ratings, lobbying, campaign endorsements, and campaign contributions than the case of the National Federation of Independent Business, an organization that claims 620,000 members and that attempts to represent the interests of small business. Whenever a bill in which the Federation is interested approaches a floor vote, it sends all legislators a letter stating its position and indicating that the issue will appear in its annual rating. At the end of each session it counts up the votes and publishes the results. The Federation declares a legislator with a score of 70 percent or better a "Guardian of Small Business," awards a pewter trophy in a public ceremony, sends out press releases to all local media, endorses the legislator for reelection, and guarantees a campaign contribution from its own PAC if he or she is in a close election. A score of less than 40 percent triggers a donation to the challenger.[45] Evidence suggests that at least some legislators search for appropriate votes related to small business to raise their scores. Just before the 1980 election, an aide to the House leadership reported that some members were watching carefully for any votes that might boost their ratings and help fend off conservative challengers. According to the aide, "More

44. Larry Sabato, "Parties, PACs, and Independent Groups," in Thomas E. Mann and Norman J. Ornstein (eds.), *The American Elections of 1982* (Washington, D.C.: American Enterprise Institute, 1983), p. 94.

45. Bill Keller, "Small Business Lobby Plays Trick or Treat," *Congressional Quarterly Weekly Report* 39 (March 21, 1981): 509.

than a few people knew where they stood, and how much they would have [to do] to come up to make 70 percent."[46]

How much legislators adjust their votes in anticipation of such scores is unknown.[47] Certainly the example of the small business lobby and the earlier example of legislators trying to keep off the list of "The Dirty Dozen" suggest that some legislators do anticipate how their own actions might affect their ratings. Group ratings can also push legislators in the opposite direction. Now that liberalism has become a dirty word in politics, some legislators intentionally try to depress their ADA scores. Senator Joseph Biden (D., Del.) admitted before a National Press Club luncheon that he sometimes votes against an ADA position because a perfect score would make him an easy target for the right wing.[48] The staff director of the Democratic Study Group suggested that other liberal legislators avoided some ADA issues for the same reason.[49]

MAKING DECISIONS

I have now made the case that legislators need to be concerned with both the positions they take and the effects they produce, and that they need to consider both the known policy preferences of attentive publics and the potential policy preferences of inattentive publics. These four sets of calculations are closely interrelated. A legislator can rouse inattentive publics either with the positions he takes or by producing displeasing effects that are traceable to his own actions. Similarly, a legislator can satisfy or provoke attentive publics either with the positions that he takes or with his connections to actual policy effects.

How do legislators combine their calculations about positions and effects, and about attentive and inattentive publics, in order to decide which side to support when a policy proposal comes before Congress?

46. Ibid.

47. There is evidence to suggest that senators moderate their issue positions strategically during the two or three years before they face reelection. See Richard C. Elling, "Ideological Change in the U.S. Senate: Time and Electoral Responsiveness," *Legislative Studies Quarterly* 7 (1982): 75–92; Martin Thomas, "Election Proximity and Senatorial Roll Call Voting," *American Journal of Political Science* 29 (1985): 96–111; and Gerald C. Wright, Jr., and Michael B. Berkman, "Candidates and Policy in United States Senate Elections," *American Political Science Review* 80 (1986): 567–588.

48. Bill Keller, "Congressional Rating Game Is Hard to Win," *Congressional Quarterly Weekly Report* 39 (March 21, 1981): 512.

49. Ibid.

How do they decide whether to follow the known preferences of attentive publics or the potential preferences of inattentive publics? Combining these calculations is actually the easy part of the analysis, for all such calculations reduce to a single metric—votes—and once reduced they can easily be summed. The more difficult part is reducing each of the separate calculations to the number of votes gained or lost.

The first thing to realize is that legislators are not beginning with a blank slate. All have faced the electorate at least once before, and some have done so repeatedly. All have a sense of who their consistent supporters are, who are consistent opponents, and who occupy the spaces in between.[50] When deciding whether to support a proposal about which group A is strongly in favor and group B is strongly opposed, the first question to ask is whether the members of these two groups tend to be consistent supporters or consistent opponents of the legislator. Most legislators play a conservative game and follow the preferences of their most consistent supporters rather than those of their past opponents.[51] It is not that they would not like to reach out and bring their former opponents into their electoral coalitions, it is just that they must wait for occasions that do not antagonize their longtime supporters. It is far easier to alienate one's longtime friends with a few very wrong votes than it is to transform one's most steadfast opponents into reliable friends with an equal number of pleasing votes.

Seldom do legislators face two opposing groups that feel equally strongly about an issue. Citizens differ in the intensity with which they hold particular preferences, and this intensity affects the likelihood that citizens might alter their opinions of legislators on the basis of legislators' positions or actions. Those who feel intensely about an issue may tolerate little deviance from their preferred path, whereas those who have more moderate preferences may never notice what a legislator is doing. All else equal, legislators follow the preferences of those who feel most intensely about an issue.[52]

We know from Chapter 2 that intensity is itself a function of several policy attributes. Intensity is particularly associated with imposing costs on citizens. Anyone who has dealt with small children knows that taking a new toy away from a child produces a reaction far more intense than providing the toy did in the first place. Alas, the same is true in

50. Richard F. Fenno, Jr., *Home Style: House Members in Their Districts* (Boston: Little, Brown, 1978), pp. 1–30; and Kingdon, *Congressmen's Voting Decisions*, p. 34.

51. Kingdon, *Congressmen's Voting Decisions*, p. 34.

52. Ibid., pp. 35–41.

politics. Legislators know that the likelihood that citizens deprived of things they have long enjoyed will look for someone to punish exceeds the likelihood that citizens with newly received benefits will look for someone to reward. Intensity is also associated with the magnitude of policy effects. Large policy effects, whether costs or benefits, produce more intense preferences than smaller effects.

Finally, legislators care about the size of the various groups that have preferences on an issue. All else equal, they prefer satisfying large groups to satisfying small ones, for the net gain in votes is greater. Sufficient size can often swamp the impact of other attributes, such as intensity. Legislators may side with large groups that have moderate preferences on visible issues, even at the risk of offending small groups with more intense preferences. Most environmental legislation, for example, is enacted as a consequence of these very calculations. Small groups can often compensate for their size, however, by offering legislators more than just their votes. Legislators often collect campaign contributions from very small groups and then use them to attract the support of larger publics on other matters.

Most of the preceding generalizations apply equally to attentive and inattentive publics. The only difference is that legislators must consider with what probability the potential preferences of inattentive publics will be transformed into real preferences, whereas attentive publics already have real preferences. When legislators consider enacting an income tax surcharge, they do not treat the potential preferences of inattentive publics any differently from the actual preferences of attentive publics, because they know it would be very easy to mobilize the inattentive publics. When they deal with the complicated rules for depreciating capital assets, however, they can easily defer to the attentive publics, knowing that it would be next to impossible to activate the inattentive publics.

To reach a decision, then, a legislator needs to (1) identify all the attentive and inattentive publics who might care about a policy issue, (2) estimate the direction and intensity of their preferences and potential preferences, (3) estimate the probability that the potential preferences will be transformed into real preferences, (4) weight all these preferences according to the size of the various attentive and inattentive publics, and (5) give special weight to the preferences of the legislator's consistent supporters. Many of these estimates will be zero for most issues, either because many people are genuinely indifferent or because it is hard to imagine how the inattentive publics could ever be activated.

When this is true, the net scores many be dominated by a few estimates—perhaps the intense preferences of a few attentive publics. If these preferences all point in the same direction, then a legislator's decision is clear. If the preferences in favor are roughly balanced by an equal number opposed, then a legislator is free to vote as he or she pleases.[53]

These calculations (for even a single vote) require substantial information and analysis. Moreover, legislators must make several hundred roll-call decisions annually. The House conducted 834 recorded votes in its peak year, 1978, while the Senate took 688 recorded votes in its peak year, 1976.[54] Is it reasonable to imagine individual legislators performing all these calculations for each and every issue that reaches the floor? Fortunately, my argument does not require each legislator to perform all these calculations alone, any more than the citizens of Chapter 3 must, on their own, acquire and process all the information required for retrospective voting. Congress is an extraordinary institution for creating, analyzing, and sharing politically relevant information; individual legislators need not duplicate one another's efforts.

The committee system is the principal vehicle for gathering and analyzing information. Committees specialize not only in policies but in the politics of those policies. They conduct extensive open hearings to determine the arguments for and against proposed programs, to identify exactly who supports and who opposes them, and to establish whether becoming associated with a program might generate political problems for some legislators. Committees encourage interest groups and other interested parties to testify and submit statements, and they commission bureaucrats and congressional staff agencies to produce even more studies. The printed hearings and the resultant committee and minority reports often represent the best guides to a program's political topography.

Legislators who are not members of the committee reporting a bill can consult the appropriate hearings and reports for guidance in making their own political evaluations. More likely, legislators rely on small staffs of legislative assistants to read and digest these volumes and recommend which alternatives best serve their employers' political inter-

53. Of course, legislators are always free to vote as they please. In my theoretical world, however, they choose to do so only if they see no significant electoral differences between supporting and opposing a particular policy option.

54. Ornstein, *Vital Statistics*, p. 168.

ests. Legislators also consult frequently with trusted colleagues who serve on the relevant committees or who otherwise have expertise to share. Colleagues are an especially valuable source because they can interpret the political significance of surprise amendments, procedural maneuvers, and other unexpected events about which committee reports are silent.[55] In fact, a perfectly reasonable way to protect one's political hide is to follow the lead of a colleague who has expertise in the proposal being considered and who has a similar constituency and supporting coalition. Kingdon reports that such cue taking is, in fact, very common in Congress.[56]

How should we conceive of this relationship between a legislator and legislative staffs or between a legislator and trusted colleagues? Is it influence? Ordinarily it is not, at least in the sense that social scientists use the term. Influence is best understood as a causal relation between one actor's preferences and another actor's behavior.[57] Yet here it is clear that legislators choose staff members and trusted colleagues whose views are fundamentally compatible with their own and who merely help legislators define which actions serve their own political interests.[58] The relationship becomes one of influence only if these informants violate that trust and recommend actions that serve their own policy preferences rather than legislators' interests. Surely this happens occasionally, but several forces keep its frequency low. Legislators have multiple sources of information, which means that no staff member who repeatedly provided poor advice would long survive. The norms of the institution also keep colleagues from misleading each other, and in any event legislators can quickly replace those who prove untrustworthy. Ordinarily, then, the use of staff members or trusted colleagues for political advice does nothing to interfere with the principal influence relation-

---

55. Such votes are increasingly common. Much of the growth in roll-call voting relates to floor amendments and procedural votes. In the 84th Congress (1955–1956) the House conducted exactly 15 recorded votes on amendments, whereas in the 95th Congress (1977–1978) there were 439 recorded votes on amendments. See Steven S. Smith, *Call to Order: Floor Politics in the House and Senate* (Washington, D.C.: Brookings Institution, 1989), p. 31.

56. Kingdon, *Congressmen's Voting Decisions*, pp. 72–109. See also Donald R. Matthews and James A. Stimson, *Yeas and Nays: Normal Decision Making in the U.S. House of Representatives* (New York: Wiley, 1975).

57. Jack H. Nagel, *Descriptive Analysis of Power* (New Haven: Yale University Press, 1975), pp. 9–22.

58. Kingdon, *Congressmen's Voting Decisions*, pp. 75–82.

ship under consideration in this book—that between citizens and their representatives.

Committees, staff members, and trusted colleagues have no monopoly on information. They are helpful especially for anticipating problems with inattentive publics and for analyzing low-salience issues. For high-salience issues and for those with attentive publics, legislators have other sources. Constituents write letters and convey their views in personal meetings. Interest groups send their agents to persuade legislators in person, and many attempt to mobilize their members back home to apply pressure from that direction.

Finally, the burden of political calculation is reduced by the fact that legislators face many of the same issues year after year. Strictly speaking, only freshman legislators must calculate the political implications of five or six hundred new issues.[59] Other legislators face fewer new issues and, thus, fewer real decisions. For the recurrent issues, they need only determine if their previous votes have been well received and whether the political terrain has changed in the interim.[60]

59. For a description of how two freshmen representatives, Peter J. Visclosky (D., Ind.) and Jim Kolbe (R., Ariz.), agonized over the tough voting decisions of 1985, see Andy Plattner, "Freshmen Fret about Potential Fallout from Casting Floor Votes on Hot Issues," *Congressional Quarterly Weekly Report* 43 (August 17, 1985): 1628–1629.

60. Kingdon, *Congressmen's Voting Decisions*, pp. 274–278.

5

Strategies for
Coalition Leaders

How do leaders assemble winning coalitions for the proposals that they put before Congress? How do they anticipate legislators' electoral needs when they design policies, fashion arguments, and choose procedures? How do leaders harness legislators' electoral ambitions to advance their own goals? This chapter examines the strategies available for building coalitions and shows how leaders choose among them. Such strategies are general plans for attracting support, both within Congress and among attentive and inattentive publics.

Building winning coalitions is hard work. Legislators who merely drop bills in the hopper and wait for something to happen are invariably disappointed. Nothing happens in Congress unless someone plans for it and works for it. Someone must define the problems, shape the alternatives, initiate action, mobilize support, arrange compromises, and work to see that Congress passes specific bills. Those who perform these duties I refer to as coalition leaders.

Coalition leaders may be drawn from both inside and outside Congress. They include rank-and-file legislators, committee and subcommittee leaders, party leaders, congressional staff members, the president, presidential staff members, executive branch officials, bureaucrats, and interest group leaders. In this chapter I seek to explain the behavior of the generic leader; I do not try to isolate the differences in the strategies and tactics of various types of coalition leaders. Of course, there are enormous differences between the resources and talents of a president like Lyndon Johnson, the average chairman of a House committee, and a freshman legislator from the minority party. Most of these differences are well known. What are not well known are the ways in which successful leaders of every variety go about anticipating and responding to legislators' electoral needs as they build winning coalitions.

My analysis begins at the point that someone decides to build a coalition for a specific proposal. I do not examine why individuals choose to become coalition leaders in the first place, why they choose to attack specific problems or advance specific remedies, or why they invest their scarce time and resources in mobilizing support. These are all interesting and important questions, but they are peripheral to my central argument.[1] As far as my theory is concerned, individuals volunteer, for reasons of their own, to champion or oppose certain causes. Once they have volunteered, the problem for theory is to explain why they adopt specific strategies to advance or retard those causes (this chapter) and why one side wins and the other side loses (the next chapter).

The supply of coalition leaders is not uniformly distributed across the range of policy problems and policy solutions. Some policy proposals attract coalition leaders in droves, while others offer few incentives to leaders of any sort.[2] Most coalition leaders have an intense interest in at least one aspect of a policy proposal—perhaps its general costs or benefits, its geographic effects, or its group effects. Proposals with concentrated geographic effects tend to acquire legislators from the affected areas as leaders. Those with concentrated group effects tend to attract bureaucrats, interest group leaders, and some legislators.[3] Proposals that are heavily laden with general costs or benefits offer mixed incentives. Those with general effects that are highly salient tend to attract coalition leaders quite easily, whereas proposals with general effects that are either less visible or long delayed often have few champions.

---

1. An earlier version of this manuscript contained an entire chapter on the incentives for policy activism for various types of coalition leaders. I eventually decided to give that chapter a decent burial after I realized that I had very little original to say on the subject, and what I did say contributed little to my central argument. The general question has not been the subject of much research, with the exception of the incentives for joining organized interest groups. On the incentives that encourage legislators to become coalition leaders, see Steven S. Smith, "Coalition Leaders in Congress: A Theoretical Perspective" (paper presented at the annual meeting of the American Political Science Association, August 1984).

2. See David E. Price, "Policy Making in Congressional Committees: The Impact of 'Environmental' Factors," *American Political Science Review* 72 (1978): 548–574; and John W. Kingdon, *Agendas, Alternatives, and Public Policies* (Boston: Little, Brown, 1984), pp. 23–47.

3. Price notes that legislators shun policies with concentrated group effects when conflict is high and public salience is low. See Price, "Policy Making in Congressional Committees."

Finally, some individuals become coalition leaders because their current positions demand it. The president, the director of the Office of Management and Budget, and the chairmen of the House and Senate budget committees, for example, are natural candidates for building coalitions on budgetary matters.

Policies that promise large, early-order benefits tend to attract coalition leaders far more easily than those that promise only later-order benefits. When a policy offers both early-order and later-order benefits, it is generally the former that stimulates activism. The push for new educational programs invariably comes from teachers or school administrators, not students or their parents. The impetus for mass transit, mental health, or welfare programs comes from the professionals who deliver such services, rather than from those who receive the services.[4] Similarly, early-order costs are a greater stimulus to activism than are later-order costs. When the Senate battled over how strong automobile bumpers must be, the coalition leaders had nothing to do with automobiles, safety, or insurance. Senator Robert Byrd (D., W.V.) promoted standards that were met more easily by steel bumpers (produced in the great state of West Virginia), while Senator Warren Magnuson (D., Wash.) held out for a standard that favored aluminum bumpers (produced in the great state of Washington).[5]

These distinctions are important because the strategies that an individual adopts depend, in part, on the individual's central interest in a proposal. Consider, for example, several of the senators involved in the Tax Reform Act of 1986. Senator Bill Bradley (D., N.J.) was primarily interested in the general benefits of tax reform. He was the principal architect of the plan and had spent years traveling across the country trying to get people interested in fundamental reform. His central con-

4. The issue is not merely one of concentrated effects, for surely students, welfare recipients, and mental patients have a great deal at stake. Nor is the issue simply one of organization, though it is true that groups organize more easily around early-order effects. The best explanation is that the incidence of early-order effects is far more certain than that of later-order effects. Those who deliver services can be fairly certain how they will profit from new infusions of money, and that knowledge encourages activism. Those who will eventually receive these services cannot know in advance exactly how they will profit, particularly as individuals. Even if students, welfare recipients, or mental patients as a class are certain to profit, today's individuals may well be replaced by others by the time a program begins delivering services.

5. Judy Sarasohn, "Titans Tangle in Senate Bumper Standards Dispute," *Congressional Quarterly Weekly Report* 37 (July 14, 1979): 1409–1410.

cern nudged him toward the few strategies that preserved the bill's general benefits.[6] Senator Russell Long (D., La.) had contrary incentives. He had very little interest in tax reform itself and a very strong concern with preserving the group and geographic benefits enjoyed by the oil companies of Louisiana.[7] Senator Robert Packwood (R., Ore.) marched to yet a different drummer. Although he had no particular interest in reforming taxes, his role as chairman of the Senate Finance Committee gave him an interest in passing a bill—any bill—that looked and sounded like reform. The political liabilities for him, both in the Senate and in Oregon, where he was running for reelection, would be too great if he allowed his committee to kill a bill that was the president's principal domestic program and that the Democratic House had already passed. Thus, it was perfectly consistent for Packwood first to push a bill laden with group and geographic benefits and then, when that bill faltered, to substitute a new bill stripped of most group and geographic benefits. At the time, each plan seemed like the best way to enact a bill.[8] It would be difficult to imagine Senator Bradley ever pushing the former bill or Senator Long the latter—even as a strategic maneuver—because the bills failed to further each senator's central interest.

Coalition leaders are free to champion whatever policy proposals they choose.[9] Presumably most leaders select proposals that advance their own central interests. Once they have chosen a specific proposal, however, they face but a small set of potentially winning strategies. Success requires them to anticipate legislators' electoral needs, which itself requires them to anticipate the possible reactions of attentive and inattentive publics. These electoral needs place severe constraints on leaders' choices among strategies.

There are no universal strategies, appropriate for any proposal under any conditions. Leaders must tailor general strategies to fit the idiosyncrasies of specific policy proposals. Leaders can choose from three

6. Jeffrey H. Birnbaum and Alan S. Murray, *Showdown at Gucci Gulch: Lawmakers, Lobbyists, and the Unlikely Triumph of Tax Reform* (New York: Vintage, 1987), pp. 23–31.

7. Ibid., pp. 227–232.

8. Ibid., pp. 176–191, 204–208.

9. Of course, there are constraints. Elected politicians do not champion proposals that they could not otherwise support, staff members cannot advance proposals without the approval of their superiors, and leaders of interest groups need to retain the support of their own members. My point is simply that most coalition leaders begin with a blank slate, rather than having to choose among paired or otherwise restricted alternatives.

strategic approaches, each of which anticipates legislators' electoral needs in a different way. *Strategies of persuasion* create, activate, or change the policy preferences of legislators, attentive publics, and inattentive publics. The intent is to shape policy preferences, both inside Congress and among relevant publics, to fit the original proposal. *Procedural strategies* attempt to influence legislators' political calculations by adroit use of legislative rules and procedures. The aim is to structure the legislative situation in a way that decreases the ability of an instigator to rouse inattentive publics or of a challenger to make a campaign issue out of a specific roll-call vote. *Strategies of modification* involve altering the various components of a policy, ranging from the policy instrument to the incidence of costs and benefits. The aim is to mold a policy so that it conforms better with legislators' and citizens' preferences and potential preferences.[10] Each of these general strategies can also be used by opposition leaders who are attempting to block a particular proposal, and both sides can combine strategies in various ways.

STRATEGIES OF PERSUASION

Persuasion involves creating, activating, or changing the policy preferences of legislators, attentive publics, and (if necessary) inattentive publics. At times coalition leaders mount large-scale campaigns to shift elite and mass opinion toward a major programmatic initiative, such as national health insurance, energy policy, or the equal rights amendment. Or leaders may confine their efforts to Washington and focus on legislators and the most attentive publics, as they shepherd a proposal through the various stages of the legislative process. Frequently coalition leaders and opposition leaders have but a few minutes

10. These three approaches do not exhaust all the strategies available to coalition leaders, although they do exhaust the ones that rely most directly on the electoral connection. *Exchange strategies*, a fourth approach, involve the trading of support across different policy areas. The aim is to persuade legislators to vote against their true interests (incurring, if necessary, modest electoral costs) in exchange for leaders' or other legislators' assistance on matters of greater importance to these legislators (including matters that pay handsome electoral dividends). *Replacement strategies* involve replacing current legislators with those holding more congenial views. This is a long-term strategy adopted only when others have failed. Opponents of abortion and proponents of the equal rights amendment are currently pursuing such strategies. On exchange strategies, see R. Douglas Arnold, *Congress and the Bureaucracy: A Theory of Influence* (New Haven: Yale University Press, 1979), pp. 47–50, 210–214.

to offer alternative interpretations of a surprise floor amendment that would change policy in some field.[11] No matter what the stage in coalition building, leaders seek to persuade legislators that a policy proposal is simultaneously a good idea *and* that it is unlikely to generate electoral problems for them. This deed can be accomplished either by generating favorable opinions among attentive and inattentive publics or by showing legislators that the program is unlikely to generate unfavorable opinions if people happen to hear about it.

An initial task for coalition leaders is to persuade people that a problem is one that government should tackle, and that the federal government should handle it. The easiest way to accomplish this goal is to link the new ends to some already well-established ends, making a new departure look like a logical extension of current policy rather than a dramatic shift in the role of government. Linkage strategies also make persuasion more economical because they build on established opinions rather than creating new opinion from scratch.

National defense has long been a favorite justification for new programs, in part because no one quibbles with defense as the premier function for national government and in part because national security really does depend on many things other than the size and composition of the armed services. Defense has been used to justify the federal government's entry into the funding of basic scientific research, space exploration, education, interstate highways, shipbuilding, and many other functions that had long been lodged in either state and local governments or the private sector.[12] For most of these programs there is at least a tenuous relationship between the proposals and national security, although sometimes there is no connection at all. In the 1950s the oil companies convinced Congress that oil import quotas were necessary to keep America from becoming dependent on foreign supplies that might become unreliable in times of trouble. The effect, of course, was to drain America first, and thus to make the nation even more dependent on foreign sources in the long run (see Chapter 9). Even when the logic of specific policies is questionable, the power of the label "defense" to help sell new policies is unquestionable.

11. For an excellent analysis of how leaders go about shaping legislators' interpretations of policy proposals, see Richard A. Smith, "Advocacy, Interpretation, and Influence in the U.S. Congress," *American Political Science Review* 78 (1984): 44–63.

12. For example, the National *Defense* Education Act (1958) or the National Interstate and *Defense* Highway System (1956).

The current favorite for linkage strategies is economic growth, productivity, and competitiveness. In fact, coalition leaders use economic productivity to justify some of the same policies that were once tied to national defense, such as education, basic scientific research, and various transportation and other infrastructure programs. The shift reflects both the increased political conflict associated with national security policy and the rise to prominence of macroeconomic policy. Today anyone who wants to create a tax loophole, change a regulation affecting industry, or establish a new program should first develop an argument about how those changes will lead to economic growth, for nothing sells better in the current political climate. The Reagan administration used this justification for cutting the top income tax rate from 70 percent to 28 percent. The argument was that if rich people pay less in taxes, they will invest their windfalls and thereby create jobs for everyone.

Equity is another favorite for linkage strategies. Here coalition leaders link a proposed policy to something else Congress has already approved, arguing that similar conditions deserve similar responses. Shortly after Congress legalized exclusive territories for soft-drink bottlers, a coalition of beer distributors began lobbying Congress for a similar antitrust exemption, using equity as a justification.[13] When activists campaigned for federal funding of heart, lung, and liver transplants, they argued that patients with nonfunctioning kidneys were already receiving free kidney dialysis and that the government should not discriminate against those with comparable needs.[14]

Linkage strategies become easier to use as the government grows in size and scope. In the beginning, when government performed only a few functions, each new proposal seemed like a major departure from current policy and, thus, required extensive debate. As governmental functions multiplied, it became increasingly easy to find well-established precedents for new proposals. The battles in the 1960s to enact federal aid to education, medical care, and civil rights were long and intense. Once enacted, they became excellent precedents for many more federal initiatives in these and neighboring fields.

The logic of linkage strategies rests, in part, on the tendency of legislators to establish consistent voting histories on recurrent issues.[15] When

13. Bill Keller, "Beer Distributors Discover Lobby Formula: Bottoms Up," *Congressional Quarterly Weekly Report* 40 (September 11, 1982): 2248–2249.

14. Elizabeth Wehr, "National Health Policy Sought for Organ Transplant Surgery," *Congressional Quarterly Weekly Report* 42 (February 25, 1984): 453–458.

15. John W. Kingdon, *Congressmen's Voting Decisions*, 2d ed. (New York: Harper and Row, 1981), pp. 274–278.

urban issues emerge legislators vote one way, when civil rights issues are on the agenda they divide along different lines, and so on for social welfare, education, agriculture, and dozens of other issues.[16] Coalition leaders for new issues attempt to exploit voting histories by attaching the proper labels to their proposals so that legislators will vote in predictable ways. Although voting histories can be taken as evidence that legislators vote ideologically, they also reflect an explicit calculation that voting in favor of (or against) a given type of policy has been good politics in the past and provides a safe course for the future.[17]

Proponents are not the only ones who use linkage strategies. Opponents attempt to derail proposals by linking them with undesirable ends. When public opinion polls revealed that the original Medicare proposal was popular, opponents claimed that it was merely the first step toward socialized medicine; they warned of bureaucrats telling patients whom to see and doctors how to practice medicine.[18] Proponents of federal funding for day care centers stressed the needs of single mothers and the problem of persuading welfare mothers to work, while opponents raised the specter of the disintegration of the American family.[19] Proponents of a bill requiring factory owners to provide workers with ninety days' notice of plant closings spoke of fairness and decency, while opponents warned that restrictions on management would further erode American competitiveness.[20] Each side of a controversy attempts to link the proposal in question to some other issue for which the distribution of opinion is both known and favorable to its position.

Linking new policy goals to established goals is not the only way to market proposals. Leaders also marshall arguments to justify the federal government's tackling a new problem. They typically offer arguments showing the extent of the problem, why neither the private sector nor state and local governments can solve it, and how the federal government might ameliorate it. The original advocates of clean air legislation,

16. Aage R. Clausen, *How Congressmen Decide* (New York: St. Martin's Press, 1973).

17. Kingdon, *Congressmen's Voting Decisions*, p. 277.

18. Richard Harris, *A Sacred Trust* (New York: New American Library, 1966); and Theodore R. Marmor, *The Politics of Medicare* (New York: Aldine, 1973). The same was true two decades earlier when national health insurance was on the agenda. See Stanley Kelley, Jr., *Professional Public Relations and Political Power* (Baltimore: Johns Hopkins, 1956), pp. 67–106.

19. Gilbert Y. Steiner, *The Children's Cause* (Washington, D.C.: Brookings Institution, 1976), p. 108.

20. Elizabeth Wehr, "Senate OKs Advance Notice of Plant Closings," *Congressional Quarterly Weekly Report* 46 (July 9, 1988): 1919–1920.

for example, attempted to show how air pollution adversely affected health, why industry would never, on its own, control it, and why the problem was beyond the capacity of state governments, given the ease with which pollutants cross state boundaries.[21]

These arguments are most effective if coalition leaders can connect them to recent public events or tragedies that can attract media coverage, dramatize the need for governmental action, and focus attention on anyone with a proposed solution. Advocates used the Soviet Union's launch of *Sputnik* to dramatize the need for NASA and the National Defense Education Act.[22] The thalidomide disaster helped produce the Drug Amendments of 1962, much as the elixir sulfanilamide scandal, which caused over one hundred deaths, contributed to the passage of the Food, Drug, and Cosmetics Act of 1938.[23] The collapse of two dams in 1972 with a loss of 350 lives helped produce the National Dam Inspection Act, although it took the collapse of two more dams and the loss of fifty more lives before Congress provided proper funding.[24]

Fortuitous events like these do not by themselves produce action. They merely create opportunities for coalition leaders to exploit. Their impact is greatest when proponents have already drafted legislation, held hearings, and prepared the way. A well-timed tragedy then forces an issue to the top of the agenda and creates the proper climate for rapid action. Leaders may even shape some events or affect their timing. Senator Estes Kefauver's staff, for example, sat on the thalidomide story until they were sure Kefauver's bill would profit from its revelation.[25] Martin Luther King, eager to pressure Congress to pass the Voting Rights Act, carefully chose Selma for his protest march because he thought its sheriff was most likely to beat the peaceful protesters.[26]

Coalition leaders also seek to persuade legislators that the proposed policy instruments will actually produce the intended effects. This task

21. Charles O. Jones, *Clean Air: The Policies and Politics of Pollution Control* (Pittsburgh: University of Pittsburgh Press, 1975).

22. James L. Sundquist, *Politics and Policy* (Washington, D.C.: Brookings Institution, 1968), pp. 173–180.

23. Paul J. Quirk, "Food and Drug Administration," in James Q. Wilson (ed.), *The Politics of Regulation* (New York: Basic Books, 1980), pp. 196–199.

24. Bob Livernash, "Congress Looking at Issue of Nation's Unsafe Dams," *Congressional Quarterly Weekly Report* 36 (June 17, 1978): 1529–1531.

25. Quirk, "Food and Drug Administration," p. 199.

26. David J. Garrow, *Protest at Selma* (New Haven: Yale University Press, 1978), pp. 222–230.

is easiest for single-stage policies whose causal logic is simple and readily understandable. No one doubts, for example, that federal programs for the construction of roads, bridges, and sewers will actually increase the supply of each. The problems emerge when leaders attempt to market policies involving long, complex causal chains. Consider, for example, how difficult it was for proponents of deregulation to sell their proposals in Congress. Economists, even though united, could not reduce their arguments about the benefits of deregulation to a few simple sentences. The case for deregulating the telephone industry was especially difficult to explain. The breakthrough occurred in airlines. New airlines that began operating inside California and Texas, beyond the reach of federal regulators, reduced their prices well below those that regulated interstate carriers were charging in the same markets. Eventually the Civil Aeronautics Board began to experiment with partial deregulation. These experiments worked, increasing service while decreasing prices, and thus helped to legitimate the basic notion of deregulation and pave the way for the complete deregulation of airlines.[27] Demonstrations are ordinarily difficult to arrange, however. Coalition leaders can either conduct long educational campaigns in an attempt to persuade people that complicated programs would work, or they can substitute other policy instruments that are easier to market.

Coalition leaders can also seek to persuade legislators of a policy's merits by altering legislators' perceptions of the incidence of costs and benefits. This strategy is most obvious for geographic benefits. Proponents carefully calculate where the benefits will be concentrated and then inform those who will receive disproportionate shares of their good fortune. The Pentagon, for example, routinely assembles a list of subcontractors for each major weapons system so that each legislator can know exactly how his district will profit if it goes into production. Similarly, advocates of grant programs estimate how each state and locality will share in the benefits. Advocates may rely on legislators to see the light, or they may mobilize local contractors, workers, and government officials to lean on their representatives.

Opponents employ complementary strategies. One approach is to identify inequities in the distribution of benefits and then sow seeds of dissension among groups and localities receiving "unjust" shares. If they choose their criteria carefully, opponents can always demonstrate

27. Martha Derthick and Paul J. Quirk, *The Politics of Deregulation* (Washington, D.C.: Brookings Institution, 1985).

injustices. If tax rates are cut by a fixed percentage, they point out that
wealthy taxpayers reap greater dollar savings. If grants are distributed
according to need, they show that some recipients receive below-
average shares. If grants are allocated on the basis of population, they
demonstrate that the truly needy receive less than they should. If contracts are awarded to traditional suppliers, they show how small businesses and minority contractors suffer.

An alternative approach is to identify those who will bear substantial
group costs and then attempt to mobilize either those groups or their
usual legislative champions. Opponents of the telephone access fee, for
example, argued that residential and small business users would pay
more so that large corporations could pay less.[28] Opponents of a bill to
regulate hospital costs convinced hospital workers that their employers
would control costs by limiting their wages.[29] Opponents of a cargo
preference bill demonstrated how much the price of home heating oil
could rise as a consequence.[30] In all three cases, opponents were successful in mobilizing the affected interests and defeating the proposals.

Coalition leaders target their appeals to those most likely to support
them while trying not to arouse potential opponents. If only a small
minority will benefit from a program, proponents may seek to mobilize
that minority as quietly as possible so that they do not alarm the even
greater numbers who might oppose their efforts. They may attempt to
resolve all conflict within a friendly subcommittee or committee so that
others do not notice what is happening.[31] They may add a small,
seemingly innocuous section to a large and popular bill, or they may
propose a floor amendment at the last minute, leaving little time for
opponents to mobilize their troops.

Opponents of a change may attempt to broaden the scope of conflict in
order to mobilize others who have contrary interests at stake.[32] They
may attempt to open committee decision making to other points of view.
If these interests are already organized, they activate those organiza-

28. Steven Pressman, "Panel Approves Phone Bill Despite AT&T Lobby Drive," *Congressional Quarterly Weekly Report* 41 (October 29, 1983): 2241.

29. Elizabeth Wehr, "Compromise Efforts Under Way on Carter's Hospital Cost Cap
Bill," *Congressional Quarterly Weekly Report* 36 (April 22, 1978): 1021.

30. "House Sinks Cargo Preference Bill," *Congressional Quarterly Almanac, 1977* 33
(1978): 534–538.

31. Kingdon, *Congressmen's Voting Decisions*, pp. 262–265.

32. E. E. Schattschneider, *The Semisovereign People* (New York: Holt, Rinehart, and
Winston, 1960), pp. 1–19.

tions. If not, opponents appeal to broader inattentive publics by holding hearings or staging other public events for the news media to cover. They may encourage journalists to write about specific proposals by providing them with easy access and free information. These moves may, in turn, encourage proponents to think about yet other groups of beneficiaries that they can mobilize to counteract the efforts of opponents.

In their arguments, proponents tend to magnify benefits and minimize costs. They market proposals as if the resulting programs were not only certain to achieve their intended ends but would also yield many pleasant by-products, such as stimulating investment, revitalizing cities, decreasing unemployment, increasing tax revenues, curbing crime, and balancing the budget. At the same time, they tend to underestimate the budgetary costs required to implement their proposals. Proponents project tiny short-term costs so that their proposals do not threaten other people's favorite programs. They also tend to underestimate the less tangible costs, ranging from compliance costs for firms to the general losses of liberty associated with an increasingly bureaucratic society. Opponents suffer from the opposite disease. They tend to minimize a program's benefits and magnify its costs.

PROCEDURAL STRATEGIES

Procedural strategies involve attempts to influence legislators' political calculations by adroit use of legislative rules and procedures. Coalition leaders may erect procedural barriers to protect legislators from strong political winds that otherwise might drive them into the opposition camp. Alternatively, they might structure the legislative situation so that the prevailing winds blow legislators into the very coalitions they are endeavoring to build. Opposition leaders use similar strategies to force legislators to support their views. Frequently, the principal battle is over whose rules shall prevail—those of the proponents or those of the opponents—because each side believes that it can win its substantive points under the proper procedures.

Procedural strategies are used to manipulate the circumstances under which legislators are forced to take public positions.[33] From legisla-

---

33. There is a growing literature that uses formal theory to understand the consequences of various congressional procedures. This literature explores, among other

tors' point of view, there is a big difference between voting in favor of an amendment that would increase by 5 percent the salaries of all federal workers and voting in favor of two separate amendments, one of which would increase legislators' own salaries and the other of which would increase the salaries of all other federal workers. The policy effects are identical, but the political effects are not. Legislators know that challengers delight in using votes on legislative salaries against them, whereas an across-the-board increase makes a poor political issue.[34] The aim of all procedural strategies is to structure the legislative situation in a way that either increases or decreases the ability of an instigator to rouse inattentive publics or of a challenger to make a good campaign issue out of a specific roll-call vote.

Coalition leaders may adopt procedural strategies that either strengthen or break the traceability chain for policy effects. Those who seek to impose large, direct, or early-order costs usually search for procedural strategies that break the traceability chain, knowing that legislators' greatest concern is that citizens might trace those costs back to their own individual actions. Those who seek to block the imposition of such costs prefer procedural strategies that strengthen the traceability chain. When the issue is delivering large, early-order benefits, the preferred strategies are reversed; proponents seek to strengthen the traceability chain while opponents seek to break it. Even when effects are not potentially traceable, both coalition and opposition leaders can employ procedures that emphasize (or camouflage) legislators' connections with popular (or unpopular) policy positions.

Weakening the traceability chain is a superb method for protecting

---

things, the ways in which rules contribute to stable legislative outcomes, the effects of closed and restrictive rules on the power of agenda setters, and the consequences of restrictive procedures for considering conference reports. For a superb review of this literature, see Keith Krehbiel, "Spatial Models of Legislative Choice," *Legislative Studies Quarterly* 13 (1988): 259–319. In this book I am more interested in explaining the *content* of legislation, and for that task I have focused on a different class of procedural strategies—those that adjust the context of congressional decision making in anticipation of the ways in which legislators will be held accountable by their constituents.

34. For example, in 1977 Speaker O'Neill pressured members to vote for an increase in congressional pay by crafting a rule that allowed only one amendment to the bill—to eliminate raises for *all* federal workers. As a consequence, members could eliminate their own raises only if they were willing to deprive everyone else of their raises. Since few members were willing to do the latter, legislators received a "pain less" pay raise. See Barbara Sinclair, *Majority Leadership in the House* (Baltimore: Johns Hopkins University Press, 1983), p. 131.

legislators from their constituents' wrath for imposing costs on them. According to the incumbent performance rule, citizens punish legislators for undesirable effects only if there are both identifiable governmental actions and visible individual contributions (see Chapter 3). It follows, then, that coalition leaders who seek to impose large, perceptible costs should either eliminate all identifiable governmental actions that produce those costs or make legislators' individual contributions as nearly invisible as possible.

One method of masking legislators' individual contributions is to delegate responsibility for making unpleasant decisions to the president, bureaucrats, regulatory commissioners, judges, or state and local officials. Congress may pass across-the-board budgetary cuts but leave it to the president or agency administrators to allocate the cuts among specific programs. Legislators thereby appear frugal while avoiding any association with specific reductions. Sometimes legislators know precisely what the executive will decide, but the process of delegation insulates them from political retribution. When Congress was unable to approve any of the standby gasoline rationing plans submitted by President Carter, presumably for fear of retrospective voting, the procedural solution was for Congress to delegate authority to the president to draft and implement a plan *without* the need for specific congressional approval. Everyone knew the president would simply affirm one of the previously rejected plans; but by delegating authority, legislators insulated themselves from any political repercussions, should a plan ever be implemented and produce unpopular effects (see Chapter 9).

A second method of masking legislators' individual responsibility is secrecy. Committees frequently work behind closed doors so that outsiders are uncertain about how to apportion responsibility. Although closed committee meetings went out of style after the reforms of 1970 and 1973, they are coming back again. They are particularly useful when committees are drafting tax bills or other controversial measures.[35] Several years ago, the Senate Finance Committee, besieged by lobbyists, fled to a small, private chamber to write a $50 billion tax increase.[36] Most of the crucial decisions about the Tax Reform Act of

35. The House Ways and Means Committee and many of the subcommittees of the House Appropriations Committee now routinely close their markup sessions to reporters, lobbyists, and the public. See Jacqueline Calmes, "Few Complaints Are Voiced as Doors Close on Capitol Hill," *Congressional Quarterly Weekly Report* 45 (May 23, 1987): 1059–1060.

36. Pamela Fessler, "Senate Panel Votes Tax Boosts," *Congressional Quarterly Weekly Report* 42 (March 17, 1984): 590

1986 were also made behind closed doors. Both the House Ways and Means Committee and the Senate Finance Committee drafted their bills in private and then approved the complete packages in public session.[37] The conference committee not only met behind closed doors, it eventually delegated to the two committee chairmen, Senator Robert Packwood and Representative Dan Rostenkowski, the task of working out the most contentious issues by themselves.[38] Unrecorded votes are also an option for interrupting the traceability chain.[39] Although they are now more difficult to arrange, unrecorded votes are still used occasionally to accomplish various difficult tasks for which no one wants to be held accountable.[40]

Eliminating identifiable governmental actions—those essential elements of retrospective voting—is also a relatively easy task. One method is to combine various proposals into a single omnibus bill so that legislators vote on an entire package rather than on each of the individual pieces. Such bills allow representatives to hide from their constituents. Legislators establish a series of nebulous positions on amorphous-sounding bills like the Clean Air Amendments of 1970, the Education Amendments of 1980, or the Omnibus Reconciliation Act of 1980, but they need never answer for the costs that specific provisions impose on particular groups or localities. Citizens affected by these provisions have a difficult time punishing their representatives, especially when legislators profess sympathy for their causes. Congress has relied increasingly on omnibus bills in the last few years, including budget resolutions, reconciliation bills, and continuing resolutions.[41] These omnibus bills are especially valuable in the fields of taxation, spending, budgetary policy, and Social Security. The giant Omnibus Budget Reconciliation

37. Birnbaum and Murray, *Showdown at Gucci Gulch*, pp. 121, 222.

38. Ibid., pp. 260, 268–276.

39. Unrecorded teller votes were once the norm in the House. The Legislative Reorganization Act of 1970 changed this, so that today twenty-five House members can demand a recorded vote. The same act also requires that committees make public all roll-call votes. Unrecorded votes are possible, therefore, only if virtually all legislators conspire to keep them that way. A disappointed minority—even a relatively small one—can always demand a roll-call vote.

40. Pamela Fessler, "Near Empty Chamber: Debt Bill Passage Surprises House Leaders," *Congressional Quarterly Weekly Report* 41 (May 21, 1983): 989.

41. Dale Tate, "Use of Omnibus Bills Burgeons Despite Members' Misgivings," *Congressional Quarterly Weekly Report* 40 (September 25, 1982): 2379–2383; and Martin Tolchin, "In the Face of Controversy, Packaging," *New York Times* (February 21, 1983): B6.

Act of 1981, for example, eliminated in a single stroke $35 billion from 232 budgetary accounts (see Chapter 7).[42] The Tax Reform Act of 1986 was itself a giant omnibus bill that modified a large portion of the tax code; House members considered the tax package as a whole, with only three minor amendments allowed.[43]

The principal tactical devices in the House for protecting omnibus bills from being split into their component parts are closed rules, which prohibit amendments, and restrictive rules, which allow only certain limited amendments.[44] The closed rule was once used routinely for tax bills and only occasionally for other bills. After the reforms of the early 1970s, the closed rule became less popular.[45] It has now largely been replaced by the restrictive rule, which limits the number, type, and content of amendments. Restrictive rules grew from 12 percent of all rules in 1977 to 45 percent in 1987.[46] They are essential for keeping large and complicated omnibus bills from unraveling.

These various methods—delegation to the executive, secrecy, and the creation of a single omnibus bill—can also be used in combination, in which case they become even more powerful. Congress has employed a combination of procedures since 1974 for drafting and enacting trade

42. The changes included a reduction of $53.2 billion in budget authority (appropriations) and $35.2 billion in annual outlays (actual spending) for fiscal year 1982. See John W. Ellwood, "Budget Control in a Redistributive Environment," in Allen Schick (ed.), *Making Economic Policy in Congress* (Washington, D.C.: American Enterprise Institute, 1983), p. 72.

43. As it turned out, the House never had a roll-call vote on the entire package. The opponents forgot to demand one during the short period between the voice vote and the final gavel. This was a genuine oversight, not an attempt to conceal the entire bill behind an unrecorded vote. See Birnbaum and Murray, *Showdown at Gucci Gulch*, pp. 174–175.

44. On the strategic use of congressional procedures, see Walter J. Oleszek, *Congressional Procedures and the Policy Process*, 3d ed. (Washington, D.C.: Congressional Quarterly Press, 1989); Stanley Bach, "The Structure of Choice in the House of Representatives: The Impact of Complex Special Rules," *Harvard Journal on Legislation* 18 (1981): 553–602; Stanley Bach, "Special Rules in the House of Representatives: Themes and Contemporary Variations," *Congressional Studies* 8 (1981): 37–58; and Stanley Bach and Steven S. Smith, *Managing Uncertainty in the House of Representatives: Adaptation and Innovation in Special Rules* (Washington, D.C.: Brookings Institution, 1988).

45. Catherine E. Rudder, "Committee Reform and the Revenue Process," in Lawrence C. Dodd and Bruce I. Oppenheimer (eds.), *Congress Reconsidered* (New York: Praeger, 1977), p. 119.

46. Janet Hook, "GOP Chafes under Restrictive House Rules," *Congressional Quarterly Weekly Report* 45 (October 10, 1987): 2449–2452; and Oleszek, *Congressional Procedures and the Policy Process*, p. 128.

agreements, a field where intense conflict over the parts can easily sink the whole endeavor. Under the procedures established in the 1974 Trade Act, executive officials first negotiate a general agreement with one or more nations, officials then present the draft in secret to the House Ways and Means Committee and the Senate Finance Committee, where small modifications are in order, and then Congress has ninety legislative days to approve or disapprove the entire package, with no amendments allowed. These procedures have been used to draft and secure approval for the 1979 Trade Act and the 1988 Canadian Free Trade Agreement.[47]

Legislators have been most creative in avoiding identifiable governmental actions when they endeavor to increase their own compensation (actually to restore what inflation has eroded).[48] Most legislators are reluctant to vote for a bill that would straightforwardly increase their salaries because they fear electoral retribution. So there is an endless search for a mechanism that avoids an identifiable action. In 1975 legislators appeared to have found a politically safe method when they voted to link their own salaries with those of other federal workers, who already received automatic cost-of-living adjustments. Unfortunately, their pay raises still required an annual appropriation, which legislators could no more support than they could support the pay raises themselves. In four of the next five years, Congress voted to block the increased appropriations. Legislators then devised a scheme that provided for automatic appropriations to match their automatic cost-of-living raises.[49] This mechanism has now delivered several automatic raises.[50]

While coalition leaders work to weaken or break the traceability chain, opposition leaders do everything in their power to strengthen it. This counter-strategy is obvious in the case of legislators' compensation. Whenever proponents of salary increases thought they had found a safe mechanism, opponents responded by creating a new identifiable governmental action for which legislators had to stand up and be counted. Under the scheme currently in force, salary increases are automatic

47. "A Secret Law," *New York Times* (May 11, 1988): A22; and Clyde H. Farnsworth, "How Congress Came to Love the Canada Free-Trade Bill," *New York Times* (June 5, 1988): sec. 4, p. 4.

48. On the politics of congressional pay, see R. Kent Weaver, *Automatic Government: The Politics of Indexation* (Washington, D.C.: Brookings Institution, 1988), pp. 118–145.

49. Irwin B. Arieff, "Congress Votes Itself New Pay, Benefits," *Congressional Quarterly Weekly Report* 39 (October 3, 1981): 1892.

50. Weaver, *Automatic Government*, pp. 129–130.

unless they are blocked within thirty days; so proponents and opponents now scramble to control the agenda during that period. In 1987 opponents did manage to obtain a vote on a motion disapproving the salary increase, but proponents delayed the vote for a day beyond the statutory limit (by adjourning the House just when opponents were about to pounce). When the House reconvened legislators voted enthusiastically against their own salary increases, knowing that it was too late to stop them.[51] Opponents of any cuts in Social Security have followed a similar strategy. Representative Claude Pepper (D., Fla.), who was both the leading defender of the Social Security system and the chairman of the House Rules Committee, was able to thwart any attempts to reduce Social Security payments by promising that no budget resolution containing cuts to the program would be allowed on the House floor without a separate vote on Social Security. No one believed that legislators would dare support a free-standing proposal such as this, and as a result, no budget resolution ever contained such a measure.[52]

Conflict over substance can quickly evolve into conflict over procedures. When the House was battling over the contents of the Omnibus Budget Reconciliation Act of 1981, which eliminated $35 billion in domestic spending, the key vote was on which rule should govern floor consideration. Conservatives wanted a single up-or-down vote on the entire package so that legislators would have to stand up and be counted as either for or against the president's economic program. Liberals wanted separate votes in six programmatic areas so that legislators would have to go on record as either for or against cuts in Social Security, school lunches, energy programs, and the like. Both sides agreed that a majority of legislators would not agree to programmatic cuts if specific reductions could be traced back to their own individual actions. Several months of conflict over what programs to reduce and how much to reduce them boiled down to a single procedural vote.[53] Once the conservatives prevailed on the procedural point (by four votes), the substantive battle was over (for complete details see Chapter 7).

Even when the policy effects are minimal, leaders can advance or retard their causes by the way they frame issues and design amendments. Positions matter, even when they are not directly connected to

51. Jacqueline Calmes, "Pay Hike for Members of Congress Takes Effect," *Congressional Quarterly Weekly Report* 45 (February 7, 1987): 219–220.

52. Weaver, *Automatic Government*, p. 84.

53. Sinclair, *Majority Leadership in the U.S. House*, pp. 190–213.

perceptible effects. One of the easiest ways to scuttle a bill is to devise several embarrassing amendments. Many proposals that might slip by if there were no recorded votes falter when legislators must stand up and be counted. Congress once rejected by voice vote an amendment that would have prohibited the Legal Services Corporation from using any funds to defend or protect homosexuality. Moments later, when Representative Larry McDonald (D., Ga.) demanded a recorded vote, legislators adopted the same amendment, 290 to 113.[54]

The annual foreign aid bill attracts more than its share of difficult amendments. Opposition leaders churn out dozens of amendments that prohibit money for controversial causes (for example, the United Nations or family planning) or unpopular countries (such as Mozambique or Syria). Many legislators feel compelled to support such amendments because they don't want to appear to favor something unpopular. Coalition leaders respond by amending the amendments. An amendment to prohibit assistance to some unpopular country is passed overwhelmingly, but an amendment to the amendment renders it harmless by allowing the president to ignore the prohibition if he decides it is "against the national interest."[55] An amendment to prohibit assistance for Vietnam, Cambodia, and Cuba is amended to refer only to direct assistance; the effect is to allow indirect assistance (the only form in existence) to continue through organizations such as the World Bank.[56] An amendment to cut one form of foreign assistance by 83 percent is then replaced by a substitute amendment that includes a cut of only 2 percent.[57]

Perhaps no issue has been more bothersome for congressional leaders than the periodic need to raise the federal debt limit to accommodate the budgetary decisions that Congress has already made. Although these bills are absolutely crucial for keeping the government solvent, few legislators enjoy supporting them because challengers routinely use their votes as evidence that legislators favor deficits.[58] In 1979 House leaders finally invented the ultimate procedural solution—a strategy that hides everybody's tracks. Under the new procedure, the House

54. Nadine Cohodas, "House Passes State, Justice Appropriations Bill," *Congressional Quarterly Weekly Report* 38 (July 26, 1980): 2139.

55. Sinclair, *Majority Leadership in the U.S. House*, p. 147.

56. John Felton, "House Sustains Carter on Africa Policy," *Congressional Quarterly Weekly Report* 37 (April 14, 1979): 725.

57. Stanley Bach, "Parliamentary Strategy and the Amendment Process: Rules and Case Studies of Congressional Action," *Polity* 15 (1983): 573–592.

58. Kingdon, *Congressmen's Voting Decisions*, pp. 49, 122, 181–182, 267.

simply assumes (1) that the debt limit should be whatever level was
included in the calculations for the most recent budget resolution, and
(2) that this debt limit is presumed to have been accepted at the moment
the House approves the conference report on the budget resolution. The
new procedure requires neither a separate bill nor a separate vote in the
House (the Senate still employs the old system).[59] In 1983 Congress
also eliminated the distinction between the "permanent" and "tempo
rary" debt limits and thereby drastically reduced the number of votes the
Senate must take.[60]

When coalition leaders are dealing with group and geographic benefits, they employ an opposite approach. Rather than attempting to break
the traceability chain, they do everything they can to accentuate the
benefits and to strengthen the traceability chain. They allow other legislators to co-sponsor legislation so that everyone can claim authorship.
They arrange frequent roll-call votes so that legislators can go firmly on
record in favor of these benefactions. They welcome "clarifying" or other
friendly amendments. Coalition leaders arrange for legislators to have a
marvelous time building records that they can proudly display to their
constituents and contributors to show the strength of their connection
to these positive effects.

Whether dealing with costs or benefits, legislators must agree to be
bound by coalition leaders' procedural strategies. Legislators are not
victims, they are co-conspirators. Coalition leaders cannot force House
members to be bound by a closed rule or a restrictive rule; they must
first persuade a majority of them to accept such a rule.[61] Coalition
leaders cannot force legislators to delegate authority to the president or
bureaucrats; they must agree to do so. Opposition leaders cannot force

59. "Debt Limit Extensions," *Congressional Quarterly Almanac, 1979* 35 (1980): 305–
307. The House still faces occasional votes on the debt limit, particularly when past
forecasts have been inaccurate and the limit must be raised before a new budget resolution
comes along.

60. Pamela Fessler, "Senate Clears Debt Limit Bill," *Congressional Quarterly Weekly
Report* 41 (May 28, 1983): 1066–1067.

61. Although the Senate does not allow closed rules, and senators can therefore introduce as many amendments as they like, it does operate on the basis of unanimous consent
agreements. Once adopted, these agreements can constrain both the number and content
of floor amendments. See Oleszek, *Congressional Procedures and the Policy Process*, pp.
177–238; Keith Krehbiel, "Unanimous Consent Agreements: Going Along in the Senate,"
Journal of Politics 48 (1986): 541–564; and Steven S. Smith and Marcus Flathman,
"Managing the Senate Floor: Complex Unanimous Consent Agreements since the
1950s," *Legislative Studies Quarterly* 14 (1989): 349–374.

House members to face lots of embarrassing amendments, for a simple majority could demand a closed rule. When coalition leaders propose restrictive rules, and when legislators accept those rules, it must be because the rules serve their joint purposes.[62]

STRATEGIES OF MODIFICATION

Strategies of modification involve altering the various components of a policy, ranging from the policy instrument to the incidence of costs and benefits. The aim is to mold a policy so that it conforms better to legislators' and citizens' preferences and potential preferences. Although coalition leaders can modify their proposals in dozens of ways, they can accept only a limited number of changes and still have a bill that serves their own central interests. They have every incentive to choose their modifications carefully so that they manage to strengthen a program's supporting coalition without sacrificing whatever it was that persuaded them to build a coalition in the first place.

One of the most productive approaches is to modify a proposal in ways designed to attract additional coalition leaders, who can then work to persuade others to join the cause. Whenever a program's initial coalition leaders come from outside Congress, they have no choice but to convince several legislators to join the team. Building coalitions is too complex for outsiders alone. They particularly need to acquire members of the appropriate House and Senate committees and make them enthusiastic about a program—enthusiastic enough to invest their scarce resources in its future. The Johnson administration, for example, was unable to find an appropriate manager for its model cities bill until it inserted a provision guaranteeing the selection of some small cities; this change finally persuaded Senator Edmund Muskie (D., Me.) to lead the effort.[63] The Reagan administration was extraordinarily attentive to the leaders of the two tax-writing committees as it transformed its first tax reform plan (Treasury I) into the plan that the president actually sent to Congress.[64]

---

62. House members do defeat some restrictive rules, but the occasions are rare. Between January 1981 and August 1985 the House rejected exactly six rules. See Andy Plattner, "Rules under Chairman Pepper Looks Out for the Democrats," *Congressional Quarterly Weekly Report* 43 (August 24, 1985): 1674.

63. Robert B. Semple, Jr., "Signing of Model Cities Bill Ends Long Struggle to Keep It Alive," *New York Times* (November 4, 1966): 44.

64. Birnbaum and Murray, *Showdown at Gucci Gulch*, pp. 76–95.

Proponents may also modify their proposals to dissuade potential opposition leaders from actively working against them. It is far cheaper to
buy off a few lieutenants before they start their work than it is to ward off
the legions that they would otherwise mobilize. Committee chairmen
often accommodate the needs of their ranking minority members so that
they can present a united front both in committee and on the floor.
Bureaucrats sometimes allocate disproportionate geographic benefits to
opposition leaders, intending either to convert them or at least to mute
their opposition. Those who awarded model cities grants, for example,
were especially generous with those committee and party leaders who
had previously opposed the program's funding.[65] Coalition leaders may
also sow seeds of disunity among interest group leaders. Robert Strauss
helped to enact the Trade Act of 1979 by including substantial rewards
for steel and textile workers; these rewards helped to split the AFL-CIO
and thereby forced it to remain neutral.[66]

Coalition leaders often begin with plans to enact comprehensive programs or to institute fundamental reforms in some policy area. Wouldn't
it be nice, they ask, to enact national health insurance, to reform the
welfare system, to dismantle some regulatory commission, to redesign
the tax system, or to expand assistance to college students so that everyone could afford college? Ordinarily coalition leaders must scale back
such ambitious plans. Large new expenditure programs are particularly
troublesome, for they quickly bump against the perpetual shortage of
governmental funds. It makes little difference whether the budget is in
surplus or deficit, because new claims on the federal treasury are potential threats to current claimants, to those who wish to expand current
programs, and to those who wish to enact their own grandiose schemes.

Legislators are often willing to take a few small steps toward some
distant goal, but they are usually reluctant to attempt the whole distance
in a single leap. Small steps are less risky than grand leaps. The strategic
response to their fears is to scale back policy proposals so that they
appear cautious, limited, and experimental. Proponents of complete
deregulation of financial institutions decide to push for modest reforms,
to be phased in gradually. Advocates of national health insurance settle
for less ambitious programs—first Medicare and Medicaid, then some
form of catastrophic insurance, and so on. Even during the heyday of the
Great Society, the Johnson administration sent Congress a lot of small,

65. Arnold, *Congress and the Bureaucracy*, pp. 179, 192.

66. Bob Livernash, "Congress Faces Hard Choices on Trade Liberalization Pact," *Congressional Quarterly Weekly Report* 37 (April 14, 1979): 678–683.

limited programs that individually appeared to cost little.[67] Coalition leaders hope that modifications to their proposals are temporary and that Congress will later expand limited programs into the comprehensive ones they originally wanted.[68]

Although it often makes sense to push for incremental rather than comprehensive reforms, "thinking small" is not always appropriate. One risk is that by solving the most egregious problem, one removes the political pressure for solving the broader problem. Establishing Medicare may have addressed the most serious problem in the financing of health care, but it also eliminated the most potent argument for national health insurance. Over the past two decades senior citizens have pushed hard to improve Medicare benefits for themselves, but they have had little interest in pushing for a broadened program that would include other classes of citizens. A second risk is that incremental reforms, especially of tax and regulatory systems, cannot deliver enough benefits to make them worth the trouble. For two decades proponents of tax reform attempted to cleanse the tax system one loophole at a time. They failed miserably. Eliminating a single provision could neither make the system noticeably more equitable nor generate much revenue, yet each loophole had its passionate defenders. It took comprehensive reform to make the benefits of tax reform worth the pain (see Chapter 8). It may well be that one can create small programs and watch them grow incrementally, but one cannot reduce or reform these programs with anything less than a comprehensive attack.[69]

67. Even Medicare, the most expensive of the Great Society programs, was projected to be relatively affordable. See Sundquist, *Politics and Policy*, p. 320; and Marmor, *The Politics of Medicare*, p. 67. The projections were a bit optimistic. Whereas in 1967 Medicare cost only $2.7 billion, which was less than 2 percent of federal spending, two decades later it totaled $72 billion, or more than 7 percent of federal spending. See U.S., Office of Management and Budget, *Historical Tables: Budget of the United States Government, FY 1988* (Washington, D.C.: Government Printing Office, 1987), table 3.3.

68. Sometimes Congress does expand programs to fit the original design. Social Security is a sterling example. After a long series of incremental additions spread over four decades, the original designers achieved almost everything they intended. See Martha Derthick, *Policymaking for Social Security* (Washington, D.C.: Brookings Institution, 1979), pp. 295–377. These incremental changes transformed Social Security from a $781 million program in 1950, which consumed less than 2 percent of the federal budget and less than 0.3 percent of GNP, to a $199 billion program in 1986, which consumed 20 percent of the federal budget and nearly 5 percent of GNP. See Office of Management and Budget, *Historical Tables*, tables 1.2 and 3.1.

69. On the difference between creating new policies and rationalizing old policies, see Lawrence D. Brown, *New Policies, New Politics* (Washington, D.C.: Brookings Institution, 1983).

Coalition leaders must somehow deal with the problem of costs. Costs are what inspire people to oppose changes in policy, and coalition leaders need to allocate costs carefully in order to minimize opposition. Concentrating all costs on a small minority of groups or localities, and thus leaving the majority unburdened, may seem like a winning strategy. Unfortunately, concentration inspires the victims to work actively against the policies, and determined minorities can frequently overpower majorities in a legislative arena noted for its many choke points (including the senatorial filibuster). Dispersing costs widely is often the safer strategy, for it minimizes the intensity of opposition.

Consider the differences in how Congress handled the disposal of two types of nuclear waste. After several months of amiable debate, Congress passed a bill in 1980 that required each state to take responsibility for disposing of its own low-level nuclear waste, either within its own borders or by forming voluntary compacts among neighboring states.[70] By comparison, legislators fought for over a decade about how to handle high-level nuclear waste (which for technical reasons cannot be stored in every state). After four years of wrangling Congress did pass the 1982 Nuclear Waste Policy Act, which delegated to the president the responsibility for choosing one or more sites for high-level wastes, but only after legislators filled the bill with provisions designed to preclude the selection of their own states.[71] Over the next few years legislators from the areas most likely to be chosen continued to maneuver to keep their own states off the list. When the Department of Energy finally narrowed its search for a western site down to Nevada, Washington, and Texas, coalition leaders finally had the nucleus for an unbeatable coalition. Legislators from Washington and Texas, joined by those from eastern areas still under consideration, ganged up on tiny Nevada. They proposed that Nevada should be the nation's *only* site for high-level waste and inserted their plan in the 1987 reconciliation bill, one of the few bills protected by Senate rules from a filibuster.[72] Except for Nevada's two senators and two representatives, most legislators thought it was a splendid solution. Notice, however, that this solution, which seems so obvious to armchair

70. Andy Plattner, "Congress Passes Low-Level Nuclear Waste Bill, Leaves Broader Solution for Future," *Congressional Quarterly Weekly Report* 38 (December 20, 1980): 3623–3625.

71. "Chronology of Action on Nuclear Power," *Congress and the Nation, 1981–1984* (Washington, D.C.: Congressional Quarterly, 1985), pp. 361–366.

72. Joseph A. Davis, "Nevada to Get Nuclear Waste, Everyone Else Off The Hook," *Congressional Quarterly Weekly Report* 45 (December 19, 1987): 3136–3138.

theorists, required nearly a decade for Congress to accept.[73] Concentrating costs on the tiniest group or area is seldom the easiest way to build a coalition in Congress.

A second solution to the problem of costs is to compensate some of the victims for the group or geographic costs they would otherwise incur. Actually coalition leaders for the nuclear waste bill attempted to compensate Nevada for being chosen as the sole site for the waste repository. They originally authorized a $100 million annual payment for Nevada, effective once the repository opened for business; but when the state continued to resist, they scaled back the payment to $20 million annually and made it contingent upon the state accepting the repository without further legislative or judicial challenges.[74] Other coalition leaders have been more successful in buying off potential opponents. Given the expense of compensatory schemes, coalition leaders ordinarily reserve compensation for the most vocal groups. Throughout the 1970s organized labor was especially skillful at obtaining various protections as its price for supporting policy changes. Examples include protection for railroad workers hurt by the formation of Conrail and Amtrak, compensation for loggers who worked in forests incorporated into the Redwood National Park, protection for airline workers displaced by the deregulation of airlines, and compensation under the trade adjustment assistance program for workers injured by lowered trade barriers.[75]

A third solution to the problem of costs is to make them as nearly invisible as possible. Most expenditure programs are financed through general taxation so that a decision to establish a new expenditure program does not directly increase anyone's taxes. The financial costs of these expenditure programs are essentially general costs. The two large programs that have dedicated taxes—Social Security and Medicare—have more visible costs, but these programs were cleverly designed so that only half of their costs are apparent to most voters. Workers see the portion of the payroll tax that is deducted from their own wages, but not

73. It also required a convenient shift in the balance of power. In 1987 Senator Paul Laxalt (R., Nev.), perhaps the president's closest friend in Congress, had just retired, and Nevada's four remaining legislators held no important positions and had virtually no seniority (two were elected in 1982, and two in 1986). Texas and Washington not only had size, committee positions, and seniority on their side, they were also the home states of Speaker Jim Wright and House Majority Leader Thomas Foley.

74. Davis, "Nevada to Get Nuclear Waste," p. 3138.

75. Robert S. Goldfarb, "Compensating Victims of Policy Change," *Regulation* 4 (September 1980): 22–30.

the half paid on their behalf by their employers.[76] The politics of Social Security would undoubtedly be much more contentious if the entire payroll tax (currently 15 percent) were deducted from each worker's pay check. Conflict would be especially high if workers paid these taxes directly (in quarterly payments, say, like property taxes) rather than through automatic withholding.

Perhaps the most common way to keep the costs of a program relatively invisible is to use the tax code rather than the budget for delivering benefits. Most changes in the tax code are written in technical language and are relatively obscure to all except those who will use them, whereas all direct subsidies are listed prominently in the federal budget. Perhaps that is why tax deductions and tax credits have been the favorite devices for delivering benefits to corporations and wealthy groups in society. Consider the case of the All Savers Certificate, a small provision in the 1981 tax bill. The nation's savings banks were seeking help from the government at a time when they were losing a great deal of money because of the high rates they had to pay on deposits. Their proposed solution was to invent a new form of savings deposits that would be tax exempt for all depositors, thus allowing banks to reduce their rates. The Treasury Department, the Congressional Budget Office, and the Joint Tax Committee warned Congress that the program would produce a revenue loss of $5 to $7 billion, but their warnings made little difference.[77] Legislators wanted to help the ailing savings banks, and this proposal seemed like a politically safe method of doing so.[78] Imagine how different the politics would have been if Congress had been asked to *appropriate* $5 to $7 billion for the savings banks, just a few weeks after it had agonized over cutting domestic programs by $35 billion. If expressed as appropriated dollars, the costs would have been too visible.

Finally, coalition leaders may modify the incidence of group or geo-

76. Up until 1984 self-employed people—the one group that sees the full charge—paid at a lower rate than those who are employed by others (75 percent of the combined employee and employer rate). The 1983 reform bill eliminated this preferential rate (with the usual single vote on the entire omnibus package). See Paul Light, *Artful Work: The Politics of Social Security Reform* (New York: Random House, 1985), pp. 186, 190, 209–212.

77. The cost estimate is reported in Robert D. Reischauer, "Getting, Using, and Misusing Economic Information," in Allen Schick (ed.), *Making Economic Policy in Congress* (Washington, D.C.: American Enterprise Institute, 1983), p. 50.

78. The Senate Finance Committee approved the provision unanimously, and the entire Senate joined in, 86 to 10. See Pamela Fessler, "All-Savers Plan: Some Second Thoughts," *Congressional Quarterly Weekly Report* 39 (July 11, 1981): 1214.

graphic benefits in order to attract additional supporters. When allocating benefits leaders face a dilemma similar to the one they face when allocating costs. Concentrating benefits by group or geographic areas may produce some very intense supporters, but too much concentration yields too few supporters to constitute a majority. Dispersing benefits more widely helps to attract additional supporters, but excessive dispersion may make the individual shares so small that both legislators and the affected publics become indifferent to a program's continued existence. Coalition leaders need to find an acceptable middle position between placing all their chips on one small group or locality and spreading their chips uniformly across all members of society.

Modifying the incidence of geographic benefits is one of the most direct methods for enticing reluctant legislators to support an expenditure program.[79] It gives legislators a pleasing answer to the age-old question, "What's in it for me?" When promoting proposed programs, coalition leaders have only a few geographic strategies available, since they do not yet have any specific benefits to promise individual legislators. All they can do is try to affect legislators' general expectations by modifying a program's character. First, they can enlarge a program's geographic scope so that more localities will be eligible for benefits and, as a consequence, more legislators will see opportunities for acquiring shares for their districts. Eligibility requirements for an urban program can be redefined so that even the most rural district will have at least one large town that qualifies for benefits. Second, they can multiply the number of shares to be allocated so that the probability of an individual legislator obtaining a share will increase. Legislators can better afford to remain indifferent when only a few shares will be distributed than when there are several hundred. The principal limitation on these two strategies is the size of a program's budget. Unless proponents can increase a program's proposed budget at the same rate they increase the number of shares to be allocated, the value of each share will decline and so too will each legislator's willingness to support the proposal.

Once a program is passed, the problem shifts from shaping legislators' expectations to satisfying those expectations. Most geographic benefits are allocated by bureaucrats, and the evidence shows that they are extraordinarily attentive to legislators' needs.[80] Bureaucrats are careful

79. For further analysis of how leaders modify the incidence of geographic benefits, see Arnold, *Congress and the Bureaucracy*, pp. 46–47.
80. Ibid.

to disperse geographic benefits widely across all eligible areas so that most legislators have a stake in a program's continuance. Bureaucrats may also concentrate extra benefits on those who are especially crucial to a program's supporting coalition, including coalition leaders, opposition leaders, and members of the appropriate committees. If a program's supporting coalition continues to appear weak, they may further expand a program's geographic scope. This is essentially the story behind the expansion of urban renewal and the economic development administra tion until each provided benefits to nearly all congressional districts.

Excessive expansion of a program's geographic scope can undermine its entire supporting coalition. Eventually legislators come to realize that their individual shares are too tiny to give them a real interest in its continuance. This was the fate of the Urban Development Action Grant program, which began as a narrowly focused proposal providing up to $675 million annually for distressed urban areas. The first time Congress acted on the program it reserved a quarter of all funds for nonurban areas.[81] Over the next decade it modified the allocational formula so that funds were spread more evenly across the country, including urban and rural areas and both distressed and relatively healthy areas. Each of these changes helped to shore up a fragile coalition; but over time these changes also diminished the intensity of support among the program's core supporters, whose own localities no longer received very large shares. Congress finally terminated the program in 1988, transferring its resources to programs that were more popular.[82]

BUILDING COALITIONS

How do coalition leaders choose among these various strategies? On what do their choices depend? In ordinary circumstances strategies of persuasion are best, both because they are more effective at building long-term support and because they do not require coalition leaders to modify their most preferred policies. Coalition leaders usually seek to enact policies that can survive future battles over budgetary

81. Jerry A. Webman, "UDAG: Targeting Urban Economic Development," *Political Science Quarterly* 96 (1981): 189–207; and R. Douglas Arnold, "The Local Roots of Domestic Policy," in Thomas E. Mann and Norman J. Ornstein (eds.), *The New Congress* (Washington, D.C.: American Enterprise Institute, 1981), pp. 272–273.

82. Phil Kuntz, "UDAG Bites the Dust," *Congressional Quarterly Weekly Report* 46 (June 25, 1988): 1754–1756.

priorities, appropriations, and reauthorizations, and the best insurance of clear sailing ahead is to convince both legislators and citizens of a program's basic merits.

Although strategies of persuasion may be best in the long term, they are often very costly in the short term. Convincing legislators and citizens that the federal government should provide federal aid to education, or that it should regulate the sources of air and water pollution, or that it should regulate the design of automobiles for safety and energy efficiency (and creating opinions that were strong enough to overpower the many groups opposed to such policies)—all this took many years of effort and the combined talents of legislators, presidents, and the leaders of various public and private interest groups. Moreover, strategies of persuasion may be inappropriate for some policies. It is generally very difficult to convince people that they should favor policies that would impose large and direct costs on them in the short term, even for things that will in the longer term greatly benefit them. Perhaps during war or some other major crisis it can be done, but it is far easier to adopt procedural strategies or strategies of modification when large, early-order costs are involved. It is also very difficult to convince people that scarce governmental resources should be lavished on the rich and powerful. Apparently coalition leaders never even considered appropriating $5 to $7 billion to protect the stockholders of savings banks in 1981, for it would have been difficult to defend direct subsidies to this group just weeks after Congress had decimated several social welfare programs. It was far easier to provide the benefits as inconspicuously as possible through a complicated change in the tax code.

Procedural strategies are most attractive when legislators decide to impose costs on either attentive or inattentive publics. Delegating such tasks to the executive, or fashioning policies in secret that are then packaged in omnibus bills and protected by restrictive rules, helps to break the traceability chain and protect legislators from the wrath of their constituents and contributors. It should come as no surprise that procedural strategies were essential for approving gasoline rationing, deregulating prices for both petroleum and natural gas, cutting domestic spending at the start of the Reagan administration, and enacting comprehensive tax reform (see Chapters 7, 8, and 9).

Strategies of modification allow leaders to target the publics that will benefit or suffer as a result of a policy, so they are especially useful for acquiring the support of particular legislators or groups. They are unsurpassed early in the coalition-building process, either for acquiring additional coalition leaders or for silencing potential opposition leaders. They are also excellent general strategies for dealing with programs that provide bundles of group or geographic benefits. Most tax bills are passed by carefully modifying the group benefits until the bill appeals to a majority of legislators. Most grant programs are passed by carefully manipulating the geographic benefits.

Coalition leaders need not choose a single strategy to advance their cause. These three general strategies (and all their variants) complement one another nicely. Leaders may begin by holding hearings to dramatize the need for a new program and to shape elite and mass opinion on the subject, they may then make small modifications to meet the objections of several groups who see their interests threatened, and they may eventually structure the legislative situation in a way designed to protect legislators from either attentive or inattentive publics who might be displeased with the final outcome. A typical bill may have to be modified several times as it passes through all the stages in the legislative process, each time moving further away from coalition leaders' original proposal.[83]

Coalition leaders differ widely in their abilities to employ the various strategies. Committee chairmen are often in a good position to influence the opinions of attentive publics by carefully orchestrating congressional hearings on a new subject. Presidents enjoy an advantage both for influencing inattentive publics and for mobilizing public opinion for comprehensive reforms. Procedural strategies, largely beyond the control of presidents, require the cooperation of both committee and party leaders. Presidents and interest group leaders may be able to modify proposals before they start their travels through Congress, but once they are launched on their way the legislative committees are in charge.

How large a coalition do leaders seek to build? Do they aim for a minimum winning coalition, or do they seek to build a grand coalition that includes all legislators?[84] All else equal, leaders prefer large coalitions because they provide the best insurance for the future. Each pro-

83. Most bills still reflect coalition leaders' preferences far more than they do the preferences of other participants. See Barry S. Rundquist and Gerald S. Strom, "Bill Construction in Legislative Committees: A Study of the U.S. House," *Legislative Studies Quarterly* 12 (1987): 97–113.

84. For previous arguments on this subject, see William H. Riker, *The Theory of Political Coalitions* (New Haven: Yale University Press, 1962); David R. Mayhew, *Congress: The Electoral Connection* (New Haven: Yale University Press, 1974), pp. 111–114; and Arnold, *Congress and the Bureaucracy*, pp. 43–44, 52.

posal must survive a long series of majoritarian tests—in committees and subcommittees, in House and Senate, and in authorization, appropriations, and budget bills. Large majorities help to insure that a bill clears these hurdles with ease. Moreover, large majorities are often required to overcome filibusters, presidential vetoes, and other obstructions that determined minorities may erect. Finally, once programs are passed and implemented, they need annual appropriations and occasional reauthorizations. Again, oversized majorities protect programs in the long run against defections, the retirement or defeat of habitual supporters, or changes in the mood of Congress.

But all else may not be equal. The real question is how much coalition leaders must sacrifice to gain solid majorities. When the marginal costs of attracting members are small, leaders can easily afford to build large coalitions. As these marginal costs increase, however, they tend to become content with more modest majorities. Marginal costs are easiest to calculate when strategies of modification are employed. Although coalition leaders are reluctant to make major modifications in their proposals once their majorities achieve minimum size, they are often eager to accommodate legislators who request only modest changes.[85]

85. Elizabeth Drew, *Senator* (New York: Simon and Schuster, 1979), p. 158.

6

Policy Decisions

Now that I have laid out in separate chapters the several aspects of my proposed explanation of decision making in Congress, it is time to return to the question posed at the outset and consider the theory as a whole: Why does Congress enact the policies that it does? Under what conditions does Congress approve proposals that serve organized interests or that deliver narrowly targeted geographic benefits? Under what conditions does Congress break free of parochial concerns and enact bills that serve more diffuse or general interests? In this chapter I argue that congressional decisions depend partly on what citizens will allow, partly on what coalition leaders propose, partly on what strategies coalition leaders and opposition leaders adopt, and partly on what legislators themselves prefer.

Both attentive and inattentive citizens set limits on congressional action. At times they keep legislators from supporting proposals that are unpopular or that would impose large and direct costs on them. At times they force legislators to support a particular alternative, either because they would profit from it or simply because they like the sound of it. Citizens set limits on congressional action whether or not they happen to have policy preferences at the time Congress acts. Both existing preferences and potential preferences can be a powerful constraint when legislators are deciding which side to support in a policy dispute.

Citizens' preferences and potential preferences can constrain legislators' actions, however, only if issues are framed in a way that allows citizens to reward and punish their representatives for specific deeds. If legislators hide their tracks by delegating authority to the executive, by combining all actions into a single omnibus bill, by meeting behind closed doors, or by acting without a recorded vote, then citizens cannot reward or punish their legislators for their individual actions. In contrast, if legislators are forced to take public positions on specific programs, citizens can hold their legislators accountable for the positions they take and, under the proper conditions, for the effects they produce.

What determines whether legislators will hide their tracks or whether they will leave a visible trail for citizens, instigators, or future opponents to follow? Responsibility for how legislation is considered is shared by coalition leaders, opposition leaders, and legislators themselves. Coalition leaders play the largest role, for they design policy proposals and shape the initial strategies. Some proposals have direct and simple causal chains, which facilitate traceability, while others offer complicated causal mechanisms, which help to obscure it. A proposal to assist steel makers by offering federal subsidies is clear and direct; a proposal to help them by tinkering with the rules for depreciating capital assets is clear enough for attentive steel makers to understand but complicated enough that inattentive citizens from areas that do not produce steel will neither notice it on their own nor be easily roused by instigators or future challengers. Coalition leaders also choose how and when a proposal will first be considered. It is far easier to enact a corporate tax break by tacking it on to the next large omnibus tax bill that comes along than by pushing forcefully for a separate, free-standing bill. The latter is simply too visible.

The availability and talent of both coalition leaders and opposition leaders also leaves a large imprint on congressional decisions. When one side is staffed by enthusiastic and talented leaders while the other attracts few leaders of any sort, the first side is powerfully advantaged. The oil depletion allowance survived for years under the careful protection of the Texas delegation, the Ways and Means Committee, and the Senate Finance Committee. Opponents of the depletion allowance enjoyed neither institutional position nor the strong incentive for action that drove the proponents. Opposition leaders did not emerge in force until 1969, when they became part of a broader movement toward tax reform.[1]

Finally, legislators themselves help to determine how visible their own tracks will be. Coalition leaders may propose delegating a difficult task to the executive, but legislators can easily reject the proposal and insist that Congress itself make policy. Coalition leaders may insert a

1. Bruce I. Oppenheimer, *Oil and the Congressional Process* (Lexington, Mass.: D. C. Heath, 1974), pp. 104–112.

potentially controversial program in the middle of a huge omnibus bill, but opponents can demand a separate vote on the program. Coalition leaders may request a restrictive rule and the House Rules Committee may grant it, but the House is not bound by the rule until a majority of legislators approve it. Legislators are not victims of leaders' procedural strategies, they are co-conspirators.

The conclusion is now inescapable. Even in a theoretical model where legislators are totally dedicated to the quest for reelection, the decisions that Congress makes are partly dependent on legislators' own personal policy preferences. This is trivially true when legislators calculate no electoral advantage or disadvantage from supporting or opposing a specific policy. It is also true for some of the major policy questions of the day. Their own policy preferences matter because legislators first choose the procedures under which they shall operate, and their choices on procedural matters are rarely constrained by electoral considerations.[2] Consider how the Senate Finance Committee handled the Tax Reform Act of 1986. At first it held its markup sessions in a huge hearing room, where lobbyists could watch every decision and every vote. Quite predictably committee members voted to save most tax preferences, and even to invent some new ones.[3] Eventually senators decided to abandon all public sessions and to draft a new reform plan in total secrecy. All of a sudden the special interests were at a serious disadvantage, for they could no longer see who was responsible for terminating their favorite tax provisions. The crucial decision concerned whether or not to draft a bill behind closed doors. When the senators decided to do so, they were essentially declaring that they were *personally* in favor of tax reform. If they really preferred the status quo (or more tax loopholes), all they had to do was to insist on open covenants, openly arrived at. Electoral calculations would then have guaranteed that an open bill would not be a reform bill.

Congressional decisions, then, depend on four factors: what proposals coalition leaders introduce, what strategies proponents and opponents employ, what actions attentive and inattentive citizens will allow, and

2. At times electoral calculations affect even the procedural votes. The crucial procedural vote on President Reagan's 1981 budget bill is an example. See Chapter 7. See also Barbara Sinclair, *Majority Leadership in the House* (Baltimore: Johns Hopkins University Press, 1983), pp. 206–213.

3. Jeffrey H. Birnbaum and Alan S. Murray, *Showdown at Gucci Gulch: Lawmakers, Lobbyists, and the Unlikely Triumph of Tax Reform* (New York: Vintage, 1987), pp. 199–203.

what policies legislators themselves prefer. Legislators are partly manipulated by the decisions of coalition leaders and opposition leaders, they are partly constrained by anticipating the actions of citizens in future elections, and they are partly acting as free agents who can manage both the degree to which they are manipulated from above and the extent to which they are constrained from below. The existence of these four factors makes for a certain indeterminacy in congressional action. A minor change in a single factor (for example, legislators rejecting a closed rule by a single vote) can switch legislators' electoral calculations completely and make them reject what they would otherwise approve.

Despite this indeterminacy, there is still a large role for theory. Although one cannot predict with certainty whether Congress will pass a specific program, one can still set forth the conditions under which Congress may approve a proposal that serves organized interests or that delivers narrowly targeted geographic benefits, and the conditions under which Congress may break free of parochial concerns and enact a bill that serves more diffuse or general interests. Before setting forth those conditions, I should remind readers that this book focuses on only two of the four factors. I do not explain why individuals decide to become coalition leaders or why they decide to champion particular proposals. I also do not explain legislators' own personal policy preferences. My focus is on how legislators anticipate and respond to citizens' policy preferences and how coalition leaders design their strategies in anticipation of legislators' electoral needs.

GROUP COSTS AND BENEFITS

Why does Congress sometimes approve proposals that serve organized interests and sometimes approve those that serve a wider public? Explaining why concentrated interests so often triumph is the easier task. People who share a particular interest are usually attentive to what is happening in Washington, and they are often organized into groups. Operating through lobbyists and political action committees, these groups communicate precise policy messages both to coalition leaders and to legislators. Attentive publics possess considerable information about what legislators are doing to advance their causes, and because the stakes are relatively high, their members have strong incentives to reward and punish legislators for their actions.

If concentrated interests enjoy such advantages, why would Congress ever approve proposals that serve more diffuse interests? Even more difficult to explain, why would Congress first deliver narrowly concentrated benefits to some group in society and then suddenly switch sides, imposing costs on the previously advantaged group and delivering benefits to those whom it had long neglected? Position changes are actually quite common. For several decades Congress created new tax deductions, credits, and loopholes, and then it turned around and terminated many of them in 1986. Oil policy in the 1950s and 1960s served producers' interests, while oil policy in the 1970s served consumers' interests. Congress sided with natural gas producers in the 1940s and 1950s, sided with consumers in the 1960s and early 1970s, and then pursued a middle course on natural gas beginning in 1978. Congress first regulated and then deregulated the airline, telecommunications, and trucking industries.

As a first cut at the problem, allow me to recount briefly how Congress has made policy toward two agricultural commodities over the past half century. These two stories help to reveal both the conditions that encourage legislators to satisfy attentive publics and the conditions that force them to consider inattentive publics. In the case of sugar, Congress first served the interests of sugar producers, then consumers, and then producers once again. In the case of milk, Congress has served the interests of dairy producers exclusively.

From 1934 to 1974 American sugar policy served the interests of sugar producers, and little attention was paid to the interests of ordinary consumers.[4] The Jones-Costigan Act of 1934 introduced a system of quotas that reserved portions of the American market for specific domestic and foreign producers. The act had two effects. First, it stabilized American sugar prices, though at a higher level than the more volatile world price. Second, it made the setting of specific quotas crucial to the sugar producers, for they allowed producers to sell sugar at a price above the market level. Every few years Congress revised the quota system, expanding some quotas while reducing others, and each time the battle was intense. Congress acted as referee in a zero-sum conflict among domestic producers of sugar cane (mainly in Louisiana and Florida), domestic producers of sugar beets (mainly in western states), and for-

---

4. For an analysis of the politics of sugar, see David E. Price, *Who Makes the Laws?* (Cambridge: Schenkman, 1972), pp. 123–138. Price concludes: "Very few policy areas can be named where the major interest groups involved have a freer hand to write their own legislative ticket" (p. 135).

eign producers of sugar cane located in more than thirty countries (with each represented by a well-paid lobbyist).[5] Although the battles were intense, legislators heard exclusively from organized and attentive publics. Legislators had little to fear from consumers as long as domestic prices remained stable and affordable. In 1965 Senators Albert Gore, Sr. (D., Tenn.) and Paul Douglas (D., Ill.) condemned the entire sugar program for maintaining artificially high prices at consumers' expense, but their arguments had little impact on legislators.[6] For the general public, sugar policy was one of the great nonissues of the day, and it was difficult to imagine how it might ever become salient to them.

In 1974 all these relationships were turned upside-down.[7] Suddenly many legislators cared very much about how consumers would perceive their actions, and they seemed quite willing to ignore the preferences of organized producers. The impetus for change was the tripling of retail sugar prices in the early months of 1974, a reaction to worldwide shortages. Consumers quickly noticed the galloping prices, consumer activists organized boycotts, and President Ford urged everyone to reduce consumption. For the first time sugar policy was front-page news, and just at the time Congress was drafting a five-year extension of the quota system. Suddenly proponents of quotas were at a severe disadvantage. In an attempt to build confidence in the program, the House Agriculture Committee drafted its bill in public session—the first time ever for a bill involving sugar quotas. In an attempt to appear open and conciliatory toward consumers' interests, the committee brought its bill to the floor under an open rule—the first time in the forty-year history of the program.[8] The House took advantage of this new openness and amended the bill six times, before it then rejected the entire bill, 175 to 209. The reason was simple: many legislators from nonagricultural areas were reluctant to support *any* bill that could somehow be connected with higher prices. Legislators were not necessarily reacting to citizens' existing policy preferences, for most citizens were still unaware of the precise nature of American sugar policy. Legislators were anticipating

---

5. Sugar refiners were also active. Some specialized in sugar beets, others in sugar cane, and still others were largely dependent on imported cane; all had an interest in how quotas were allocated among producers.

6. Price, *Who Makes the Laws?*, pp. 134–135.

7. For the complete story of the sugar program's demise, see "Sugar Act Extension Killed in the House," *Congressional Quarterly Almanac, 1974* 30 (1975): 225–230.

8. Ibid., p. 226.

how easy it would be for a future challenger to make a campaign issue out of a vote that could easily be connected with higher prices.

The quota system expired on December 31, 1974, and for the next seven years the United States maintained a relatively free market for sugar. Although Congress approved a two-year program of price supports for domestic producers in 1977, the support price was set so low that it did little to disrupt the market. Throughout this period sugar producers lobbied heavily for a new sugar program, but Congress was no longer receptive to their pleas. The House rejected one sugar bill in 1978 (177 to 194) and another in 1979 (158 to 249). Opposition leaders were especially skillful at portraying these bills as inflationary, and with inflation accelerating, legislators were reluctant to vote for any bill with that label.[9]

Proponents finally established a new sugar program in December 1981—seven years after the earlier one had expired. Although House members continued to oppose assisting sugar producers, voting 213 to 190 to delete the proposed program from a farm bill, they were eventually outmaneuvered.[10] Coalition leaders concentrated on the Senate, which overrepresents rural areas and was thus a friendlier forum, and grafted a new program of price supports onto a huge omnibus farm bill. When the House deleted the program, House and Senate conferees, who were themselves drawn from the friendly agriculture committees, simply restored it. Then the conference report was kept off the House floor until two hours before Congress adjourned for the year. The House was given the option of accepting or rejecting the entire farm bill, for it was too late to return it to the conference committee for further deliberation. Under the pressure of adjournment, House members approved the omnibus bill, 205 to 203, and thus reestablished a highly restrictive sugar policy.[11] It took skill and patience to reestablish a program that

9. Bob Livernash, "Consumer-Labor Votes Kill House Sugar Bill," *Congressional Quarterly Weekly Report* 37 (October 27, 1979): 2396.

10. Elizabeth Wehr, "House Repudiates Peanut, Sugar Programs," *Congressional Quarterly Weekly Report* 39 (October 17, 1981): 2031.

11. Elizabeth Wehr, "House Passes Farm Bill by Two-Vote Margin," *Congressional Quarterly Weekly Report* 39 (December 19, 1981): 2481–2485. Although President Reagan was philosophically opposed to both price supports and sugar quotas, he eventually approved both. In 1981 he promised several legislators from Louisiana and Florida that he would sign a sugar bill if they would support his overall budget cuts. They did, and he kept his promise. In 1982 Reagan used his administrative authority to impose quotas on sugar imports, in an attempt to reduce the direct costs of the price support program. Despite the

costs American consumers between \$1 and \$4 billion annually (depending on world prices).[12]

In contrast, American dairy policy has always favored producers. Dairy policy rests on three legs: the Capper-Volstead Act of 1922, which gives immunity from antitrust laws to farmers who join milk cooperatives; the Agricultural Adjustment Act of 1933, which allows the Department of Agriculture to set minimum prices for milk; and the Agriculture Act of 1949, which requires the federal government to purchase surplus milk at a guaranteed price.[13] Throughout the 1950s, 1960s, and 1970s, Congress made frequent changes in these dairy programs, generally making them more favorable to producers and less favorable to consumers and taxpayers. The effects of these programs are clear. Dairy farmers sell their milk at prices above the market level, with consumers paying the difference.[14] Higher prices then encourage farmers to produce more milk than the market can bear because farmers know that the federal government will buy it and that the taxpayers will foot the bill.

The politics of milk is very similar to the (ordinary) politics of sugar. Both programs are supported by producers who reap enormous group benefits, while inattentive citizens pay the costs. Unlike sugar subsidies, however, American dairy programs have escaped any sort of consumer backlash. First, policy makers allowed milk prices to drift upward very gradually so that there was never a price shock that could be used to rouse inattentive consumers. Second, an increasing share of the costs were general costs, hidden in the vast federal budget, rather than higher

---

fact that sugar quotas cost consumers about four times as much as price supports, the president preferred that the program's costs not be listed in the federal budget. Note how some conservative politicians prefer large and invisible costs to small and visible ones. See Dale Tate, "Wheeling, Dealing, and Accommodation," *Congressional Quarterly Weekly Report* 39 (July 4, 1981): 1169; and Elizabeth Wehr, "Administration Dairy, Sugar Plans Draw Fire," *Congressional Quarterly Weekly Report* 40 (May 8, 1982): 1071.

12. For cost estimates, see the following editorials: "A Shameful Sugar Policy," *New York Times* (May 10, 1982): A20; and "The Sour Politics of Sugar," *New York Times* (June 22, 1982): A26.

13. On the politics of dairy programs, see R. Kent Weaver, *Automatic Government: The Politics of Indexation* (Washington, D.C.: Brookings Institution, 1988), pp. 146–172; and Martha Derthick and Paul J. Quirk, *The Politics of Deregulation* (Washington, D.C.: Brookings Institution, 1985), pp. 224–233.

14. Retail prices are between 7 and 22 percent higher than what they would be in the absence of regulation. See Paul W. MacAvoy (ed.), *Federal Milk Marketing Orders and Price Supports* (Washington, D.C.: American Enterprise Institute, 1977), p. 111.

prices imposed directly on consumers. Third, dairy policy is immensely complicated, resting as it does on antitrust immunity, marketing orders, and price supports. Dairy policy doesn't provide a very good campaign issue (outside areas with dairy farms) because it is so intricate, thus making it difficult for consumers to trace specific costs back to legislators' individual actions.

Dairy programs had their own crisis in the early 1980s, but everything was resolved quietly within the agricultural community.[15] The problem was that the budgetary costs of dairy price supports began to increase rapidly, rising from $300 million in 1979, to $1.1 billion in 1980, to $1.9 billion in 1981. Although these increases had no direct impact on consumers, they eventually put dairy price supports in direct conflict with other agricultural programs for scarce budgetary resources. By 1981 dairy price supports consumed 47 percent of the total budget for all agricultural price supports. In response to this problem, Congress revised the support program several times to control (though not to reverse) these budgetary increases. Note, however, that this debate occurred mainly within the agricultural community, and it was resolved by the agricultural committees. It was not a battle between producers and consumers that spilled over to the floors of the House or the Senate, for all of the costs were general costs and were therefore invisible to inattentive publics. While budgetary costs were increasing by a factor of six, the increase in consumer prices was quite modest (a percent or two above the general rate of inflation).

The changing fortunes of sugar policy and dairy policy show how subtle differences in programs can have profound effects on who wins and who loses. The two programs appear quite similar; both deliver large, concentrated benefits to agricultural producers while imposing only small and diffuse costs on the public at large. As long as these costs remained small, both programs prospered and few citizens knew of their existence.[16] When the costs multiplied, however, the differences between the two programs became evident. Citizens noticed when the costs of the sugar program tripled because they paid these costs directly at the supermarket. In contrast, when the costs of the dairy program

15. For the politics of this period, see Weaver, *Automatic Government*, pp. 146–172.

16. Few citizens would have noticed when the programs were first created either. Both programs were created during the 1930s, when farm prices were declining. They had the effect of denying consumers lower prices for sugar and milk, but they did not increase the customary prices for these two commodities.

increased by a factor of six, citizens remained unaware that anything was happening because these were general costs hidden in the vast federal budget. In the first case, prudent legislators anticipated citizens' potential preferences because they knew that sugar prices would make a wonderful campaign issue for challengers, whereas in the second, little chance existed that the general costs of dairy programs could ever be used against legislators.

I shall now posit two necessary conditions for forcing legislators to serve the interests of inattentive publics. First, legislators feel electorally pressured to serve inattentive citizens only if an issue is salient or potentially salient to substantial numbers of those citizens. Second, legislators feel electorally pressured to serve inattentive citizens only if there are talented leaders in Congress who will champion the interests of inattentive citizens by introducing the necessary amendments, demanding roll-call votes at the proper time, and doing everything that is procedurally necessary to create a connection between legislators' individual actions and both the collective actions of Congress and the resulting policy effects. In the case of sugar, both conditions were quickly satisfied in 1974. The tripling of retail prices not only made sugar policy highly salient, it also created incentives for some legislators to become opposition leaders.[17] Once opposition leaders demanded roll-call votes, many legislators felt compelled to side with consumers, because if they did not higher prices could then be traced to their own individual actions. In the case of dairy policy, however, there was nothing to make milk salient to the average voter. Throughout this period milk prices increased very slowly, and no other policy shocks occurred with which one might rouse inattentive citizens. Although the news media enjoyed reporting on government warehouses overflowing with surplus cheese, the stories were not of the sort to make people demand action from their legislators.

If an issue is salient or potentially salient to substantial numbers of inattentive citizens, then legislators must consider the possibility that instigators or future challengers might eventually turn their constituents against them. We know from Chapter 2 that the probability that a program will become salient to citizens depends on the magnitude and the timing of its costs and benefits, the proximity of other people who are

17. For an analysis of how salience affects the incentives for activism, see David E. Price, "Policy Making in Congressional Committees: The Impact of 'Environmental' Factors," *American Political Science Review* 72 (1978): 548–574.

similarly affected, and the availability of talented instigators. Programs with large, concentrated, early-order costs become salient to inattentive citizens far more easily than those with small, diffuse, later-order effects. Potential salience by itself cannot guarantee that legislators will heed citizens' potential preferences. The second requirement is that there must be leaders in Congress who will create occasions where legislators must stand up and be counted as either for or against a specific program. Without those occasions, the prospects for retrospective voting disappear, and so too do the incentives for legislators to anticipate citizens' potential policy preferences.

These two conditions are necessary but not sufficient conditions for the triumph of inattentive publics. Legislators could have continued to favor sugar producers in 1974 if they had been relatively united in their inclination to do so; all they had to do was to adopt procedures that camouflaged their own individual contributions and destroyed the traceability chain. The relative talents of coalition leaders and opposition leaders also makes a difference. Those championing the interests of sugar producers eventually outmaneuvered their opponents and re-established a restrictive sugar policy. They did so by doing their dirty work in a conference committee where opposition leaders had no voice and by offering legislators a last-minute choice between accepting an omnibus farm bill that contained sugar price supports or rejecting the entire package.[18] Not only did they manage to destroy any traceability chain between sugar prices and legislators' individual actions, they also made it difficult for opposition leaders to challenge their procedures by placing their handiwork in a conference report.

A similar pair of conditions forces legislators to serve the interests of attentive publics. Legislators feel electorally pressured to serve attentive citizens only if (1) an issue is both important to those attentive citizens and not potentially salient to substantial numbers of inattentive citizens, and (2) there are talented leaders in Congress who will champion the issue by introducing the necessary amendments, demanding roll-call votes at the proper time, and doing everything that is procedurally

18. This is but another example of how legislative committees can use conference procedures to advance their own policy preferences rather than those of the majority. See Kenneth A. Shepsle and Barry R. Weingast, "The Institutional Foundations of Committee Power," *American Political Science Review* 81 (1987): 85–104. On the extra advantages that accrue to conference committees in the closing days of a Congress, see Shepsle and Weingast, "Why Are Congressional Committees Powerful," *American Political Science Review* 81 (1987): 937–938.

necessary for attentive citizens to hold legislators accountable for their actions.

Examples abound of congressional action to serve attentive publics when both conditions are satisfied. In 1980 soft drink bottlers obtained an antitrust exception so that they could have exclusive franchises in specific geographic areas, thus eliminating any competition from alternative suppliers of identical soft drinks. They did so by forcing legislators to stand up and be counted on a bill that was highly salient to local bottlers and yet not even potentially salient to consumers. Members of both House and Senate supported the bottlers overwhelmingly (377 to 34, and 89 to 3).[19] In 1982 used car dealers obtained an exemption from regulation by the Federal Trade Commission by forcing roll-call votes in both House and Senate. Most legislators sided with used car dealers, who were both attentive to congressional action and large financial contributors, rather than with used car purchasers, who were unaware of what was happening and who could hardly be roused by an issue with such indirect effects. Both House and Senate supported the auto dealers (286 to 133, and 69 to 22).[20] The story of the 1981 All Savers Certificate shows a similar deference to attentive publics. Once again the issue was very important to savings banks, but not potentially salient to ordinary voters (see Chapter 5).

The reader will notice that coalition leaders employ exactly the same techniques for forcing legislators to serve either attentive or inattentive publics. In both instances, a coalition leader first creates an identifiable governmental action and then forces legislators to stand up and be counted on that issue. The only difference is whether or not an issue is salient or potentially salient to inattentive citizens. If an issue is potentially salient to inattentive citizens (as sugar policy was in 1974), those who champion their interests demand a roll-call vote in order to force

19. Nadine Cohodas, "House Judiciary Reports Bill to Protect Bottlers from Antitrust Challenges," *Congressional Quarterly Weekly Report* 38 (June 21, 1980): 1766; and Nadine Cohodas, "House Action on Soda Pop," *Congressional Quarterly Weekly Report* 38 (June 28, 1980): 1815.

20. Judy Sarasohn, "Senate Overwhelmingly Acts to Block FTC Used-Car Rule," *Congressional Quarterly Weekly Report* 40 (May 22, 1982): 1187–1188; and Judy Sarasohn, " FTC's Car Rule Falls Victim to First Congressional Veto," *Congressional Quarterly Weekly Report* 40 (May 29, 1982): 1259. The Consumers Union challenged the constitutionality of this congressional veto of an FTC rule and obtained a Supreme Court ruling that overturned it. See Elder Witt and Judy Sarasohn, "Legislative Veto Ruling Reiterated," *Congressional Quarterly Weekly Report* 41 (July 9, 1983): 1406.

legislators to anticipate and respond to citizens' potential preferences. If an issue is not potentially salient to inattentive citizens (the example of soft drink territories in 1980), those who champion the interests of attentive publics demand a roll-call vote in order to force legislators to respond to the intense preferences of these groups.

These two sets of conditions show how legislators can be forced to serve the group interests of either attentive or inattentive citizens. They also suggest ways in which legislators can *escape* serving the interests of either attentive or inattentive citizens. Although the congressional friends of organized interest groups may be able to force legislators to support new tax preferences by introducing amendments and by demanding roll-call votes, legislators can escape such pressures by meeting behind closed doors, by drafting omnibus bills, and by reporting them to the floor under restrictive rules. Legislators did all these things in 1986 when they enacted tax reform (see Chapter 8). In similar fashion, although the friends of inattentive citizens may be able to force legislators to support more diffuse interests by introducing amendments and demanding roll-call votes on potentially salient issues, legislators can also escape these pressures by meeting behind closed doors, by drafting omnibus bills, and by reporting them to the floor under a restrictive rule. Legislators did these things in 1981 when they reestablished a restrictive sugar policy.

Secrecy, unrecorded votes, and restrictive rules do not necessarily favor either attentive or inattentive citizens. Under the proper conditions, they can be used to benefit either concentrated or diffuse interests. Reform-minded people in the 1950s and 1960s first observed that these techniques were often used to benefit organized interest groups, so they advocated opening up congressional procedures and letting the sunshine in. Two decades later, after the advent of sunshine laws, we know better. Open markup sessions often give organized interests a powerful advantage over inattentive citizens, for they can monitor exactly who is doing what to benefit and to hurt them.[21] Recorded votes are just as likely to force legislators to serve attentive citizens as inattentive citizens.[22] Omnibus bills are convenient vehicles for imposing group costs and delivering general benefits, just as they are useful for protect-

21. See Jacqueline Calmes, "Few Complaints Are Voiced as Doors Close on Capitol Hill," *Congressional Quarterly Weekly Report* 45 (May 23, 1987): 1059–1060.

22. Bill Keller, "Congressional Rating Game Is Hard to Win," *Congressional Quarterly Weekly Report* 39 (March 21, 1981): 512.

ing group benefits from attack.[23] Restrictive rules allow legislators to serve both diffuse interests and concentrated interests.

Although the conditions under which legislators feel forced to serve attentive or inattentive publics are easy to specify, these conditions provide only partial explanations for who wins and who loses. First, legislators feel forced to serve a particular side only if there are coalition leaders who frame the issue appropriately and who arrange procedures favorable to that side. Unfortunately, neither the existence nor the talent of coalition leaders is explainable within the current model. Second, legislators can sometimes escape from the pressures to serve one side or the other by agreeing among themselves to follow alternative procedures—procedures that favor neither attentive nor inattentive publics. Unfortunately, legislators' personal policy preferences are also not explainable within the current model.

To say that these conditions provide only partial explanations of congressional action does not imply that they have no predictive value. To be sure, these conditions cannot explain (nor could they have predicted) why President Reagan and Chairman Rostenkowski chose to champion a particularistic tax bill in 1981 and a tax reform bill in 1986. They do explain how these two leaders were able to pass such dissimilar bills (see Chapter 8). They also predict how legislators might react if future coalition leaders adopted similar strategies for similar bills. That they cannot predict the exact outcomes in such cases is partly a consequence of the differing skills and talents of the various proponents and opponents. Like all great games, politics is a sport in which who wins and who loses depends on the relative talents of the players on each side, and talent is as yet unexplainable within any theoretical model in the social sciences.

GEOGRAPHIC COSTS AND BENEFITS

Why does Congress sometimes approve proposals laden with geographic benefits and sometimes approve those that have few geographic benefits of consequence? Under what conditions do legislators evaluate proposals by their geographic consequences, and under what

23. Dale Tate, "Use of Omnibus Bills Burgeons despite Members' Misgivings," *Congressional Quarterly Weekly Report* 40 (September 25, 1982): 2379–2383; and Martin Tolchin, "In the Face of Controversy, Packaging," *New York Times* (February 21, 1983): B6.

conditions do they focus more on group and general effects?[24] Once
again, it is easier to explain legislators' fascination with geographic
effects than it is to show why geographic concerns do not dominate
congressional decision making. Legislators are elected from geographic
districts, and they have a natural concern with how specific programs
affect their constituents. Obtaining benefits for their districts also
creates opportunities for free publicity and credit claiming, and both are
valuable in the quest for reelection. Finally, most legislators seek to
avoid issues that could be used against them in subsequent elections,
such as supporting programs devoid of geographic benefits for their
districts or opposing programs that would favor their districts.

If legislators care so much about geographic benefits, why do they
sometimes approve proposals that offer few geographic benefits of consequence? Perhaps more puzzling, why has Congress spent the past
decade reducing programs that are heavily laden with geographic benefits while expanding those with lesser concentrations of such benefits?
From 1978 to 1988, for example, Congress reduced intergovernmental
grants from 17.0 percent of federal outlays to 10.4 percent of outlays.[25] It
completely dismantled several large grant programs, including the
fourth largest grant program in existence (revenue sharing). Congress
continued to reduce spending on water projects—everybody's favorite
example of pork-barrel politics.[26] Meanwhile, Congress expanded defense programs, where geographic benefits play a lesser role, and protected many programs with no geographic effects at all, such as transfer
payments to individuals.

The conditions under which geographic considerations come to dom-

24. This section, which relies heavily on my previous work on the geographic allocation
of benefits, attempts to show how the results of that work fit within the broader framework
presented in this book. It also attempts to account for the termination of specific programs
in the 1980s, whereas my previous work focused on the creating and sustaining of programs. For further details, see R. Douglas Arnold, *Congress and the Bureaucracy: A
Theory of Influence* (New Haven: Yale University Press, 1979); "Legislators, Bureaucrats, and Locational Decisions," *Public Choice* 37 (1981): 107–132; and "The Local
Roots of Domestic Policy," in Thomas E. Mann and Norman J. Ornstein (eds.), *The New
Congress* (Washington, D.C.: American Enterprise Institute, 1981), pp. 250–287.

25. U.S., Office of Management and Budget, *Historical Tables: Budget of the United
States Government, FY 1988* (Washington, D.C.: Government Printing Office, 1987),
table 12.1.

26. Expenditures on water projects that were constructed by the Army Corps of Engineers and the Bureau of Reclamation continued their long-term decline from 1.7 percent
of federal outlays in 1948 to 0.66 percent in 1968, 0.44 percent in 1978, and 0.25 percent in
1988. Ibid., tables 1.1 and 9.4.

inate congressional decision making are easy to specify. First, geographic considerations become paramount when programs provide copious
geographic benefits but only meager group or general benefits. Legislators focus on the geographic effects because there is little else to capture
their attention. Second, geographic considerations increase in importance when legislators are asked to make explicit choices about the
geographic allocation of costs or benefits. Legislators are especially attentive to constituency concerns when they must vote publicly on alternative allocational schemes, for such votes allow both challengers and
constituents to connect real effects to legislators' individual actions.

Intergovernmental grants and public works projects are the clearest
examples of programs that provide abundant geographic benefits but
relatively few group and general benefits. When legislators consider
whether to create (or renew) a program like revenue sharing, it is quite
natural for a legislator to ask, "What's in it for me?" Revenue sharing was
designed to channel funds directly to state and local governments to be
used as they saw fit, so there were no particular groups advantaged by
the program. Although one could argue that revenue sharing served
important general interests, such as strengthening local governments
and decentralizing power, these attractions were minor and were not
sufficient to overshadow legislators' greater interest in the geographic
allocation of benefits. Most other grant programs do offer somewhat
greater group and general benefits than did revenue sharing, but even
so the politics of intergovernmental grants usually revolves around the
careful allocation of geographic benefits. Legislators may value the general benefits associated with health, educational, or environmental programs, but these alone are insufficient reasons for supporting them
when legislators discover that money is being spent in other legislators'
districts rather than in their own.

When programs provide meager group and general benefits, the careful allocation of geographic benefits becomes the key to coalition building. Interior and public works bills include water projects for every
imaginable type of district—flood control projects for coastal communities, navigation projects for inland waterways, and reclamation projects
for arid lands. Intergovernmental grant programs are often conceived as
efforts to target needy communities, but they inevitably evolve into
broad-based programs offering something for everyone. The original
proposal to name a dozen model cities quickly evolved into a program
funding 151 cities spread over 227 congressional districts.[27] Congress

27. Arnold, *Congress and the Bureaucracy*, pp. 165–206.

established the Economic Development Administration in 1965 and authorized it to make grants to economically depressed communities, encompassing about 12 percent of the population. As enthusiasm for the Great Society waned, coalition leaders simply broadened the eligibility criteria to keep legislators interested. By 1982, when President Reagan proposed abolishing the entire program, 80 percent of the country fit the eligibility criteria for economic development grants—more than enough to sustain the program against the president's repeated attacks.[28]

Many intergovernmental grant programs pass through a similar life cycle. Proponents begin by proposing a program that would concentrate benefits in those communities most in need of a particular form of assistance. Legislators from those communities often become enthusiastic supporters, and some of them volunteer to become coalition leaders. Proponents quickly learn that programs that offer concentrated geographic benefits but few group or general benefits are not very popular in Congress. To persuade a majority of legislators to join the coalition, proponents broaden the distribution of benefits. In subsequent years coalition leaders may continue to broaden the eligibility criteria so that more and more legislators feel a part of the program. Such strategies create large but unenthusiastic coalitions. Legislators from the communities originally targeted for assistance become less enthusiastic because their districts receive much smaller shares than they imagined. Legislators from the newly included districts are also unenthusiastic because benefits are not a high priority for their districts (they merely insist that if a program is to exist, they want to share in the booty). Programs resting on large and unenthusiastic coalitions may survive for a long time, but they are always vulnerable to attack. Even if they are not terminated, their budgets may dwindle, or they may be combined with similar programs. For example, urban renewal, model cities, and water and sewer grants no longer exist, and the successor program that provides block grants for community development has been whittled down to half its previous size.

Geographic considerations increase in importance when legislators are asked to make explicit choices about the geographic allocation of expenditures. When legislators must stand up and be counted on geographic allocations, they are careful to vote their districts' immediate interests. To do otherwise would be to hand future challengers an easy

28. Harrison Donnelly, "Reagan Opposition Threatens EDA Development Program," *Congressional Quarterly Weekly Report* 40 (September 18, 1982): 2295–2296.

issue to use against them. Consider how House members divided in 1979 over two alternative formulas for allocating fuel assistance grants among the states. Members from frostbelt districts were practically unanimous (93 percent) in favor of a formula weighted toward colder states, while those from sunbelt districts voted overwhelmingly (96 percent) for one weighted toward warmer states.[29] Perhaps legislators just happened to divide this way on the merits of the proposal, but the more powerful explanation is that they felt compelled to vote for the formula that maximized the flow of funds to their own districts. Voting for the less generous formula would allow a challenger to campaign up and down a district charging, "The incumbent voted against a proposal that would have given the citizens of this district an extra $3 million to help pay their heating bills, and in favor of a proposal that channeled the same funds to other districts. Isn't it time we had a representative in Washington who would fight for *our* interests?" Few incumbents willingly give challengers such easy lines.

Geographic benefits alone provide a poor foundation for a supporting coalition, but when combined with group benefits they offer a much firmer base. A brief comparison of the $700 million impact aid program providing grants to school districts that enroll many students living on tax-free federal property (for example, military installations) with the $5 billion revenue-sharing program supports this conclusion. Both programs allocated their funds by formula. The principal difference was that impact aid was concentrated in a few school districts—at least one in each state and at least one in about 90 percent of all congressional districts—whereas revenue sharing was spread relatively evenly across all states and localities and used for a multitude of purposes—a bit toward police salaries, a bit toward tennis courts, a bit toward street sweeping, and so on. The impact aid program, first created in 1950, has survived repeated attacks from presidents of both parties. The secret is that the funds constitute a considerable fraction of school budgets in some areas. Terminating the program would impose large and perceptible costs on teachers, students, parents, and taxpayers in these areas, costs that would be directly traceable to legislators' votes. Legislators have repeatedly protected impact aid from the presidential attacks.

The revenue-sharing program, created in 1972, has led a more trou-

29. Kathy Koch, "Congress Clears $30.3 Billion in Interior, Energy Funding after Regional Fuel Aid Fight," *Congressional Quarterly Weekly Report* 37 (November 17, 1979): 2593–2595; and Arnold, "Local Roots of Domestic Policy," p. 277.

bled life. Congress allowed inflation to erode the value of its benefits throughout the 1970s, it removed all states from the program in 1980, and it terminated the entire program in 1986.[30] The political problem was that benefits were spread so thinly across virtually all groups in society that citizens hardly noticed when funds first arrived, and they were unlikely to notice when the funds were withdrawn. Legislators had little to fear in terminating such a program[31] and much to gain by shifting the funds to other, more politically compelling programs.

The story of revenue sharing demonstrates that programs with geographically divisible benefits enjoy no special privileges in Congress. They compete with other programs for scarce funds, and sometimes they lose. The strongest coalitions are those in support of programs that deliver large and regular funds to the same citizens year after year. Once citizens become addicted to a flow of benefits, legislators cannot bear to be associated with terminating them. That was certainly the case with impact aid. Coalitions are considerably weaker when programs deliver benefits to an ever-changing cast of recipients. For example, the urban development action grant program, which allocated grants on a one-time basis to developers who were proposing to build specific projects, was relatively easy to terminate in 1988.[32] Legislators may have disappointed future beneficiaries planning to apply for grants, but they never had to impose costs on current beneficiaries. Once again Congress willingly terminated a program and shifted the funds to more politically compelling programs.

The distinction I have been drawing between revenue sharing, urban development action grants, and impact aid is one based on the likelihood that citizens might trace perceptible costs back to legislators' individual actions. Legislators could terminate both revenue sharing and urban

30. On the recent politics of revenue sharing, see Diane Granat, "State Aid, Formula Change among Issues to Be Debated in Revenue Sharing Renewal," *Congressional Quarterly Weekly Report* 41 (April 2, 1983): 659–663; and Steve Blakely, "Revenue Sharing: Ups and Downs," *Congressional Quarterly Weekly Report* 44 (September 27, 1986): 2264.

31. Of course, mayors and governors were disappointed by the loss of revenue sharing because they had to readjust their own budgets as federal funds were withdrawn. Perhaps in an earlier era when local officials controlled significant electoral resources, legislators would have been more attentive to their needs; but under current conditions, most legislators have little to fear from disappointed local officials.

32. Phil Kuntz, "UDAG Bites the Dust," *Congressional Quarterly Weekly Report* 46 (June 25, 1988): 1754–1756.

Table 6.1. Reductions in intergovernmental grant programs, 1978–1988 (in millions of 1982 dollars)

Type of grant	1978	1988	Percent reduction
Revenue sharing	9,700	0	100
Construction projects[a]	16,812	8,065	52
All other grants	74,976	68,854	8
Total grants[a]	101,488	76,919	24

a. Does not include trust fund expenditures for highway or airport construction.
Source: U.S., Office of Management and Budget, *Historical Tables: Budget of the U.S. Government, FY 1988* (Washington, D.C.: Government Printing Office, 1987), tables 9.5, 12.1, and 12.3, as adjusted for inflation with the composite deflator in table 1.3.

development action grants with little fear of electoral retribution, whereas they repeatedly protected impact aid from cuts out of fear that citizens might hold them accountable for cutting off their regular flow of benefits. This basic distinction also helps to explain why Congress, during a period of fiscal austerity, severely cut some intergovernmental grant programs while sparing many others. As Table 6.1 reveals, Congress eliminated more than half of all grants for construction projects between 1978 and 1988 while cutting other grant programs by less than one percent per year. The logic of most construction projects is identical to that of urban development action grants. Curtailing such programs would impose costs on future beneficiaries, who are relatively harmless, rather than on current beneficiaries, who can be very dangerous. The logic of most other grant programs resembles that of impact aid. Curtailing these programs would impose large and traceable costs on current beneficiaries, thus putting them in a vengeful mood.

That legislators would voluntarily cut or terminate programs that fund construction projects is a counterintuitive conclusion, given that legislators derive so much political joy from obtaining these projects for their districts and from presiding at the inevitable ground breakings, cornerstone layings, ribbon cuttings, and grand openings. The explanation is very simple, however, if one considers the relative probabilities for retrospective voting. Few political costs are associated with voting to terminate programs that provide one-time construction grants, whereas very real political risks are associated with voting to cut either entitlement programs like Social Security or grant programs that provide regular operating funds like impact aid. In times of fiscal austerity, when legislators must cut something, it is less risky to reduce future opportunities for credit claiming than it is to be associated with terminating constituents' regular supply of group or geographic benefits.

Geographic considerations fade in importance when programs provide abundant group and general benefits. Most legislators support or oppose medical research, the national park system, and defense expenditures for their general benefits, not because their own districts contain research labs, parks, or defense installations. Similarly, most legislators support the veterans' hospital program for the large group benefits offered to veterans, regardless of whether they have hospitals within their own districts. This is not to say that legislators do not care deeply about such geographic benefits, for they continue to compete vigorously for everything from veterans' hospitals and military installations to research facilities and federal office buildings. The point is simply that legislators do not make their support for these programs contingent on favorable allocational decisions. The competition for geographic benefits is kept separate from debates about the nature and size of the programs.

How much geographic considerations intrude on congressional decision making depends on how successful coalition leaders are in keeping questions about the geographic allocation of benefits off the floor. Consider how a small change in procedures affected the ability of the Department of Defense to close surplus and obsolete military bases. Between 1952 and 1974 a simple understanding between Pentagon officials and members of the military committees in Congress allowed officials to close 125 major military bases, representing 41 percent of all bases in operation.[33] The simple understanding was that military officials could close bases as long as they spared those located in districts represented on the military committees. In return, members of the military committees worked to keep off the congressional agenda proposals to allow greater congressional involvement in decisions about base closings.

After this cozy arrangement was circumvented in 1976, the effects were dramatic. It all began when the Pentagon announced its periodic

---

33. These data refer to Army and Air Force installations that employed at least one thousand civilian and military personnel. The Navy also closed many installations during this period, though I do not have a similar count. In addition, all three services closed several hundred smaller installations. On the politics of base closings from 1952 to 1974, see Arnold, *Congress and the Bureaucracy*, pp. 95–128.

round of base closings in early 1976, an event which stimulated a revolt on the floor of the House. Members from the Northeast charged that Pentagon officials had repeatedly selected northern bases for closure and spared southern bases. They proposed an amendment on the floor, approved over the objections of the military committees, requiring the Pentagon to notify Congress when it was considering closing specific bases and to prepare environmental impact statements for each listed base.[34] Both provisions gave affected legislators ample time to combine forces to protect their local bases. Over the next decade Pentagon officials continued to propose closing military bases, but not a single proposal survived the new procedures and not a single major base was actually closed. Among other things, legislators from affected areas began attaching to appropriations bills amendments that denied funds for closing or consolidating specific bases that the Pentagon had announced it was studying. Once Congress became involved in these decisions, it obeyed the first law of congressional behavior: never impose costs on one's constituents that might be directly traced to one's own individual actions.

Although the short-run costs associated with keeping a few extra bases open are minimal, these costs mount over time as more and more bases are spared the budgetary axe, and they become especially noticeable when the Pentagon finds its entire budget under serious pressure. This was the case in 1988 when Representative Dick Armey (R., Texas) devised a new approach to base closings, an approach that cleverly protected individual legislators from going on record in favor of specific base closings and that also prohibited a return to the earlier system in which members of the military committees enjoyed special advantages.[35] Under the new law, Congress waived most laws governing base closures and delegated to a special bipartisan commission the authority to select bases for closure. The Secretary of Defense was then given the authority to close all or none of the chosen bases, and his decision was final, unless Congress passed a joint resolution blocking the entire package.[36] Thus, neither Congress nor the Secretary of Defense could play their usual political games. Armey's strategic breakthrough was to devise a method that allowed legislators to vote for the general benefit of

34. The story is recounted in "Revised Military Construction Bill Cleared," *Congressional Quarterly Almanac, 1976* 32 (1977): 311–318.

35. John H. Cushman, Jr., "An Impossible Dream May Soon Be Possible," *New York Times* (May 3, 1988): A32.

36. Pat Towell, "Conferees Accept Bill to Ease Closing of Old Military Bases," *Congressional Quarterly Weekly Report* 46 (October 8, 1988): 2808–2809.

military efficiency without ever having to support a plan that directly imposed large and traceable geographic costs on their constituents. Both House and Senate passed the bill overwhelmingly, the commission recommended a list of 91 institutions to be closed, the Secretary of Defense accepted their recommendations, and the House rejected a resolution that would have blocked implementation.[37]

Competition for geographic benefits has only modest effects on the shape of public policy when programs provide abundant general benefits. Legislators may compete vigorously for shares of geographic benefits when programs are first created, but they seldom support programs simply because they wish to obtain such benefits, nor do they redesign them in order to spread out the benefits. The policy effects are actually greater on the downside—when geographic benefits are to be curtailed—because legislators have a stake in the continued provision of those benefits. We have already seen how legislators struggled to retain military bases in their districts. To the extent they are successful, legislators reduce somewhat the efficiency and the effectiveness of the military services. The policy effects are still greater when legislators mobilize to keep the assembly lines running and producing weapons that the military no longer needs or wants, simply because they wish to keep their local economies booming.[38]

GENERAL COSTS AND BENEFITS

I have already alluded to some conditions under which Congress seems to ignore particular interests in favor of the general. In this

---

37. House members voted as they pleased when the question was creating the commission, but most voted their districts' interests when they were asked to accept or reject the entire package. On the first vote, House members who eventually had bases closed or reduced in their districts were nearly as supportive of the commission idea as other legislators (81 percent vs. 93 percent). On the second vote to accept or reject the commission's recommendations, 97 percent of House members who gained military employment (through transfers from other bases) supported the package, as did 92 percent of those who were unaffected by the recommendations, whereas only 39 percent of those who were scheduled to lose military employment supported the package—even though the vote was on the entire list of 91 installations, not on each installation separately. For a list of installations by district, see Mike Mills, "Base Closings: The Political Pain Is Limited," *Congressional Quarterly Weekly Report* 46 (December 31, 1988): 3625–3629. For the individual votes, see *Congressional Quarterly Weekly Report* 46 (October 15, 1988): 3018–3019; and *Congressional Quarterly Weekly Report* 47 (April 22, 1989): 926–927.

38. Arnold, "Local Roots of Domestic Policy," pp. 259–264.

section I set forth both the conditions that *force* legislators to take into account more general interests and the conditions that merely *allow* them to do so.

Legislators feel forced to serve diffuse or general interests only if a program's general costs or benefits are salient or potentially salient to substantial numbers of citizens, and only if coalition leaders employ procedures that encourage traceability for general effects rather than for group or geographic effects. The salience of an issue is itself a variable. It may fluctuate in reaction to changes in objective conditions and in response to coalition leaders' efforts at persuasion. The general costs associated with sugar quotas became an issue only after the retail price of sugar tripled. Issues related to the environment and automobile safety became salient only after proponents of federal action worked to educate people about the dangers of inaction. Salience is also directly related to the magnitude of the general costs and benefits. Large effects are simply easier to see than smaller ones.

The extent to which legislators anticipate citizens' preferences about general costs and benefits depends on the relative size and visibility of those general effects compared with the size and visibility of the group and geographic effects. Consider how legislators might respond to two proposed amendments, each of which would yield identical general benefits by reducing the federal deficit $10 billion annually. The first amendment proposes to cut $10 billion from the Medicare budget by increasing the deductible that patients must pay for each hospital visit, while the second proposes that the budget of each federal agency should be reduced by one percent, with each administrator responsible for allocating the cuts among his agency's programs. Despite the identical general benefits, most legislators would ignore the general benefits in the first case while considering them very seriously in the second. The first vote is overwhelmingly about Medicare. Legislators have good reason to believe that if they support the amendment, millions of beneficiaries would notice the increased costs and trace their new burdens to legislators' votes. The second vote is essentially about economy in government and fiscal responsibility. Legislators suspect that conservative groups and future challengers might use their votes against this amendment as evidence that they are not serious about controlling spending (while the recipients of governmental assistance would hardly notice such small across-the-board cuts).

The battle between those seeking to produce general benefits and those interested in group and geographic benefits often reduces to a battle over how an issue is to be framed. Coalition leaders interested in general benefits attempt to design both their proposals and procedures so that citizens and legislators focus their attention on the general benefits, with scant attention given to the associated group and geographic costs. The sponsors of the 1985 Gramm-Rudman-Hollings bill to control the federal budget succeeded brilliantly at this strategy by forcing legislators to vote on a plan that mandated annual reductions in the federal deficit while deferring all specific reductions until another day (see Chapter 7). The strategy was brilliant because legislators felt electoral pressure to support a proposal that promised a balanced budget in five years; yet if legislators weakened when it came time to make specific reductions, the bill simply mandated uniform across-the-board cuts. If the Supreme Court had not objected on constitutional grounds, the plan would have imposed severe group and geographic costs without legislators ever having to vote for them.

When general benefits are highly salient and group and geographic costs appear negligible, legislators often feel compelled to support whatever proposals are put before them. Such considerations have been important in the congressional consideration of many environmental and safety bills, as well as the federal funding of medical research (see Chapter 4). Similarly, when general costs are highly salient and group and geographic benefits appear negligible, legislators often feel pressure to oppose the proposals put before them. Such considerations frequently dominate votes on foreign affairs, where group and geographic benefits are inherently limited. Many senators voting on the Panama Canal treaty in 1978, for example, believed that voters might hold them accountable for the general costs associated with giving away a priceless American asset. Similarly, many legislators have trouble supporting foreign assistance bills because the general costs are so much more visible than the general benefits.

Creating conditions that force legislators to consider general costs and benefits is often impossible, either because the general effects are too small for citizens to notice or because the causal connections between governmental policy and these general effects are too long and complicated for citizens to appreciate. In such cases coalition leaders can still create environments that encourage legislators to consider the general effects. They can do so by working to break the traceability chain for group and geographic effects. This approach helps to eliminate any political costs associated with voting for such proposals and allows legislators to vote purely on the merits. Coalition leaders employ the usual procedural devices for breaking the traceability chain, including delegation to the executive and the use of omnibus bills and restrictive rules.

General benefits can also increase in importance when coalition leaders place groups in direct conflict with each other, so that the influence of one helps to neutralize that of the other. Consider how Representative Les Aspin (D., Wis.) encouraged Congress to consider the general costs of the system of military pensions by putting current recipients of group benefits in direct competition with future recipients. Under long-established practice the government allowed military personnel to retire on half pay after twenty years of service. Since the costs were not incurred for at least two decades, no one in Congress had much incentive to work to reduce the system's future costs (despite the fact that accrued liabilities amounted to more than half a trillion dollars). Championing change in the system was thought to be especially risky because both current and future beneficiaries liked their generous pensions. Aspin began his campaign quietly in 1983 by arranging to have the accounting system changed so that each year the government had to place money in a trust fund to cover all pension liabilities generated during that year. No one objected to this innocuous-sounding change in bookkeeping, and soon the budget began listing pension contributions as an annual expense. Several years later Aspin proposed a change in the entire pension system that would reduce the pensions of future retirees and reduce the annual federal contribution by $4 billion. By transferring a quarter of the savings to current retirees, he completely neutralized the opposition—current retirees profited at the expense of future retirees. With the opposition divided, Congress focused on the plan's general benefits, which included not only $3 billion in annual savings but a more rational retirement system that encouraged skilled personnel to reenlist for up to thirty years of service.[39]

THE DYNAMICS OF CONGRESSIONAL DECISION MAKING

In Part Two I use the theory developed in Chapters 1 through 6 to explain congressional decision making in the fields of economic, tax, and energy policy over the past several decades. My aim is not to

---

39. For the entire story, see "Mr. Aspin Slays the Monster," *New York Times* (April 1, 1986): A30.

"test" the theory in the scientific sense, but rather to show that it yields reasonable explanations for the dynamics of policy decisions over a reasonably long period.

I have chosen these three policy areas because they are important in their own right and because political scientists have not yet developed adequate explanations for congressional decision making in these areas. They are troublesome for political scientists because each contains one or more shift points when Congress has rejected some established policy (which seemed inevitable at the time) and replaced it with a brand-new policy that imposed costs on those who were previously advantaged. Chapter 7 explains several puzzles related to economic policy, including why Congress often ignores the macroeconomic consequences of its actions and yet sometimes enacts policies that are explicitly designed to produce more pleasing macroeconomic outcomes. Chapter 8 explains why Congress devoted so many years to creating particularistic tax provisions and then suddenly switched course and enacted comprehensive tax reform. Chapter 9 explains why Congress first regulated petroleum and natural gas prices, allowed those regulations to persist for several decades, and eventually deregulated both fuels just when everybody agreed that deregulation was impossible.

These three chapters illustrate how the theory can be used to explain the dynamics of congressional decision making. The applications are not designed to test the theory in any rigorous sense. Within each of the policy areas I have intentionally chosen some cases in which Congress has served organized interests or delivered narrowly targeted geographic interests and some cases in which Congress has served more diffuse, general, or unorganized interests. I have not attempted to select a random sample of all congressional decisions in each policy area, for basing a research strategy on a random sample would invariably produce too few examples of Congress's shift points. At this point my principal goal is to understand the conditions under which legislators serve interests of various types. Only after I am more confident that I have identified such conditions would I consider devising techniques for testing those conditions or estimating the frequency of their occurrence.

Although I have attempted to create a fairly general theory of congressional decision making that is applicable to all areas of policy, the empirical chapters do not draw evenly on all portions of the theory. Instead I emphasize several aspects of the theory. Partly this reflects my choice of policy areas. If I had chosen to analyze intergovernmental, environmental, and social welfare policy, I would have employed different elements from the theory. It also reflects a conscious choice to emphasize what I believe is new, distinctive, or counterintuitive in the theory and to pass over elements that appear to be more commonplace. For example, I repeatedly show how coalition leaders employ several procedural strategies that I believe are underappreciated by congressional analysts, whereas I devote little attention to the more obvious strategies of persuasion. For similar reasons I emphasize (1) the degree to which legislators worry about the effects they produce and not simply the positions they take, (2) the degree to which legislators feel constrained by inattentive publics and not simply by organized interest groups, and (3) the importance of general costs and benefits, and not simply group and geographic costs and benefits, in congressional decision making.

Part Two

The Theory Applied

7

Economic Policy

What kind of imprint does Congress leave on macroeconomic policy? Is Congress basically a responsible partner in government, working diligently to enact sound fiscal policies? Or is it an irresponsible meddler, repeatedly interfering with the best-laid plans for macroeconomic policy and restrained only by the combined actions of veto-wielding presidents and independent-minded members of the Federal Reserve Board? The truth actually lies somewhere in between. Congress displays both admirable strengths and understandable weaknesses in the field of macroeconomic policy. It appears to be neither more nor less responsible than the president.

In this chapter (and the next) I attempt to explain why Congress makes the macroeconomic decisions that it does. My aim is not only to explain the broad patterns of decisions on taxing and spending but to inquire about the impact of electoral calculations on these budgetary decisions. Does the quest for reelection inspire legislators to enact sound economic policies, to keep the economy relatively healthy, and to give citizens one of the few general benefits on which they can all agree? Or does the electoral quest have more perverse consequences, encouraging legislators to spend more than they can raise, to enact both taxing and spending programs that are a drag on the national economy, and to deny citizens economic outcomes that all would prefer?

A prevailing interpretation of legislative politics emphasizes the negative consequences of the electoral quest. Many careful scholars have argued that a Congress filled with legislators interested in reelection and lacking the discipline of strong parties is inherently biased in favor of particularism, deficit spending, and governmental growth, and that all three have undesirable effects on the performance of the economy.[1] To be sure, there is much truth in these observations. Legislators do create and sustain programs filled with group and geographic benefits, and this tendency toward particularism leaves an obvious imprint on both the tax code and the federal budget. Legislators do find it easier to approve new expenditure programs than to impose the taxes to support them. And Congress has participated in both the creation of deficits and in the expansion of the size and scope of government.

A fair assessment of Congress, however, must also recognize several contrary themes. Although Congress has enacted many particularistic tax bills, it has also passed genuine tax reform. Although Congress has created many new expenditure programs, it has also terminated some of these programs and reduced many others. Although legislators find it difficult to pass tax increases, they have somehow managed to do so. Although legislators have participated in cutting taxes, they have usually done so in response to presidential requests (and often reluctantly). Although Congress has lately had trouble balancing the budget, it regularly balanced the budget throughout most of American history.

THE POLITICS OF ECONOMIC POLICY

The principal problem for theory is to specify both the conditions under which Congress enacts responsible economic policy and those under which it adopts less responsible policies. The problem is complicated by the fact that so much of what happens in Congress affects the general health of the economy. Everyone would agree that Congress makes macroeconomic policy when it decides how large the deficit should be. So, too, does Congress influence the general health of

1. On particularism, see Kenneth A. Shepsle and Barry R. Weingast, "Legislative Politics and Budget Outcomes," in Gregory B. Mills and John L. Palmer (eds.), *Federal Budget Policy in the 1980s* (Washington, D.C.: Urban Institute Press, 1984), pp. 343–367; on deficit spending, see James M. Buchanan and Richard E. Wagner, *Democracy in Deficit: The Political Legacy of Lord Keynes* (New York: Academic Press, 1977); on governmental growth, see Morris P. Fiorina, "Legislative Facilitation of Government Growth" (paper presented at the conference on the causes and consequences of public sector growth, Dorado Beach, Puerto Rico, November 1978), with portions reprinted as "Universalism, Reciprocity, and Distributive Policymaking in Majority Rule Institutions," in John P. Crecine (ed.), *Research in Public Policy Analysis and Management: Basic Theory, Methods, and Perspectives* (Greenwich, Conn.: JAI Press, 1981), pp. 197–221.

the economy whenever it makes lesser decisions concerning the size, purpose, and nature of federal expenditures, the basic character of the tax code, the conditions for competition in specific industries, or the extent of environmental, health, or safety regulation. The only difference is that some decisions affect the economy in large and immediate ways while others have more indirect and cumulative effects.

In these two chapters I assume that practically every policy that Congress considers has both a macroeconomic component and a noneconomic component. The macroeconomic component is the total effect that a policy would have on economic growth, unemployment, and inflation, both in the short run and in the long run. The noneconomic component includes all other effects. Thus, a billion-dollar program to train high school dropouts to hold semiskilled jobs has several possible economic effects—contributing a billion dollars to the deficit in the short term, decreasing unemployment by some fraction several years down the line, and possibly stimulating economic growth and decreasing the deficit in the long run—in addition to the obvious noneconomic effects.

These two components then give rise to two types of policy decisions: explicit economic policy and derivative economic policy. An *explicit economic policy* is a policy that someone proposes in an effort to solve a specific macroeconomic problem. The economic component of the policy provides the impetus for action. Explicit economic policies include fiscal policy, monetary policy, wage and price controls, investment tax credits, countercyclical public works, or a revision of the tax code to stimulate work, savings, or investment. A *derivative economic policy* is a policy that someone proposes to ameliorate some other condition, although it also has macroeconomic effects. For these policies, the noneconomic component provides the impetus for action. Derivative economic policies include all expenditure programs, all attempts to modify the tax code to achieve noneconomic goals, and all regulatory or incentive programs that unintentionally alter the way individuals work or save or the way firms invest.

The politics of economic policy differs significantly depending on whether Congress is considering explicit economic policy or derivative economic policy. For derivative economic policy, legislators pay greater attention to the noneconomic components, which tend to be relatively large, than to the economic components, which are usually much smaller. For explicit economic policy the emphasis is reversed. Legislators focus more on the economic components and give proportionally less attention to the noneconomic components. In both cases legislators' calculations reflect the way in which the issues might enter citizens' assessments in future elections.

Consider how legislators might calculate the political advantages and disadvantages associated with voting for a derivative economic policy. First, imagine a case in which legislators are asked to terminate a $5 billion program that provides grants and loans to college students. The political costs of termination are obvious. Students and parents would bear large, early-order costs that could easily be traced to legislators' recorded votes. By comparison, the political benefits are considerably fewer. Voting to terminate the program would allow legislators to claim that they were working hard to trim the deficit and help them create or maintain voting records that would appear fiscally responsible. Despite these attractions, most legislators would consider that the political costs would far exceed the political benefits. Such is the power of retrospective voting.[2]

The political evaluation shifts somewhat if we consider a case in which legislators are asked to create a brand-new program that would provide grants and loans to college students. Legislators have much less to fear from students and parents in this case. Most students and parents would never notice that a proposed program had failed to pass, and most challengers would be unable to rouse them into action by alerting them to potential benefits forgone (rather than actual benefits abolished). To be sure, many legislators would still have good political reasons for favoring the program, but the political benefits of being associated with a new program are sufficiently modest to be overshadowed by economic considerations (at least under the proper conditions).

Calculations about the economic components of a derivative policy depend on the size of the economic effects, the state of the economy, and the nature of current fiscal policy. Legislators can easily discount economic effects when they consider creating a $5 million program, for this is mere noise in the federal budget. Creating a $5 *billion* program is another matter. Voting in favor of such a large program can, under the proper conditions, be evidence of fiscal irresponsibility, and the damage will be magnified if the vote is part of a pattern of support for excessive spending.[3] No legislator wants to face a challenger who can argue that

2. A reminder from Chapters 3 and 4 that, unless otherwise modified, I use the term *retrospective voting* to refer to citizens using the incumbent performance rule or to legislators anticipating that citizens might reward or punish them for their individual connections with real effects.

3. Consider, for example, the National Taxpayers Union, which constructs its legislative ratings by incorporating every recorded vote that could possibly affect the size of federal

"the incumbent voted in favor of twenty separate programs that would have increased the deficit by over fifty billion dollars!" Legislators become especially cautious about providing challengers with votes that suggest anything other than fiscal prudence when the budget is already far out of balance or when inflation is rampant. It is obviously much easier to create a large new subsidy program when the budget is in balance or when the economy is in deep recession.

Despite the fact that legislators' political calculations usually revolve around the noneconomic components of derivative economic policy, the economic components can still play an important role in their decisions, especially if coalition leaders work to raise legislators' consciousness about a vote's economic (and political) implications. Presidents often attempt to label certain votes as budget busters, both to heighten legislators' attention to the economic components of the policy and to provide a campaign issue to be used against those who fail to heed the warning. The budget committees perform similar functions within Congress. Senator Edmund Muskie (D., Maine), for example, first established the power of the Senate Budget Committee in 1975 by crafting several floor votes against the expansion of the school lunch program and against an increase in the military procurement budget (both were enormously popular at the time).[4] In each case Muskie managed to transform a programmatic vote into one in which the economic component dominated legislators' calculations.

Legislators' political calculations change once again when they deal with explicit economic policy. Here the economic components are both larger and more prominent than the noneconomic components. Usually they get top billing and provide the names by which the policies are known. No one can doubt that votes on wage and price controls, a president's economic recovery program, or a major budget resolution are votes on macroeconomic policy, however much they may affect other ends. At a minimum, legislators can be held accountable for the positions they take on these economic policies. In some cases there is also the potential for retrospective voting, with citizens tracing real economic effects back to legislators' votes.

The potential for retrospective voting is greatest when programs promise large economic effects. Consider, for example, a legislator who

---

spending. Legislators who support every spending program that comes along earn a rating of zero, while those who oppose all forms of spending attain a perfect score.

4. Bernard Asbell, *The Senate Nobody Knows* (Garden City, N.Y.: Doubleday, 1978), pp. 142–163, 268–279.

is deciding whether to support a president's economic recovery program that promises to restore the nation's economic health (such as President Reagan's 1981 program). If a legislator opposes the economic program, if Congress fails to enact it, and if the economy continues in ill health, then she and the other opponents are vulnerable to the charge that *they* are responsible for economic conditions because they blocked the president's remedy without enacting something better. On the other hand, if a legislator supports the program, she can either claim partial credit if the economy improves or blame the president for offering an inadequate program if it does not. A similar logic prevails for a legislator deciding whether to give the president standby authority to impose price controls during a time of high inflation. Opposing such a program leaves a legislator open to blame for rapidly increasing prices, whereas supporting it transfers blame to the president for either imposing unpopular controls or failing to impose any controls at all.

One uncertainty is that legislators never know exactly what economic issues will arise in the next election for which they might be blamed. Consider, for example, how legislators scrambled from side to side in 1979 and 1980 as they saw either inflation or recession as the more likely economic issue for the 1980 election.[5] Early in 1979 inflation seemed the greater danger and House members passed a first budget resolution that promised to reduce the deficit to $23 billion for fiscal year 1980. Several months later signs of impending recession encouraged them to increase spending by $16 billion in the second budget resolution. After the consumer price index soared to an annual rate of 18 percent in January 1980, legislators switched sides again and adopted a first budget resolution that provided a small surplus ($500 million) for fiscal year 1981. By summer a recession was under way and Congress passed a second budget resolution that included a $30 billion deficit and called for a $30 to $40 billion tax cut in calendar year 1981. These four reversals in policy occurred over an eighteen-month period, as legislators struggled both to foresee where the economy would be on election day and to imagine how their positions on the budget would look to voters on that day of judgment.

Exactly how legislators evaluate policy options, then, depends on how those policy options are packaged. If legislators are asked to terminate a popular spending program, they quite naturally consider the possibility that affected citizens might trace their loss of group benefits back to

5. *Congress and the Nation, 1977–1980* (Washington, D.C.: Congressional Quarterly, 1981), pp. 220–230.

legislators' individual actions and hold them accountable for those actions. If legislators are asked to balance the federal budget by shaving 2 percent from all spending programs, they are more likely to consider the possibility that citizens might trace future economic effects back to their votes and hold them accountable. In both cases, legislators are anticipating the effects of retrospective voting and adjusting their behavior accordingly. The only difference is that in the case of derivative economic policy, legislators expect citizens to focus more on the group costs than on the general costs, whereas in the case of explicit economic policy the emphasis is reversed.

In many other cases legislators have little to fear from retrospective voting because they see little possibility that citizens could trace either group effects or general effects back to individual actions. They may still feel electoral pressure to support one side or the other, but the pressure has more to do with their policy positions than with the effects they produce. On the one hand, some legislators may enjoy voting for new or increased group benefits in the hopes that group members will reward them at the polls. On the other hand, legislators do not enjoy creating records of fiscal irresponsibility that can then be used against them. Exactly how they balance these conflicting demands depends both on how the issues are framed and on the current state of the economy.

In what follows I employ these basic ideas and the arguments of previous chapters to explain how Congress has made fiscal choices between 1946 and 1988. My aim is to show how electoral calculations leave their imprint on congressional decisions, at times encouraging legislators to enact sound macroeconomic policy and at times making such choices virtually impossible. I shall try to re-create the context of congressional decision making so that we can understand how legislators estimated the electoral consequences of specific economic decisions. Their calculations depend both on the nature of economic problems and on what other actors (particularly the president) are doing to shape citizens' views of congressional action. Legislators know that there is a big political difference between supporting a small tax increase after urgent appeals from the president and enacting the same increase over the determined opposition of a popular president.

BALANCED BUDGETS

Most governments have difficulty balancing their budgets. Even without all the messy complications of democratic institutions, the resources available to governments are inherently limited while the demands for governmental services are practically boundless. Democratic institutions complicate matters because elected politicians believe that spending money yields electoral dividends and that imposing taxes generates political costs. Although both legislators and elected executives are subject to the temptation to spend more than they raise, the conventional wisdom holds that executives are better at balancing budgets than legislators. Executives stand alone before all the voters and thus can plausibly be held accountable for expenditures, taxes, deficits, and the general performance of the economy; individual legislators face only their own constituents, among whom they can claim credit for popular spending programs and argue how blameless they are as individuals for the increased taxes and deficits that others have produced.

On the surface the argument that congressional politics exacerbates governmental tendency toward deficits makes sense. The empirical evidence, however, is less than compelling. Executives certainly deserve their share of blame for deficits. President Reagan's 1981 economic program, for example, managed to double the national debt in only five years. And President Johnson's simultaneous pursuit of Great Society programs and the war in Vietnam did much to fuel the inflation of the late 1960s and early 1970s. Furthermore, Congress is frequently more fiscally conservative than the president, as demonstrated by its long reluctance to approve President Kennedy's tax cut, its deep skepticism toward President Reagan's tax cut, and its quick enactment of the Gramm-Rudman-Hollings bill, which would have automatically reduced both defense and nondefense expenditures in the pursuit of a balanced budget. In fact, the most careful empirical study of postwar budgets has shown that Congress appropriated just about exactly what presidents requested.[6] From 1947 to 1984 Congress actually appropriated about $1 billion dollars per year *less* than presidents requested, with an average of $3.4 billion in reductions under Democratic presidents more than balancing an average of $1.9 billion in increases under Republican presidents. To be sure, Congress frequently alters presidential priorities *among* programs. Total spending, however, reflects presidential requests, not a peculiar legislative tendency toward deficits.[7]

6. Paul E. Peterson, "The New Politics of Deficits," in John Chubb and Paul Peterson (eds.), *The New Direction in American Politics* (Washington, D.C.: Brookings Institution, 1985), pp. 365–397.
7. At least this is the case for appropriated accounts (which are what Peterson exam-

How does Congress manage to approve a budget that, if not in balance, nevertheless reflects a president's fiscal policy? How does Congress resist the temptation to increase total spending or cut taxes? My analysis begins with an examination of the last period in which the federal government balanced its budget. This account provides a baseline for my analysis of how Congress and the president created first modest and then massive deficits.[8]

The last period in which the federal government balanced its budget was from 1946 to 1961. In this period the government accumulated surpluses in seven years and ran deficits in the other nine, with average annual receipts exceeding outlays by a tiny margin (0.2%).[9] How did Congress manage what, in retrospect, seems an amazing feat? Three factors contributed to this performance. First, most citizens and most politicians believed that governments should balance their budgets, the possible exceptions being years of war or depression.[10] The Keynesian notion of intentional deficits was becoming increasingly popular among economists, but few politicians believed that deficits were desirable, and many were convinced that their constituents would not look kindly upon those who produced them.[11] Second, presidents generally proposed balanced, or nearly balanced, budgets for Congress to consider.

---

ined). As Ellwood notes, the case *might* be different for entitlement accounts. Although there are as yet no careful empirical studies of entitlements, my own sense is that Congress and the president probably share the blame equally for them too. See John W. Ellwood, "Budget Authority vs. Outlays as Measures of Budget Policy" (paper delivered by the 1986 Annual Meeting of the American Political Science Association), pp. 19–22.

8. None of my analysis assumes that Congress should balance the budget annually. Even if economists, legislators, and presidents agreed that an unbalanced budget would be desirable and that a specific deficit or surplus would be optimal, legislators must still achieve that target. The political puzzle of how legislators resist the temptation to overspend or undertax is unchanged whether they are seeking a truly balanced budget or one with an agreed-upon surplus or deficit.

9. These calculations are based on the accounting rules used today. See U.S., Office of Management and Budget, *Historical Tables: Budget of the United States Government, FY 1988* (Washington, D.C.: Government Printing Office, 1987), table 1.1. At the time the so-called administrative budget, which did not count trust funds such as Social Security, was more commonly reported. Under the administrative budget, the federal government had six years of surpluses and ten years of deficits, with average outlays exceeding receipts by 3.7 percent. See *Congress and the Nation, 1945–1964* (Washington, D.C.: Congressional Quarterly, 1965), p. 392.

10. On the idea of a balanced budget, see James D. Savage, *Balanced Budgets and American Politics* (Ithaca, N.Y.: Cornell University Press, 1988).

11. James Sundquist, *Politics and Policy* (Washington, D.C.: Brookings Institution, 1968), pp. 13–56.

Third, the House Appropriations Committee had evolved into a careful watchdog of the treasury, allowing expenditures to grow only within the revenue constraint.[12] Not only did the House place some of its most fiscally conservative members on this committee, but the chairman assigned members to subcommittees where their districts had no special group or geographic interests at stake. Moreover, with few entitlement programs other than Social Security, the Appropriations Committee directly controlled a large fraction of federal spending.

These factors help to explain why legislators did not create unbalanced budgets as a matter of explicit economic policy. Legislators' own beliefs in a balanced budget made it unlikely that they would propose creating deficits, and their sense of citizens' opinions on these matters suggested that supporting deficit spending would be politically risky. In the midst of the worst postwar recession (1958), for example, only one senator used Keynesian language to justify a proposed tax cut to stimulate the economy.[13] The senator was Paul Douglas (D., Ill.), a former professor of labor economics at the University of Chicago. Despite the deep recession and despite legislators' presumed attraction to cutting taxes, his amendment failed, 71 to 14. Neither the economics nor the politics of the idea made sense to most legislators.

The three factors provide a less convincing explanation for legislators' failure to overspend by adopting a whole series of programmatic amendments. Wouldn't most legislators have felt some electoral pressure to support an amendment increasing expenditures for highways, or dams, or veterans' benefits, or Social Security? Wouldn't a whole collection of programmatic amendments, spread over the entire year, have created a substantial deficit? Presumably most legislators would have felt electoral pressure if they were asked to vote publicly on these kinds of amendments. During this entire period, however, the House operated under a system of rules that made it easy to propose an amendment but very difficult to demand a roll-call vote.

Most amendments were disposed of quietly and without a recorded vote. The only way to obtain a roll-call vote on the floor of the House was first to have an amendment approved in the Committee of the Whole,

---

12. By happy coincidence, this period of balanced budgets is almost exactly the period covered by the most exhaustive study of appropriations politics in Congress (1947–1962). So we know a great deal about how legislators managed to achieve fiscal balance. See Richard F. Fenno, Jr., *Power of the Purse* (Boston: Little, Brown, 1966).

13. Sundquist, *Politics and Policy*, pp. 20–28.

whose quorum was only one hundred members. When attendance was sparse, as it often was, the fifty members of the Appropriations Committee had a distinct advantage. Moreover, all votes in the Committee of the Whole went unrecorded, which helped both to break the usual electoral connection and to increase the power of committee and party leaders who carefully watched how legislators voted.[14] Over this entire sixteen-year period, House members faced only thirty-six roll-call votes on amendments to appropriations bills (out of 547 proposed).[15] Thus, they had only about two occasions per year in which the usual electoral logic might impel them to vote for increased spending.

In principle, it was easy to enact programmatic amendments and to increase spending beyond what the Appropriations Committee had proposed. All that was required was that a large and committed majority show up on two separate occasions—once for an unrecorded vote and again later for a roll-call vote. The catch was that an amendment had to survive both stages to be approved, whereas the electoral incentive affected only the second stage. At the first stage, legislators felt no electoral pressure to attend because attendance was not recorded, and they felt no electoral pressure to vote a particular way because their positions were not recorded. These floor procedures protected legislators from their worst impulses and allowed them to do what they all believed was both good policy and good politics—keeping the budget in balance.

FISCAL ACTIVISM

President Kennedy was the first executive to propose that Congress increase the deficit as an explicit economic policy.[16] Kennedy was hardly a natural-born Keynesian. He had voted against the Douglas tax cut in 1958, and he had campaigned for the presidency as a strong believer in balanced budgets. His economic advisors, however, were all committed Keynesians, and they eventually convinced him that a tax cut would stimulate the sluggish economy and that the resultant growth

14. Fenno, *Power of the Purse*, pp. 432–435.

15. Ibid., p. 464.

16. I am assuming that previous presidents tolerated deficits in order to advance other programmatic ends (for example, relief appropriations during the Depression), but that they did not intentionally create deficits. See Donald T. Critchlow, "The Political Control of the Economy: Deficit Spending as a Political Belief, 1932–1952," *Public Historian* 3 (1981): 5–22.

would quickly erase the short-term deficits that were required as a catalyst. Convincing Congress to pass the cut was far more difficult. President Kennedy first proposed cutting taxes in early June 1962. Congress finally enacted the Revenue Act of 1964 nearly twenty-one months later under President Johnson.[17]

The administration persuaded Congress to cut taxes without ever convincing legislators of the Keynesian rationale. In fact, the administration's strategy was to make tax cuts politically palatable to legislators rather than intellectually appealing. This feat was accomplished both by creating lots of group benefits that would be attractive to legislators, citizens, and corporations, and by maneuvering so that legislators would not be closely associated with any disagreeable economic effects. The administration carefully distributed the benefits across every segment of society—rich and poor, organized and unorganized, large firms and small—so that legislators could deliver substantial benefits to each of their taxpaying constituents.

The administration was especially effective in persuading the business community to support the tax cuts. Some business leaders were convinced by their own newly acquired economic advisors that tax cuts could spur the economy to greater health; others were interested in how the bill would reduce taxes on both corporate income and their own personal incomes. The business community's strong support for the plan helped to take the political sting out of voting to cut taxes at a time when the budget was already slightly out of balance. Republican legislators in particular were persuaded that supporting it would not alienate their strongest supporters.[18]

The administration also convinced conservative leaders such as Wilbur Mills (D., Ark.) and Harry Byrd (D., Va.), the chairmen of the two tax-writing committees, that the alternative to tax reduction was to increase government spending at the start of the next recession. In essence, the administration threatened to dangle politically appealing group and geographic benefits in front of susceptible legislators—proposals that conservative leaders knew would be irresistible whenever recession struck—if they could not agree on tax reduction. The economic consequences of the two alternatives were equivalent, and thus the administration could afford to appear indifferent. Conservative

17. For the best single account of the tax bill, see Sundquist, *Politics and Policy*, pp. 34–53.

18. Ibid., pp. 47–48.

leaders, however, much preferred reducing taxes to increasing spending.[19] Finally, everyone kept the proposal carefully identified as an administration program, which helped to insulate legislators who wanted
to vote for it from electoral retribution. If the program failed and the
economy weakened, it was the president's fault. If it succeeded, legislators could share in the glory. Together these strategies helped to focus
legislators' attention on the group benefits, which always make tax
cutting so irresistible, rather than on the economic rationale or the
short-term deficits, both of which the administration made more firmly
traceable to itself than to individual legislators.

Legislators fretted for nearly two years about whether to cut taxes.
Two years after doing so, however, there was little about which legislators might worry. The economy performed spectacularly. Real gross
national product grew by 5.3 percent in 1964 and 5.8 percent in 1965,
unemployment fell by more than a point, and consumer prices were
virtually unchanged. As predicted, the deficit increased in 1964 (to 5
percent of federal outlays); but then it magically shrank the following
year (to 1.2 percent of outlays) as the booming economy generated
higher revenues at lower rates. The comparisons between the last four
years of the Eisenhower Administration and the first four years of the
Kennedy/Johnson Administration were even more telling (see Table
7.1). The fiscal activists beat the fiscal conservatives on every count.
Real growth was twice as fast, unemployment was nearly a point lower,
and inflation was lower by a fraction. Perhaps most surprisingly, the net
deficit was smaller under those who advocated intentional deficits than
under those who attempted to balance the budget every year.

Exactly how much (if at all) the tax cut contributed to this economic
boom is not important to the analysis. The economy prospered exactly as
the fiscal activists had predicted, and this, more than anything else, gave
fiscal activism credibility in Washington. Legislators also discovered
that supporting an activist policy did not produce a negative reaction
among their constituents. To the best of my knowledge, no legislators
suffered from their association with the 1964 tax cut. Legislators never
became vulnerable to the charge that they had voted to produce greater
deficits because the deficits increased for only a few quarters and then
declined sharply as the economy entered a period of sustained growth.
Instead they found that a growing economy quickly filled governmental
coffers, providing funds for both new expenditure programs and more

19. Ibid., pp. 46, 49–51.

Table 7.1. Fiscal and economic performance by period and presidential administration, 1946–1988

Fiscal years[a]	President submitting budget	Deficit or surplus as percent of total outlays[b]	Percent change in real GNP	Unemployment rate (%)	Percent change in consumer price index
A. Period of fiscal conservatism					
1946–49	Truman	+6.0	−4.5	4.4	+7.4
1950–53	Truman	−1.2	+6.7	3.5	+3.0
1954–57	Eisenhower	+1.0	+2.0	4.5	+1.3
1958–61	Eisenhower	−5.1	+2.5	6.0	+1.5
Mean for period		+0.2	+1.7	4.6	+3.3
B. Period of fiscal activism					
1962–65	Kennedy/ Johnson	−4.3	+5.1	5.1	+1.3
1966–69	Johnson	−5.1	+3.8	3.6	+3.9
Mean for period		−4.7	+4.5	4.3	+2.6
C. Period of inflation and stagnation					
1970–73	Nixon	−7.2	+3.2	5.2	+4.9
1974–77	Nixon/Ford	−12.8	+2.0	7.1	+8.1
1978–81	Carter	−11.3	+2.4	6.5	+10.7
Mean for period		−10.4	+2.5	6.3	+7.9
D. The Reagan years[c]					
1982–85	Reagan	−21.8	+2.8	8.4	+4.3
1986–88	Reagan	−17.3	+3.5	6.2	+3.3
Mean for period		−19.9	+3.1	7.4	+3.9

a. Data for administrations and periods are averages of annual data.
b. Budgetary data are for fiscal years; economic data are for calendar years.
c. Performance of Reagan administration is based on data for only 7 years.
Sources: Data compiled by the author from U.S., Office of Management and Budget, *Historical Tables: Budget of the United States Government, FY 1990* (Washington, D.C.: Government Printing Office, 1989), table 1.1; and U.S., Office of the President, *Economic Report of the President* (Washington, D.C.: Government Printing Office, 1989), pp. 315, 344, 378. Data for 1988 from *Survey of Current Business* 69 (October 1989): 22; and *Monthly Labor Review* 112 (October 1989): 58, 59.

tax cuts. Legislators responded happily the following year by enacting scores of new Great Society programs and by eliminating most excise taxes.

This one experience with fiscal activism did not transform legislators into committed Keynesians. Most were never converted intellectually. The experience did, however, make legislators far more receptive to presidential budgets that contained short-run deficits, as long as they did not have to vote specifically on the issue of deficits. It also increased their susceptibility to proposals that would increase spending or decrease taxes. Such proposals were always politically attractive to politicians, given their plentiful group and geographic benefits. Now they also seemed to deliver substantial general benefits, in the form of economic prosperity, whereas before they were largely associated with general costs. The congressional system for making budgets ensured that legislators never had to vote explicitly in favor of deficits. They voted on the parts of the budget, never on the whole. Citizens still believed in balanced budgets, and legislators continued to resist any direct connection with deficits. Voting to raise the statutory limit on federal debt, for example, remained a difficult vote for most legislators because it seemed to endorse the very deficits they had been quietly producing by the creation of scores of programs voted on separately.

The flip side of Keynesianism was the recommendation that the government should at times produce a surplus, either by raising taxes or lowering spending, to cool an overheated, inflationary economy—a bitter pill for elected politicians to take. Voting to increase taxes or decrease expenditures creates group and geographic costs directly traceable to legislators, but only a diffuse general benefit—the avoidance of inflation—that will be virtually untraceable to individual legislators sometime in the murky future. This side of Keynesianism was politically explosive. When proponents of fiscal activism first introduced politicians to the joy of cutting taxes, they failed to mention that it could easily be followed by the agony of raising taxes.

Soon after cutting income taxes in 1964 and excise taxes in 1965, politicians had to face exactly that agonizing decision. By early 1966 the usual Keynesian indicators suggested that the economy was out of its slump and was now generating the seeds of inflation: unemployment had dipped below the 4 percent floor for the first time in over a decade, and wholesale prices began to increase appreciably for the first time in nearly a decade. Moreover, federal expenditures were now increasing more rapidly than revenues, and the deficit, which had shrunk to 1.2

percent of federal outlays in 1965, began to grow again. Part of this growing deficit was a consequence of the many new Great Society programs, and part was a response to the war in Vietnam. Real defense expenditures, for example, increased by 40.2 percent between 1965 and 1968.[20]

After more than a year of indecision, President Johnson proposed a 10 percent surcharge on corporate and personal income taxes in August 1967.[21] The proposal was politically unworkable. Many legislators agreed that Congress should work to reduce or eliminate the deficit but believed the pain should not be concentrated completely on taxpayers while the beneficiaries of governmental services were shielded from any reductions. They refused to support a tax increase unaccompanied by significant expenditure cuts. Their refusal compounded the political problem because legislators as a class were equally loath to have either tax increases or expenditure cuts traced to their own individual actions. Wilbur Mills (D., Ark.), the chairman of the House Ways and Means Committee, set about crafting a "share-the-pain" strategy to combine expenditure cuts with the tax surcharge. The aim was to insulate legislators from too direct a connection with either type of pain. The only problem with this procedural strategy was that appropriations and taxes were under the jurisdiction of separate committees, each jealously guarding its prerogatives. Congress had yet to develop budget committees that could report a single bill to accomplish both ends.

Congressional leaders danced gingerly around the problem for nearly a year until they found a solution that exploited the Senate's more open procedures. Senator John Williams (R., Del.) offered a single amendment, which would cut expenditures by $6 billion and increase income taxes by 10 percent, to an unrelated and innocuous House-passed bill that was already on the Senate floor. Unlike the House, the Senate had no rules about the germaneness of floor amendments, so it was possible to craft a single amendment to accomplish both purposes.[22] The Senate

20. The annual rates of growth for defense outlays were 9.1 percent in 1966, 18.8 percent in 1967, and 8.2 percent in 1968. Office of Management and Budget, *Historical Tables, FY 1988*, table 6.1.

21. For the best account of the enactment of the tax surcharge, see Lawrence C. Pierce, *The Politics of Fiscal Policy Formation* (Pacific Palisades, Calif.: Goodyear Publishing, 1971), pp. 135–172. See also *Congress and the Nation, 1965–1968* (Washington, D.C.: Congressional Quarterly, 1969), pp. 141–174.

22. The tactic demanded the forbearance of the House, since the Constitution requires that all revenue measures originate in the House. The bill on the floor, a routine measure,

passed the amendment 53 to 35 in April 1968 and sent the bill directly to a conference committee, bypassing the House. The conference committee accepted the bill as amended. The House then approved the conference report 268 to 150, in its only roll-call vote on the issue, and the president signed it in late June. House members had to vote only once on the entire matter—to approve the conference report for an omnibus bill that included both a temporary tax increase and unspecified expenditure cuts.

The overwhelming approval of the Revenue and Expenditure Control Act of 1968 demonstrates that Congress is quite capable of passing contractionary as well as expansionary fiscal policy. In fact, Congress approved a far more stringent bill than the president wanted. This example also highlights the need for a careful procedural strategy if Congress is to impose direct and traceable costs on citizens. Creating a single vote in the House and the Senate was essential to the plan, so that legislators would be forced to vote on explicit economic policy rather than on a whole series of tax and expenditure questions. Explicit economic policy allows citizens to connect economic fluctuations with legislators' recent actions and thus allows them to hold legislators accountable for deteriorating conditions. This was *the* vote on controlling inflation during the 90th Congress, and legislators knew that future challengers could use it against them if inflation continued.

The amendment also mandated $6 billion in expenditure cuts, and in ordinary circumstances this provision would have allowed beneficiaries to trace their loss of group or geographic benefits to legislators' votes. To thwart the prospect of retrospective voting, coalition leaders carefully crafted the amendment to require that the Appropriations Committee make these reductions in their upcoming review of the budget, rather than specifying the cuts in the amendment itself. Legislators were thus spared direct connection to specific expenditure cuts. Of course, taxpayers could trace the 10 percent surcharges on their income taxes to legislators' votes, since the tax surcharge was the very centerpiece of the whole bill. Anticipating this possibility, congressional leaders offered several explanations that legislators could give their constituents: (1)

---

had originated in the House, so the strict constitutional requirement had been met. Its spirit had been violated, however, and the House usually enforced the spirit of the provision too. Many people surmised that the House never objected because Wilbur Mills himself had invented the Senate tactic in order to bypass House rules that hindered what he was trying to accomplish.

the tax surcharge was temporary and would expire in fifteen months; (2) it was essential for supporting our boys in Vietnam; (3) it was essential for balancing the budget and restraining inflation; and (4) it was coupled with expenditure cuts so that everyone shared in the pain. These were good explanations, especially with both Vietnam and inflation dominating the daily headlines. Legislators could choose whatever combination of explanations best suited their own constituencies.

The 1964 tax cut and the 1968 tax surcharge show that Congress is quite capable of passing explicit economic policy, even when some of the components are intrinsically unpopular. Persuading legislators to support economic policies often requires some fancy footwork. In the case of the tax cut it required the creation of a carefully balanced package of group benefits, as well as an effort to tie future general costs to the administration's actions rather than to legislators' individual actions. In the case of the tax surcharge it required extraordinary procedures so that House members would never have to vote for the tax increase by itself and so that specific group and geographic costs could never be traced to legislators' individual votes.

INFLATION AND STAGNATION

The tax surcharge of 1968 created an immediate governmental surplus. The federal deficit, which amounted to 14.1 percent of outlays in fiscal year 1968, was transformed into a 1.8 percent surplus in fiscal year 1969—the largest one-year fiscal swing since 1951. As expected, the economy slowed considerably. Real GNP grew by only 2.4 percent in 1969—the slowest growth rate in nearly a decade. Inflation, however, failed to respond as Keynesian theory would predict. The rise in consumer prices, which had been 2.9 percent in 1967, accelerated to 4.2 percent in 1968, 5.4 percent in 1969, and 5.9 percent in 1970. Economists were quick to explain that the fiscal medicine had been applied too late and that the economy had become overheated while politicians dallied. Even so, nothing in Keynesian theory could explain how unemployment and inflation could increase in tandem, as they did for most of the next decade.

The decade of the 1970s was a difficult time for both macroeconomists and politicians. The United States suffered three major recessions (1970, 1974, and 1980), one each for the Nixon, Ford, and Carter administrations. As Table 7.1 shows, all economic indicators deteriorated during this period: unemployment increased almost 50 percent, the inflation rate tripled, and real economic growth was cut nearly in half. The simultaneous persistence of high inflation and high unemployment plagued not only the U.S. economy but that of most major industrial nations.[23] Economists struggled to explain what was happening in the economy and to develop new policy remedies. Initially, they scolded politicians for waiting more than two years before imposing a tax surcharge (as if politicians were completely free to raise or lower taxes whenever economists thought it might be a good idea).[24] Then there were the supply shocks: worldwide agricultural shortages in 1972, OPEC's 1973 decision to quadruple oil prices, and OPEC's decisions in 1979 and 1980 to triple oil prices once again. These actions (all exogenous to economists' models) could explain only the initial sources of economic distress, but not why inflation and unemployment persisted and worsened over time. Eventually economists were forced to reexamine much of macroeconomic theory in a delightful debate: there were those who were attempting to repair Keynesian theory,[25] those who sought to bury it with monetarism,[26] and those who sought to replace both Keynesianism and monetarism with something new, ranging from rational expectations to supply-side economics.[27]

Meanwhile, the president had to propose a budget every year, and the Congress had to pass one. Somehow they had to decide how much to spend, how much to raise through taxation, and how large a deficit or surplus they should produce. The only difference in the 1970s was that economists offered little consistent advice about what fiscal policies politicians should pursue. Politicians were left to their own devices, each free to choose which economic ideas to follow from year to year. Whether by design or accident (and it was a little of each), presidents and legisla-

23. Lawrence B. Krause and Walter S. Salant (eds.), *Worldwide Inflation* (Washington, D.C.: Brookings Institution, 1977).

24. See, for example, Arthur M. Okun, *The Political Economy of Prosperity* (Washington, D.C.: Brookings Institution, 1970), pp. 118–120.

25. For one of the most creative attempts, see Arthur M. Okun, *Prices and Quantities: A Macroeconomic Analysis* (Washington, D.C.: Brookings Institution, 1981).

26. See Philip Cagan, *Persistent Inflation* (New York: Columbia University Press, 1979).

27. Political scientists, sociologists, and historians also joined the debate by analyzing what economists preferred to keep exogenous. See Fred Hirsch and John Goldthorpe (eds.), *The Political Economy of Inflation* (Cambridge: Harvard University Press, 1978); and Leon S. Lindberg and Charles S. Maier (eds.), *The Politics of Inflation and Economic Stagnation* (Washington, D.C.: Brookings Institution, 1985).

tors chose the route of deficits. Between 1970 and 1981 they accrued twelve consecutive deficits, ranging from 1.5 percent of federal outlays in fiscal year 1970 to 19.8 percent in 1976 and averaging 10.4 percent per year.

How did the federal government manage to accrue such large and regular deficits? Three explanations for deficits merit investigation. Deficits could have arisen because (1) presidents proposed unbalanced budgets, (2) Congress increased presidents' proposed expenditures or decreased recommended revenues, or (3) budgetary experts predicted poorly the future course of the economy, estimated incorrectly its impact on revenues and expenditures, or both. Table 7.2 attempts to sort out the relative contributions of each factor for the Nixon, Ford, and Carter administrations.[28]

Presidents deserve the largest share of credit for deficits during this period. As Table 7.2 shows, presidents proposed average annual deficits of $39 billion (in 1982 dollars), which was more than 70 percent of the actual deficits achieved. President Nixon twice proposed small surpluses (1970 and 1971), but both disappeared under the weight of the 1970 recession. The other ten presidential budgets contained deficits

28. The estimates in Table 7.2 are very crude approximations. Columns A and D are unproblematic. Column A is derived from the president's annual budget, and column D from his budget message two years later. Both have been adjusted to 1982 dollars with the OMB's composite deflator for federal outlays. Column B is based on an exhaustive comparison of budgetary documents by Paul Peterson. Unfortunately, his study includes only annually appropriated accounts, not entitlements. My assumption is that most changes in entitlements have only small consequences for the current budget, even though their consequences may be very large for subsequent budgets. Column C is the residual of the other three. As such, it includes at least five sources of change in the size of the deficit: (1) ordinary errors in estimating complicated revenue and expenditure streams, (2) errors in estimating macroeconomic conditions that in turn affect revenue and expenditure estimates, (3) changes in macroeconomic conditions that induce presidents to alter their fiscal recommendations during the course of the year, (4) programmatic changes that presidents submit during the course of the year, and (5) programmatic changes that Congress makes in nonappropriated accounts that affect the current year's budget. My sense is that *most* of the changes are a consequence of errors in estimating macroeconomic conditions, the evidence being that the largest effects invariably occur in the midst of unforeseen recessions. I present these crude approximations with the full realization that the estimates may reveal more about the above assumptions than they do about the true effects of the president and Congress on federal spending. Unfortunately, better data are currently unavailable. John Ellwood suggests it could take "several years, if not a lifetime" to assemble the proper data series to separate all these effects (see Ellwood, "Budget Authority vs. Outlays," p. 19).

Table 7.2. Sources of federal deficits by presidential administration, 1970–1981

Fiscal years[a]	President submitting budget	A President's proposed deficit[b]	+ B Net effect of changes made by Congress	+ C Net effects from economic fluctuations and estimation errors	= D Actual deficit
1970–73	Nixon	−15.7	+12.8	−34.2	−37.1
1974–77	Nixon/ Ford	−48.0	−15.8	−2.7	−66.5
1978–81	Carter	−53.2	+21.6	−27.9	−59.5
Mean		−39.0	+6.2	−21.6	−54.4

a. Budgetary data are averages of annual data in billions of 1982 dollars. Negative numbers indicate increases in the deficit; positive numbers, decreases in the deficit.

b. Proposed deficits for 1970 and 1978 refer to revised budgets submitted by Presidents Nixon and Carter, not the original budgets submitted by Presidents Johnson and Ford just prior to leaving office.

Sources: Data compiled by the author from original data reported in U.S., Office of Management and Budget, *Budget of the United States Government* (fiscal years 1970 to 1983); U.S., Office of Management and Budget, *Historical Tables: Budget of the United States Government, FY 1988* (Washington, D.C.: Government Printing Office, 1987); and Paul Peterson, "The New Politics of Deficits," in John Chubb and Paul Peterson (eds.), *The New Direction in American Politics* (Washington, D.C.: Brookings Institution, 1985), pp. 365–397. See note 28, this chapter, for further details.

from the very start. All three presidents delivered and justified their budgets in Keynesian terms. When the economy was in recession they proposed cutting taxes and increasing expenditures. President Nixon became the first Republican president to use Keynesian language to justify fiscal policies when he reminded Congress that his proposed $11.6 billion deficit for fiscal year 1972 really contained a "full-employment surplus" of $0.1 billion. Similarly, when inflation seemed to be the greater threat, presidents recommended tax surcharges and spoke of creating genuine surpluses.

The economy was so volatile throughout the decade that presidents frequently sent supplementary budget messages to Congress, sometimes only a few months after delivering the original budget messages.

President Ford, for example, came to office ready to "Whip Inflation Now." In October 1974 he proposed cutting expenditures and imposing a 5 percent tax surcharge. Four months later he reversed course completely and proposed to stimulate the economy with a tax rebate and a budget that contained the largest deficit since World War II (even after adjusting for inflation). President Carter reversed course twice during even shorter periods. In January 1977 he proposed fiscal stimulus in the form of a $14 billion tax rebate for the current fiscal year. Ten weeks later he withdrew the whole plan, arguing that the stimulus was no longer necessary. Then, in January 1980, Carter proposed a $15.8 billion deficit for fiscal year 1981. Two months later, after the January inflation rate soared to an annual rate of 18.2 percent, he reversed direction again and recommended a $16.5 billion surplus.

Congress approved all presidential requests to incur deficits during this period. The production of deficits was, in every way, a joint endeavor for the legislative and executive branches. Contrary to public belief, however, Congress was the more fiscally conservative of the two branches. It reduced presidential deficits by more than $6 billion per year during this period, or by nearly one sixth of what presidents requested (see Table 7.2). Only during the second Nixon administration, when president and Congress disagreed fundamentally over domestic spending, did Congress make changes that increased the size of the deficit.

Why did Congress make the more fiscally conservative decisions? Why did it not merely accept the happy task of spending money up to the ceiling of the president's proposed deficit? The first line of defense was the House Appropriations Committee. To be sure, this Committee in the 1970s was not the same fiscal watchdog that Richard Fenno had observed in the 1950s and 1960s. Subcommittees were no longer filled with disinterested members, subcommittee chairmen were now elected by and accountable to the Democratic caucus, and committee doors were unlocked so that journalists, interest groups, and other legislators could watch the deliberations.[29] Although the committee was weaker than before, Allen Schick still describes it as a "subdued guardian."[30] It

29. Allen Schick, "The Three-Ring Budget Process: The Appropriations, Tax, and Budget Committees in Congress," in Thomas E. Mann and Norman J. Ornstein (eds.), *The New Congress* (Washington, D.C.: American Enterprise Institute, 1981), pp. 288–328.

30. Allen Schick, *Congress and Money* (Washington, D.C.: The Urban Institute, 1980), pp. 415–440.

still published proudly its annual record in cutting presidential requests. The second line of defense was the floor of the House, where legislators could either accept or revise the Committee's decisions. Here too there were fundamental changes. The Legislative Reorganization Act of 1970 allowed twenty or more members to demand a roll-call vote on any matter before the Committee of the Whole, whereas prior to this reform the rules permitted a roll-call vote only for an amendment that had first been approved by an unrecorded teller vote in the Committee of the Whole, and then only upon the request of forty-four or more members. The effects were dramatic. In 1970—the last year before the new procedure was in place—there were *no* roll-call votes on amendments to appropriations bills. By 1974 there were forty-nine and in 1978 there were seventy-nine (plus nineteen more on amendments to budget resolutions). Procedurally, it became relatively easy to rewrite appropriations bills on the floor of the House.

Most observers suggest that when the roll is called legislators are more inclined to increase spending over committee recommendations than to reduce it.[31] My own theory suggests a more complicated response. When legislators vote on *individual* expenditure programs, they tend to be biased in favor of increased spending. These are votes on derivative economic policy, and thus the group and geographic effects are far more traceable than the macroeconomic effects. Alternatively, when legislators face votes on explicit economic policy—for example, a one percent across-the-board reduction in federal spending—legislators are more likely to fear connection with the macroeconomic effects than with the more vague and distant programmatic effects.

To test these theoretical predictions, I examined each proposed amendment either to an appropriations bill or a budget resolution for which there was a roll-call vote in the House between 1969 and 1980.[32]

31. Ibid., p. 438.

32. I constructed the data series from the one-paragraph summaries of all 6,259 roll-call votes in the House during this period, as recorded in the *Congressional Quarterly Almanacs*, 1969 to 1980. Those relating to appropriations bills and budget resolutions numbered 1,217, of which (a) 178 were essentially procedural votes, relating to the adoption of rules, the ending of debate, and the like, (b) 384 were related to the final passage of bills, the adoption of conference reports, or attempts to override presidential vetoes, (c) 288 were on limitation amendments, which were largely restrictions on the purposes for which federal funds could be spent but which had only minimal fiscal effects, and (d) 367 were on amendments that changed the level of spending and that would have increased or decreased the deficit by at least $1 million. I regarded a recommittal motion with instruc-

As expected, legislators treated generously most proposals to increase programmatic spending (Table 7.3A). They adopted exactly half of these amendments, with average increases of $474 million per amendment. Most were for popular programs with attentive beneficiaries—for example, educational grants, veterans' benefits, or Amtrak. Legislators' decisions on all these amendments added approximately $30 billion to the deficit over the entire twelve-year period. Legislators were far less eager to approve amendments that would decrease expenditures for specific programs (Table 7.3B). They adopted only one-fifth of such proposals, with average decreases of $248 million per amendment. Typically they approved amendments to curtail activities that were relatively controversial, such as the B-1 bomber, the supersonic transport, the World Bank, or the administration of OSHA regulations. In all, these programmatic decreases saved about $7.9 billion. With programmatic increases both outnumbering and outweighing programmatic decreases, Congress managed to add about $22 billion to the deficit over the twelve-year period.[33]

Legislators were more diligent about cutting spending when they voted on explicit economic policy. Legislators faced eighty-one roll-call votes on amendments that would impose across-the-board spending cuts and approved nearly a quarter of them (Table 7.3C). Most of these amendments cut a fixed percentage from an entire bill or department—for example, the foreign aid appropriations bill or the one for the Department of Defense. At times the sponsors exempted one portion of a bill from the otherwise uniform cuts. Israel and Egypt were usually spared

tions as either a limitation amendment or a fiscal amendment (depending on the nature of the instructions), whereas I treated a recommittal motion without instructions as a procedural motion. I also coded the many votes about abortion, busing, and congressional pay as limitation amendments rather than as fiscal amendments, even though some of them might have produced more than $1 million in fiscal effects. Before constructing Table 7.3, I further subdivided the 367 fiscal amendments into those that would increase programmatic spending (129), those that would decrease programmatic spending (157), and those that would decrease spending across the board (81). I coded as "programmatic" all amendments that referred to specific programs or collections of programs that did not embrace an entire department. I coded as "across the board" all amendments that referred to expenditures at the departmental level or higher, or that referred to specific types of expenditures in all departments.

33. These calculations include only the effects of each amendment on a single year's budget. To the extent that the changes affected programs' budgetary bases, upon which future budgets are calculated, the long-term effects would be considerably larger.

Table 7.3. Net fiscal effects of floor amendments to appropriations bills and budget resolutions in the House, 1970–1981

Fiscal years	Proposed floor amendments for which there was a roll-call vote	Floor amendments adopted	Net effect on current deficit in millions of 1982 dollars[a]
A. Amendments to increase programmatic spending			
1970–1973	16	6	−3,599
1974–1977	46	32	−15,890
1978–1981	67	26	−10,856
Total	129	64	−30,345
Proportion of amendments adopted: .50			
Average size of amendments adopted: $474 million			
B. Amendments to decrease programmatic spending			
1970–1973	15	3	+478
1974–1977	54	10	+1,302
1978–1981	88	19	+6,141
Total	157	32	+7,921
Proportion of amendments adopted: .20			
Average size of amendments adopted: $248 million			
C. Amendments to decrease spending across the board			
1970–1973	5	0	0
1974–1977	26	3	+18,007
1978–1981	50	16	+13,596
Total	81	19	+31,603
Proportion of amendments adopted: .23			
Average size of amendments adopted: $1,663 million			
D. All amendments to change the level of spending			
1970–1973	36	9	−3,121
1974–1977	126	45	+3,419
1978–1981	205	61	+8,881
Total	367	115	+9,179

a. Negative numbers indicate increases in the deficit; positive numbers, decreases in the deficit.

Source: Data compiled by the author from annual volumes of the *Congressional Quarterly Almanac*, 1969 to 1980. See note 32, this chapter, for further details.

across-the-board reductions in the foreign aid bill, and veterans' pro-grams were immune from cuts in the HUD/Independent Agencies ap-propriations bill. Occasionally Congress instructed the departments to identify ways to achieve a specific level of savings. The House once reduced appropriations for the Department of Health, Education, and Welfare by $500 million, with the reduction to be taken from programs identified by the HEW Inspector General as containing "waste, fraud, and abuse." Not many legislators were willing to vote in favor of sin, and the amendment passed easily.[34] A similar amendment to a budget resolution applied to the entire government. It directed the appropria-tions committees to reduce budget authority and outlays $1.1 billion by reducing "excessive government travel, film-making, paperwork, and overtime." This amendment was a real crowd pleaser, passing 403 to 3.[35]

Across-the-board cuts go in and out of fashion. Fashion is partly dic-tated by the state of the economy and partly by legislators' sense of the mood of the people. Representative Clarence Miller (R., Ohio) made a career out of introducing such amendments, becoming known to his colleagues as "Five Percent Clarence."[36] In 1976 he proposed 5 percent cuts for each of the regular appropriations bills. He lost all ten roll-call votes by a wide margin (except for foreign aid, which was relatively close). Inflation was down, and most legislators were more concerned about the stubbornly high unemployment rate than about the deficit. In 1977 Miller was more successful, as the House passed a 5 percent reduction in the foreign aid bill. Then in 1978 lightning struck. On June 6, California's voters overwhelmingly approved Proposition 13, a con-stitutional amendment designed to limit property taxes in that state. Representatives in Congress interpreted the referendum more broadly as a popular revolt against inflation, taxes, and governmental expendi-tures, and they scrambled to make their voting records correspond with the new mood. Within days Congress was cutting everything in sight. On June 8 the House cut $1 billion from HEW to cover the infamous waste, fraud, and abuse (which was actually not a line item in HEW's budget). On June 13 it shaved an additional 2 percent from the La-bor/HEW appropriations bill, the next day 2 percent from the State/

34. *Congressional Quarterly Almanac, 1979* 35 (1980): 82H.
35. Ibid., p. 36H.
36. Alan Ehrenhalt (ed.), *Politics in America* (Washington, D.C.: Congressional Quar-terly, 1987), pp. 1186–1187.

Justice/Commerce bill and 5 percent from the legislative branch appropriations bill. Two days later it sliced 2 percent off the energy and public works bill. Within the next few weeks two foreign aid bills and the supplemental appropriations bill suffered the same fate. In two short months the House used across-the-board tactics to eliminate several billion dollars in federal spending.

Across-the-board amendments resulted in a net reduction of $31.6 billion in spending over the entire decade (and considerably more if one assumes that each change affected subsequent budgets as well). These amendments, coupled with the $7.9 billion worth of programmatic decreases, more than compensated for the effects of the $30 billion in programmatic increases. Counting all three types of amendments, the House had reduced the net deficit by about $9.2 billion (Table 7.3D). To be sure, such reductions are relatively trivial in a budget of this magnitude. Their importance is in showing that roll-call voting is not inherently biased toward increased spending, as some have argued. Legislators approve increased spending quite readily when they vote on programmatic amendments filled with group and geographic benefits, but they appear far more fiscally conservative when they are forced to take public positions on explicit economic policy.

Floor amendments in the House are not the only way Congress has to affect fiscal policy. They simply offer a nice controlled setting where one can observe legislators accepting, revising, or rejecting a fixed agenda coming to them from the House Appropriations and Budget Committees. If one wanted to observe larger fiscal effects, one would examine the complex annual process for drafting the congressional budget resolutions, which set overall targets for revenues, outlays, budget authority, and the deficit. The entire budget process is designed to focus legislative attention away from the programmatic concerns of the appropriations process and toward a more conscious concern with explicit economic policy.

Since I have already noted how Proposition 13 affected representatives' decisions when they were considering amendments to appropriations bills, it should be useful to broaden the analysis to see how the House and Senate budget committees were interpreting and reacting to these same events. Of course, Proposition 13 was not all that was happening at that time. In January 1978, when President Carter submitted his budget for fiscal year 1979, high unemployment and a possible recession were the dominant economic issues. By May, when Congress adopted its first budget resolution, no recession was in sight, unemployment was falling, and inflation was beginning to accelerate. Four months later, when Congress approved its final budget resolution, inflation was surging, Proposition 13 had been approved overwhelmingly, and everyone was talking about fiscal prudence. The budget resolutions reflected these changing conditions. President Carter proposed a $60.6 billion deficit in January, the first congressional budget resolution projected a $50.9 billion deficit, and the final resolution promised a $38.8 billion deficit. Although part of this $22 billion reduction reflected new revenue estimates and revised estimates of expenditures for entitlement programs, a considerable portion followed from legislators making hard decisions in reaction to Proposition 13. The Senate Budget Committee, for example, transformed a September vote on public works (ordinarily a very popular issue) into one on macroeconomic policy. By a vote of 63 to 21 the Senate instructed its conferees to reject completely a House plan to increase expenditures for public works by $2 billion. The Senate Budget Committee also secured approval for cutting $5 billion from a housing authorization bill, $1 billion from mass transit, and lesser amounts from public service employment, impact aid, and educational grants for handicapped and gifted students.[37] It did so by transforming programmatic issues into explicit economic policy and thus altering legislators' political calculations.

This brief examination of the congressional budget process shows that the budget committees respond to the same forces that affect legislators' decisions about appropriations amendments on the floor. The principal difference is that the budget committees can produce large effects quickly. The $22 billion reduction in the deficit during eight months in 1978 easily dwarfs the $9 billion reduction produced by all the floor amendments to both appropriations bills and budget resolutions throughout the entire decade.

Clearly, legislators behave differently depending on whether they are voting on derivative or explicit economic policy. When legislators vote on individual expenditure programs, they tend to cater to the demands of the beneficiaries and to ignore the economic effects. Observers who focus on programmatic votes quite naturally conclude that legislators are biased in favor of increased spending. The only trouble with this view is that it cannot account for the observed fact that throughout the 1970s Congress managed to reduce spending below the levels requested by presidents. The explanation for this apparent anomaly is that

37. *Congress and the Nation, 1977–1980,* pp. 218–220; Schick, *Congress and Money,* pp. 386–389.

when legislators vote on explicit economic policy they consider the economic components, and all their votes on these economic issues more than compensate for all their votes on programmatic issues.

The differences in how legislators act on derivative and explicit economic policies are consistent with the electoral explanations developed in previous chapters. Legislators focus on the programmatic effects of derivative economic policies because they fear that beneficiaries will trace any reductions in group or geographic benefits to legislators' votes and because they wish to create pleasing voting records in the hope that future beneficiaries will notice. Similarly, legislators focus on the economic components of explicit economic policies because they wish to create voting records that show serious concern with fiscal effects and because they seek to reduce their vulnerability to charges that they are responsible for economic problems.

These electoral explanations gain even greater credibility when one considers how quickly legislators modified their behavior in the light of changed political circumstances. Proposition 13 had nothing at all to do with the federal budget; it revealed simply that California's voters were upset about their property taxes. Representatives in Congress, however, reacted as if it were a warning shot meant for their ears. Congress immediately amended every appropriations bill in sight, shaving several billion dollars off the federal deficit in but a few weeks.

THE REAGAN YEARS

President Reagan came to office determined to cut taxes, reduce domestic spending, increase defense spending, and balance the budget. He accomplished the first three within eight months, but at the cost of massive deficits that continue to plague budget makers today. Increasing defense expenditures was relatively easy to achieve and requires no special explanation. A consensus had emerged during the late 1970s that the Pentagon needed more funds. Congress had already increased real defense outlays by 2.5 percent in fiscal year 1979, 3.1 percent in 1980, and 4.5 percent in 1981. President Carter recommended a 5 percent increase in his final budget (fiscal year 1982), and President Reagan simply asked an already receptive Congress to do more.[38]

38. Richard A. Stubbing, "The Defense Budget," in Gregory B. Mills and John L. Palmer (eds.), *Federal Budget Policy in the 1980s* (Washington, D.C.: The Urban Institute Press, 1984), pp. 81–110.

The toughest element in the package was the reduction in domestic spending. Presidents had regularly tried to persuade Congress to cut domestic spending, but with little success. Presidents Nixon and Ford had mounted major assaults on a wide range of governmental programs and attempted to terminate or consolidate many programs. Other presidents had been more selective, singling out specific programs for major reductions, such as impact aid, rivers and harbors projects, or hospital construction. Neither approach had succeeded. Legislators were always reluctant to cut specific programs because beneficiaries could easily trace their loss of benefits to legislators' roll-call votes (and their champions in Congress made certain to demand roll-call votes to stimulate these electoral calculations).

President Reagan ignored past failures and asked for a $48 billion reduction in domestic outlays for fiscal year 1982. Congress approved approximately $35 billion of those cuts.[39] How did President Reagan achieve such massive cuts when other presidents had been uniformly unsuccessful in obtaining smaller reductions? A full explanation would vastly exceed my limited space.[40] Here, I seek merely to show how coalition leaders structured the entire legislative situation so that a majority of legislators would see not risk but electoral profit in supporting the president's recommendation.

The principal innovation was to combine all spending cuts into a single package, to label the package as the president's economic recovery program, and then to force legislators to vote on the entire package without permitting amendments. This strategy transformed the usual programmatic votes into votes on explicit economic policy. It increased the likelihood that citizens would, at the time of the next election, connect the state of the economy with legislators' positions on the president's program. It decreased the chances that citizens might blame legislators for the loss of specific benefits.

Not all legislators would make identical electoral calculations. Most of the cuts were to be concentrated on the less fortunate in society,[41] and thus a legislator representing a poor district might expect that his con-

39. The exact total approved was probably somewhat less, given all the games both sides were playing with the numbers. See Allen Schick, "How the Budget Was Won and Lost," in Norman J. Ornstein (ed.), *President and Congress: Assessing Reagan's First Year* (Washington, D.C.: American Enterprise Institute, 1982), pp. 32–33.

40. For an excellent account, see ibid., pp. 14–43.

41. Among other things, the bill terminated various public service employment programs and reduced funds for food stamps, public assistance, subsidized housing, Medicaid, and various health and education programs.

stituents would interpret a vote in favor of the president's program as one
that deprived them of substantial benefits.[42] Many other legislators,
however, had to worry about the following scenario: What would happen
in the next election if I vote against the president's program, the program fails to pass, and the economy continues to deteriorate? Without
much doubt, a legislator in this predicament would be delivering a
powerful campaign issue to a future challenger, one that would allow
citizens to trace deteriorating economic conditions directly to the legislator's recorded vote. The risk was especially great for those who represented areas filled with President Reagan's supporters, for they were
more likely to believe that the president's program would improve the
economy and to blame those legislators who refused to give the program
a chance. Voting in favor of the program helped to protect legislators
from these retrospective evaluations. As one senior Democrat put it after
voting for the Reagan budget in 1981, "I don't see how this can hurt me.
If it doesn't work, I'll run against it. And if it does work, nobody's going to
be mad at me."[43]

The administration launched its strategy in the Senate, where the
Republicans had just gained control for the first time in twenty-six
years. Republican leaders moved quickly and in March brought a budget resolution before the Senate that incorporated most of the president's recommendations. Democrats and a few moderate Republicans
proposed thirty separate amendments that attempted to break the bill
into more identifiable parts. Most Republicans and conservative Democrats stood firm, arguing that any amendment that was not revenue
neutral would permit the entire fabric to unravel. They maintained that
anyone who supported such an amendment was actually voting against
the president's economic recovery program. In fact, the Senate approved
exactly one amendment, a revenue-neutral proposal that transferred
$200 million from foreign aid to the school lunch program.[44]

42. This was exactly the predicament in which Margaret Heckler (R., Mass.) found
herself in 1982 when she was thrown into the same district as Barney Frank (D., Mass.),
after Massachusetts lost one House seat in the 1980 reapportionment. Frank made a big
issue of Heckler's vote in favor of Reagan's economic program (which he had opposed) and
detailed how it had affected the depressed portions of her new district. Frank won with 60
percent of the vote. See Ehrenhalt, *Politics in America*, pp. 689–690.

43. As quoted in *Congressional Quarterly Weekly Report* 42 (October 13, 1984): 2501.

44. See Gail Gregg, "GOP Senators Successful in Heading Off Attempts to Restore
Veterans' Funds," *Congressional Quarterly Weekly Report* 39 (March 28, 1981): 547–
550; and Gail Gregg, "Senate Orders $36.9 Billion in Budget Cuts," *Congressional Quar-
terly Weekly Report* 39 (April 4, 1981): 602–603, 610–613.

The House, which was still controlled by the Democrats, was less receptive to the president's plan. House procedures, however, were far more accommodating to a strategy that required an up-or-down vote on the entire proposal. The House, unlike the Senate, allows complicated legislation to come to the floor under a closed rule that prohibits any amendments, the only stipulation being that the House must first approve the rule. Democrats on the House Budget Committee first adopted a budget resolution in May that required authorizing committees to reduce annual outlays by only $15.8 billion—far less than the president had requested. The Rules Committee then offered a rule that would prohibit floor amendments to this budget resolution but that would allow for three substitute resolutions, one of which, the Gramm-Latta substitute, was essentially the president's economic program requiring a $36.6 billion reduction in outlays. Legislators were given the choice between voting for the president's economic program or for the Democrats' more symbolic and token cuts. Sixty-three conservative Democrats joined all 190 Republicans in approving the president's program.[45]

Floor procedures were even more important in June when the House approved the Omnibus Reconciliation Act of 1981, specifying exactly which programs would be cut to achieve a $35 billion reduction in outlays. Once again the House Budget Committee offered its own reconciliation bill, while conservatives prepared a substitute known as Gramm-Latta II. This time the Rules Committee designed a rule, very favorable to the Democrats, that would have split the substitute resolution into six amendments, thus forcing legislators to vote explicitly to cut (1) Social Security and public assistance, (2) school lunches and student loans, (3) energy and commerce programs, (4) food stamps, (5) subsidized housing, and (6) cost-of-living adjustments for federal employees' salaries and pensions. The intention was to transform a single vote on explicit economic policy into six programmatic votes with readily identifiable group and geographic costs. Leaders on both sides agreed that under such a rule the House would never approve the president's economic program. The administration and Republican leaders in the House worked feverishly to convince legislators to vote against an other-

45. See Dale Tate and Gail Gregg, "Congress Set for Showdown on First Budget Resolution," *Congressional Quarterly Weekly Report* 39 (May 2, 1981): 743–745; and Dale Tate, "House Provides President a Victory in the 1982 Budget," *Congressional Quarterly Weekly Report* 39 (May 9, 1981): 783–785.

wise routine procedural motion "to order the previous question on the rule" (thus ending debate). This became the key vote in 1981 on the president's entire economic program. Twenty-nine conservative Democrats joined the united Republicans in defeating the motion, 210 to 217. The House then adopted, 216 to 212, a Republican-sponsored rule that allowed for a single vote on the entire economic package and then approved, 217 to 211, the Gramm-Latta II substitute.[46]

It is easy to explain why legislators, once the House adopted the Republican-sponsored rule, approved the entire package of spending cuts. They were voting on the president's economic recovery program, and many of them were afraid that citizens would hold them accountable if they voted to block the president's program. It is not so obvious why legislators would agree to the rule in the first place, rather than accepting the original rule that would have required six separate votes. Ordinarily one expects that legislators are not heavily constrained by electoral considerations when they act on procedural matters (see Chapter 6). In this case, however, the administration worked to activate electoral considerations by making this procedural vote the key test of whether a legislator supported the president's program. The administration transformed what was usually an obscure procedural matter into a very visible vote on the president's economic program, thus guaranteeing that future challengers could use this vote as if it were really a substantive vote on explicit economic policy. In addition, some legislators wanted to approve the president's program but could not do so without the protection of a closed rule.

Forcing legislators to vote on explicit economic policy was the key to the administration's entire political strategy. The administration also offered extra group and geographic benefits to crucial legislators who were severely cross-pressured. Moderate Republicans acquired $350 million for Medicaid, $400 million for home-heating subsidies, $260 million for mass transit, and $100 million for Amtrak. Conservative Democrats obtained an extra $400 million for veterans' hospitals, additional funds for the Clinch River breeder reactor, and an administration

46. Barbara Sinclair, *Majority Leadership in the U.S. House* (Baltimore: Johns Hopkins University Press, 1983), pp. 190–213; Dale Tate, "Republicans Press Reconciliation Drive," *Congressional Quarterly Weekly Report* 39 (June 20, 1981): 1079–1087; Dale Tate, "House Ratifies Savings Plan in Stunning Reagan Victory," *Congressional Quarterly Weekly Report* 39 (June 27, 1981): 1127–1129, 1160–1161; and Dale Tate, "Reconciliation Conferees Face Slim Choices," *Congressional Quarterly Weekly Report* 39 (July 4, 1981): 1167–1178, 1198–1199.

promise to support higher sugar price supports.[47] Several legislators were absolutely crucial for final victory, and the administration was willing to pay handsomely for their support. James Jones (D., Okla.), chairman of the Budget Committee, said after the key procedural vote, "The Democratic cloakroom had all the earmarks of a tobacco auction."[48]

The incumbent performance rule helps explain why legislators' political calculations changed when coalition leaders transformed a series of programmatic votes into a single vote on explicit economic policy. Other electoral forces also contributed to the president's success in 1981. The party performance rule helps explain why Republican legislators remained unified throughout the entire year. A half-century ago economic policy had made the Republicans the minority party, and many Republicans considered that economic policy was the key to their restoration in the 1980s. President Reagan based his 1980 campaign on economic policy and then declared his landslide victory to be a mandate for action. Republicans in the Senate were eager to show that 1980 was not a fluke and that they deserved to retain control of the Senate. Republicans in the House prepared for their own restoration in 1982. Rather than distancing themselves from their party, Republicans in 1981 worked hard to look economically responsible in hopes that voters would reward them as a team with a generation in power, much as the Democrats had profited from concerted action in the 1930s.[49]

Congress gave the president just about everything he requested in the first eight months: increased defense spending, decreased domestic spending, and a massive tax cut (see Chapter 8). Unfortunately, the three did not add up to a balanced budget. Instead, they created the largest peacetime deficits in American history—doubling the national debt in five years and setting the stage for a tripling within the decade. Annual deficits averaged 19.9 percent of federal outlays during the first seven years of the Reagan administration, compared with 4.7 percent during the Kennedy and Johnson administrations and 10.4 during the Nixon, Ford, and Carter administrations (see Table 7.1).

Most economists argued from the very beginning that the president's proposals would not produce balanced budgets. Why, then, would the

47. William Greider, *The Education of David Stockman and Other Americans* (New York: Dutton, 1982), pp. 34, 43, 53, 54; Sinclair, *Majority Leadership*, pp. 210–211.
48. Sinclair, *Majority Leadership*, p. 210.
49. Schick, "How the Budget Was Won and Lost," pp. 16–19.

president propose and the Congress approve such fundamentally incompatible policies? Explaining presidential behavior is beyond my competence. One explanation is that the president actually believed that supply-side tax cuts would so stimulate the economy that deficits would quickly disappear. He certainly used supply-side rhetoric to justify his recommendations, but it is hard to know for sure how much supply-side theory influenced his actions in the first place.[50] A second explanation is that balancing the budget was always less important to the president than achieving his first three goals. Again, there is little evidence about the president's initial priorities, but subsequent behavior strongly supports this view. Throughout the rest of his administration President Reagan stood firm in protecting both defense increases and tax cuts from those who sought to sacrifice one or the other to reduce the deficit, while using the existence of massive deficits as continual justification for further cuts in domestic programs.

Explaining congressional action is considerably easier. Congress had never before attempted to fashion its own fiscal policy in opposition to the president. From the very beginning of self-conscious, macroeconomic policy making, presidents designed fiscal policy. Congress might decide to make marginal changes in a president's proposals, or it might reject them completely in favor of the status quo; but as a large, decentralized institution it was poorly equipped to design coherent policy on its own. As I have already argued, rejecting the president's program in favor of the status quo was politically dangerous for legislators, especially given the administration's superb political tactics. They were left with only one viable option—approving the president's plan with only marginal changes.

Shortly after Congress passed the president's economic programs, the administration started to project increasing deficits "as far as the eye can see." This prediction, coupled with the start of the nation's worst postwar recession in late 1981, broke the president's spell over Congress. Legislators had given the president practically everything he had requested, but deficits increased when the administration had promised decreases and the economy stalled when the administration had predicted immediate growth and prosperity. Before long Democrats

---

50. See Hugh Heclo and Rudolph G. Penner, "Fiscal and Political Strategy in the Reagan Administration," in Fred I. Greenstein (ed.), *The Reagan Presidency: An Early Assessment* (Baltimore: Johns Hopkins University Press, 1983), pp. 21–47; and Greider, *Education of David Stockman*, pp. 93–110.

stopped worrying about realignment and Republicans stopped dreaming about capturing the House in 1982. Legislators no longer feared having to face their constituents as opponents of the president's economic programs; it was the president's supporters who paid the ultimate political price. Republicans lost twenty-six House seats in the 1982 midterm election—the worst defeat for any party two years after regaining the White House since 1922.[51]

The shift in congressional sentiment was immediate and dramatic once the economy turned sour. Within a few weeks after Congress passed both the Omnibus Reconciliation Act of 1981 and the Economic Recovery Tax Act of 1981, the stock market plunged and the administration reluctantly admitted that there was no end in sight for deficit increases. In September 1981, the president proposed a second round of appropriations cuts totaling $13 billion. Among other things, he proposed cutting some programs that had been used as sweeteners to attract support for the first round of cuts. Congress refused to consider the proposal. Eventually Congress did accept a $4 billion across-the-board cut in most domestic programs, but only after the president vetoed an earlier plan and forced a temporary governmental shutdown.

Congress and the president made little progress toward balancing the budget for the remainder of the Reagan administration. The president spoke eloquently about the need for a constitutional amendment to compel government to balance its budget, but lacking this coercive measure he chose not to propose either a balanced budget or a series of budgets that had a realistic chance of eventually achieving balance. Moreover, he refused to consider, even as part of a compromise plan, reducing the defense budget (defense outlays grew by 41 percent in real terms during Reagan's first five years in office). He repeatedly promised to veto any increases in tax rates. He refused to consider reductions in Social Security benefits, especially after one of David Stockman's trial balloons in this area was rejected unanimously by the Senate.[52] The only changes the president found acceptable were further cuts in domestic spending. Unfortunately, it would have required the elimination of more than two-thirds of all domestic spending to balance the budget.[53]

51. Phil Duncan, "House Vote: Major Midterm Setback for the Republicans," *Congressional Quarterly Weekly Report* 40 (November 6, 1982): 2780.

52. Greider, *Education of David Stockman*, p. 45.

53. In 1983, for example, the deficit was 25.8 percent of total outlays. After protecting defense spending (25.9 percent of outlays), Social Security and retirement benefits (25.6

Through the next several years Congress attempted to fashion its own budgetary and fiscal policies—a genuine first. The Senate began the task in early 1982, when it rejected unanimously the president's fiscal 1983 budget, which proposed cutting domestic expenditures another $46 billion. Instead, the Senate crafted a genuinely new budget that, after revision in the House, cut annual entitlement expenditures $5.8 billion, reduced regular domestic spending $4.4 billion, and increased revenues by $32.8 billion. Although the president accepted the tax increase, he attempted to reimpose his will on spending by vetoing an omnibus appropriations bill, arguing that Congress should provide more for defense and less for social programs. Both the House and Senate overrode the veto decisively. In subsequent years Congress often ignored the president's budget from the very start; even loyal Republicans were known to label it dead on arrival. Each year Congress crafted its own budget, often with little input from the administration.

Congress entered the business of making its own budgets because almost everyone believed that the president's budgets were politically unrealistic, including those who shared his preferences. Unlike the president, leaders of the budget committees operated under the premise that their job was to design budgets that Congress would pass. The real surprise, however, was that the budgets they proposed were often more fiscally prudent than those they replaced. Enacting these budgets required, once again, some clever strategies.

Consider, for example, how congressional leaders managed to raise taxes in 1982—in the middle of a recession and only two months before the midterm elections. Republicans in the Senate took the lead in designing a new tax bill and persuading the president to support their proposal. The Senate acted before the House, in part because senators were better insulated from immediate electoral retribution (only one-third of the Senate is up for reelection at a time), and in part because the Senate was controlled by Republicans who were in a better position to negotiate with the administration. Much as they had done in 1968, senators circumvented the constitutional requirement that revenue measures must originate in the House by attaching their entire plan to a minor tax bill that the House had passed a year earlier. The Senate approved the bill 50 to 47, with only one Democrat in favor and three Republicans opposed. The plan itself involved accelerating the collec-

---

percent), and interest payments (11.1 percent), the president would have had to eliminate 70 percent of all other spending (which constituted only 37.4 percent of total outlays) to balance the budget. *Historical Tables, FY88,* tables 1.1 and 3.3.

tion of corporate taxes and eliminating several tax breaks for businesses created in 1981. It was largely a tax on the Republican party's core constituency—or, more accurately, a reduction in the gains they were awarded in the 1981 tax bill (see Chapter 8). As distasteful as Republican senators found it to vote for such tax increases, this vote was essentially one on controlling the deficit, about which Republicans were both sensitive and vulnerable, given how they had allowed the deficit to multiply under their brief stewardship.[54]

The House found itself completely unable to write a tax bill during an election year and instead voted to go straight to conference on a bill they had never considered. The conference committee reported a bill that was very similar to the original Senate proposal, raising taxes by $98.3 billion over the following three years. As the conference report came to the floor of the House, the crucial vote was on an attempt to modify the closed rule so that members could vote on the individual provisions in the tax bill rather than on the entire economic package. The effort was defeated 220 to 110, which paved the way for the House to adopt the conference report, 226 to 207. As usual, electoral concerns were paramount for House members. Democrats were convinced that their votes in favor of the bill would be used against them in the fall elections. The president eventually offered them insurance policies, in the form of personal letters that thanked them for their support.[55]

Although Congress found it difficult to raise taxes in an election year, it nevertheless did so. Coalition leaders accomplished this feat by always structuring the process so that legislators voted on explicit economic policy rather than on specific tax provisions. The taxes themselves were imposed on corporations, who cannot vote, rather than on individuals. Moreover, business leaders had nowhere else to turn. No one believed they would suddenly favor Democratic candidates simply because Republicans had worked to rescind some of the tax breaks they so generously provided the previous year. Finally, coalition leaders protected

54. Pamela Fessler, "Divided Finance Committee Approves Tax-Increase Plan," *Congressional Quarterly Weekly Report* 40 (July 3, 1982): 1575–1576; Pamela Fessler, "Finance Tax Bill Is Likely Outline for House," *Congressional Quarterly Weekly Report* 40 (July 10, 1982): 1646–1648; and Pamela Fessler, "Spending Cuts, Record Tax Hike Pass Senate," *Congressional Quarterly Weekly Report* 40 (July 24, 1982): 1747–1749.

55. Pamela Fessler, "House Sends Tax Bill Directly to Conference," *Congressional Quarterly Weekly Report* 40 (July 31, 1982): 1808; and Dale Tate, "Congress Clears $98.3 Billion Tax Increase," *Congressional Quarterly Weekly Report* 40 (August 21, 1982): 2035–2046.

House members—the most vulnerable legislators just a few months before election day—from any involvement until the very end, at which point they were asked simply to affirm or reject the conference report.

Working by itself, Congress was unable to tame annual deficits of $200 billion. Each year Congress accepted some of the president's proposals for reductions in domestic spending; but with all of the easy cuts made during the first year, legislators were unwilling to accept drastic reductions in the more popular programs. Each year legislators scaled back the president's proposals for increased defense spending. In 1983 Congress almost passed a tax increase completely on its own, but House members were so leery of raising taxes without the president's support that they defeated the procedural motion that would have brought the committee's bill to the floor. In 1984, Congress passed a tax bill that increased revenues by $50 billion over three years, but only after the president promised not to veto it. In subsequent years, although there appeared to be substantial sentiment in Congress for major tax increases, few legislators were prepared to take the lead in raising taxes only to see the president veto their bills. Walter Mondale established decisively in the summer of 1984 that outsiders advocating tax increases are no match for an incumbent president who declares that such increases are unnecessary.

Finally, exasperated by the endless deficits and fearful of the political consequences of doing nothing, Congress passed the Gramm-Rudman-Hollings amendment in December 1985. Proponents forced legislators to act by attaching the amendment to a routine but crucial bill raising the ceiling on the national debt.[56] This amendment had its origins in electoral politics, as twenty-two Republican senators up for reelection in 1986 balked at voting to increase the debt ceiling unless they could also show that they were doing something about the deficit.[57] Gramm-Rudman-Hollings met their needs perfectly. The plan would have mandated annual reductions in the federal deficit until the budget was balanced five years later. If Congress and the president failed to achieve the mandated level of reductions on their own, the new law would have implemented them automatically by imposing across-the-board cuts in all programs, with the exception of Social Security and interest on the

56. On the politics of adoption, see Darrell M. West, "Gramm-Rudman-Hollings and the Politics of Deficit Reduction," *Annals* 499 (1988): 90–100.

57. Steven V. Roberts, "Politics of the Deficit: Economic Move Tied to Election," *New York Times* (October 28, 1985): A15.

national debt. The plan was politically irresistible, for it allowed senators to vote publicly on a plan to reduce the deficit without having to vote on specific reductions. The timing was also exquisite, given that automatic cuts would not occur until just after the 1986 election, lest voters connect specific reductions to senators' roll-call votes. After disposing of several embarrassing amendments that would have required automatic cuts just before the election or that would have cut spending or raised taxes immediately, the Senate adopted the budget proposal, 75 to 24.[58]

The entire proposal went directly to a conference committee, where Democrats from the House worked to modify its provisions.[59] Among other things they insisted that half of the automatic cuts fall on military spending and half on all other programs not explicitly exempted. In addition to Social Security and interest, they exempted six poverty programs and two veterans' programs and limited cuts to 2 percent annually for five health programs. These exemptions reflected the balance of power among the House conferees. House members also invented an elaborate system for calculating automatic cuts involving the Office of Management and Budget and the Congressional Budget Office, with the General Accounting Office acting as referee, in order to keep the administration from politicizing that which they insisted should remain an automatic procedure.[60] The House and Senate then adopted the conference agreement, 271 to 154, and 61 to 31.[61]

58. Elizabeth Wehr, "Support Gains for Balancing Federal Budget," *Congressional Quarterly Weekly Report* 43 (October 5, 1985): 1975–1978; and Elizabeth Wehr, "Senate Passes Plan to Balance Federal Budget," *Congressional Quarterly Weekly Report* 43 (October 12, 1985): 2035–2042.

59. The House never acted on the amendment directly because it changed its procedures in 1979 so that House members would never again have to endure the painful ritual of voting to raise the statutory limit on the national debt. Legislators had always been reluctant to support these increases, given how both interest groups and challengers used them as evidence of fiscal imprudence. Under the new procedure, the approval of the House is absolutely automatic (requiring neither debate nor formal vote) for whatever level of debt is assumed in the conference report for the most recently passed budget resolution. *Congressional Quarterly Almanac, 1979* 35 (1980): 305–307.

60. Elizabeth Wehr, "Conferees Strive to Fathom Senate Budget-Balancing Plan," *Congressional Quarterly Weekly Report* 43 (October 19, 1985): 2091–2094; Elizabeth Wehr, "House OKs Democrats' Budget-Balancing Plan," *Congressional Quarterly Weekly Report* 43 (November 2, 1985): 2191–2193; Elizabeth Wehr, "Fiscal Crisis, Partisanship Push Budget Conferees," *Congressional Quarterly Weekly Report* 43 (November 9, 1985): 2267–2275; and Elizabeth Wehr, "Congress Enacts Far-Reaching Budget Measure," *Congressional Quarterly Weekly Report* 43 (December 14, 1985): 2604–2611.

61. In the beginning, President Reagan was an enthusiastic supporter of the bill, which would have given him broad powers to cut federal programs while protecting most defense

Senators and representatives embraced Gramm-Rudman-Hollings because it met their political needs. They could vote for sound economic policy and for a balanced budget without ever having to vote to reduce specific group and geographic benefits. Legislators need never fear that constituents might trace their loss of specific benefits to legislators' individual actions, for they never had to make such decisions. They avoided doing so when they adopted Gramm-Rudman-Hollings, and they avoided having to do so in the future because the procedure was automatic and self-executing.

The plan began as an insurance policy for legislators who were reluctant to face their constituents without doing something about the deficit. It evolved into a sophisticated plan to force both the president and Congress to deal realistically with the budget as a whole. Its principal innovation was to alter the status quo in budgetary politics. If Congress and the president did nothing, federal spending would shrink instead of grow. If legislators refused to cut programs selectively, automatic formulas would do it indiscriminately. If the president resisted cuts in the military budget, opponents need only stall to achieve the same result. If Congress and the president genuinely wanted to continue spending money at the same rate, they simply had to bite the bullet and increase taxes. Few of those who designed the law expected that the automatic cuts would ever be imposed after the first year or so. Their aim was to create an action-forcing mechanism that would make stalemate more painful than confronting the real trade-offs between taxing and spending, between domestic and military expenditures, and between entitlement and discretionary programs. Their intention was to create a more level playing field, a field on which few programs would enjoy special advantages. Not even Social Security would be truly protected from cuts once legislators started to search for funds to forestall across-the-board reductions everywhere else.

Gramm-Rudman-Hollings was based on a sophisticated understanding of what it would take to force the president and Congress to make hard choices. In July 1986, however, the Supreme Court removed the law's keystone and the structure collapsed. The Court ruled unconstitutional a portion of the law that gave the comptroller general (an official of

spending. By the time it emerged from conference, with half the cuts targeted on defense and with little presidential discretion in any area, the president was a closet opponent. He signed it reluctantly. See Elizabeth Wehr, "Conference Accord Is Possible on Budget-Balancing Measure," *Congressional Quarterly Weekly Report* 43 (November 16, 1985): 2346–2349.

the legislative branch who cannot be removed by the president) the power to administer the automatic cuts. Although the law contained a fallback procedure for implementing spending cuts if the automatic provision did not survive judicial review, this procedure required both president and Congress specifically to approve all the cuts. This result was exactly what elected politicians sought to avoid. Gramm-Rudman-Hollings without a truly automatic trigger proved to be business as usual for the next fifteen months.

The crash of the stock market in October 1987 finally persuaded both congressional leaders and the president to devise unusual procedures to forge and enact a budget compromise. Among other things, they agreed to reestablish an automatic trigger, this time giving the Office of Management and Budget the sole power to make cuts. Congress and the president also reached a two-year agreement designed to reduce the deficit by $33 billion in 1988 and $43 billion in 1989. The agreement was drafted in a summit meeting of fourteen congressional and executive leaders who worked behind closed doors to apportion the pain across defense expenditures, nondefense programs, entitlements, and taxes. Legislators were then given the opportunity to accept or reject the fiscal decisions in two separate bills designed to implement the plan. The proposed reconciliation bill bypassed both the House committees and the House floor and went directly to a conference committee. House members had exactly one opportunity to vote on this reconciliation bill, when they were asked to accept or reject the conference report. Thirteen separate appropriations bills were also combined into a single $600 billion bill that ran for more than 2,100 pages. This bill was also sent to the House floor under a restrictive rule that allowed only seven amendments, none of which affected the division of pain among functional areas.[62]

This final act from the Reagan years shows a Congress perfectly capable of making difficult fiscal choices. Even after legislators had approved all the easy programmatic cuts in the early 1980s, they still proved themselves capable of approving further reductions in expenditures. Even when taxes were emerging as a difficult political issue, legislators

62. Elizabeth Wehr, "Turning Budget Pact into Law Won't Be Easy," *Congressional Quarterly Weekly Report* 45 (November 28, 1987): 2929–2933; Jacqueline Calmes, "House Passes All-in-One Appropriations Bill," *Congressional Quarterly Weekly Report* 45 (December 5, 1987): 2972–2977; and Janet Hook, "Budget Deal Enacted at Last, Congress Adjourns," *Congressional Quarterly Weekly Report* 45 (December 26, 1987): 3183–3192.

approved additional tax increases. All that was required was that these programmatic cuts and tax increases had to be combined into a single economic package, so that legislators were forced to vote on explicit economic policy rather than on a series of programmatic changes.

MAKING ECONOMIC POLICY

The portrait I have been painting of Congress and macroeconomic policy differs in fundamental ways from the prevailing interpretation of legislative politics. Many scholars have argued that a Congress filled with legislators interested in reelection is inherently biased in favor of particularism, deficit spending, and governmental growth. My own view is that the electoral quest inspires both a concern with group and geographic benefits, which when pursued to excess can produce deficits, and a concern with some of the general costs and benefits associated with governmental spending. Although the exact balance between these two forces varies from issue to issue, over time these twin forces largely cancel each other out. The result is that Congress enacts fiscal policies that appear remarkably similar to those which presidents propose. If there is a systematic difference between the two, it is that legislators' decisions tend to be *more* fiscally conservative than presidents' recommendations.[63]

The examples cited in this chapter show Congress working to control particularism, deficit spending, and governmental growth and endeavoring to enact responsible fiscal policy. We have seen legislators resist, although eventually approve, Keynesian tax cuts (1964) and supply-side tax cuts (1981).[64] We have watched Congress enact four tax increases (1968, 1982, 1984, 1987), each time adopting a more fiscally conservative policy than the president requested. We have observed House members first approving particularistic amendments to appropriations bills and then adopting across-the-board reductions that more than outweighed the particularistic increases (1970s). We have seen legislators adopt the Gramm-Rudman-Hollings amendment in an attempt to impose fiscal discipline on both themselves and the president. We have observed Congress approving a presidential request for massive cuts in domestic spending (1981). The overall image is not of a spendthrift

---

63. Peterson, "New Politics of Deficits," pp. 365–397.
64. See Chapter 8 for a discussion of the 1981 tax bill.

Congress overpowering a more prudent executive, but rather one of a large legislative institution attempting to satisfy citizens' often contradictory preferences for general benefits as well as group and geographic benefits.

Enacting particularistic policies is relatively easy. A single senator proposing a floor amendment to a tax or appropriations bill is often all that is necessary to invoke legislators' calculations about group or geographic benefits. Enacting sound economic policies, and especially those that restrict group or geographic benefits, is considerably more difficult. Coalition leaders must first frame an issue as explicit economic policy, in order to invoke legislators' calculations about general benefits, and then develop and enforce procedures that ward off particularistic amendments. This chapter has shown that although enacting such policies requires talented leaders and clever strategies, it is far from impossible. It is, in fact, a regular occurrence on Capitol Hill.

8

Tax Policy

How can one account for the general shape of the federal tax code? How have legislators managed to create a tax system that extracts one-fifth of the gross national product for governmental use without ever placing their own careers in jeopardy? Why did legislators first create such a complicated tax code, filled with special exemptions, deductions, and credits, and then suddenly switch course in 1986 and enact a tax reform bill that eliminated many of these particularistic provisions? In the previous chapter I explained how Congress adjusts the level of tax revenues in the pursuit of explicit fiscal policy. This chapter attempts to explain the evolution of the income tax over the past several decades and shows how legislators have left their unmistakable imprint on the tax code.

Clearly, elected politicians do not like to impose taxes on their constituents. Few politicians campaign for office by promising to raise taxes, and those who do are seldom rewarded with office.[1] Once in office, however, politicians do sometimes increase taxes. Do voters then punish them at the polls? The only evidence on the question concerns gubernatorial elections. The best study shows that governors who imposed tax increases between 1948 and 1974 were twice as likely to be defeated at the next election as those who held the line.[2]

Do legislators suffer a similar fate when they vote to impose new taxes

---

1. Walter Mondale, who promised to raise taxes during the 1984 presidential campaign, is a good example.

2. See Theodore J. Eismeier, "Budgets and Ballots: The Political Consequences of Fiscal Choice," in Douglas W. Rae and Theodore J. Eismeier (eds.), *Public Policy and Public Choice* (Beverly Hills, Calif.: Sage Publications, 1979), pp. 121–149.

or raise existing levies? No systematic evidence exists on the question, in part because legislators have created a system that helps to shield them from electoral retribution. The creation of this system actually provides some of the best evidence that legislators fear electoral retribution when they act on tax matters. Their fear seems perfectly justifiable in the case of direct taxes, because all three conditions required for retrospective voting generally exist. Direct taxes impose perceptible costs on those who pay them; the costs can be traced to identifiable governmental actions because no tax may be imposed without an act of Congress; and legislators are required to take public positions on most tax bills (because someone usually demands a roll-call vote). The anticipation of retrospective voting helps to focus legislators' attention on the possible electoral consequences of voting to increase taxes even when they hear little from their constituents in advance of congressional action.

THE DEVELOPMENT OF THE INCOME TAX

If legislators are reluctant to be associated with either creating or increasing taxes, then how can one account for the existence of such a vast and effective system for taxing personal and corporate income? Actually, the establishment of the income tax occurred long before the rise of a careerist legislature filled with reelection-minded politicians, so there is no need for a theory about the contemporary Congress to explain anything about the origins of the income tax. Even so, much of the early political history of the income tax is consistent with the present theory. There is little evidence to suggest that legislators incurred significant electoral risks by establishing an income tax.

New taxes are usually created in times of crisis, and the income tax was no exception.[3] Crises increase the need for governmental revenue, make citizens more tolerant of new taxes, and encourage politicians to take greater than usual risks. Congress adopted the first income tax in 1861 to finance the Civil War and then terminated it a decade later after the financial need had passed. It created a second income tax in 1894 to

---

3. On the early development of the income tax, see Roy G. Blakey and Gladys C. Blakey, *The Federal Income Tax* (New York: Longmans, Green, 1940); and John F. Witte, *The Politics and Development of the Federal Income Tax* (Madison: University of Wisconsin Press, 1985), pp. 67–130.

deal with a major depression that had severely reduced governmental revenue. The Supreme Court overturned this tax in 1895 on constitutional grounds. Congress enacted yet a third income tax in 1913, just after the Democrats returned to power (and after the Sixteenth Amendment had been added to the Constitution). Given that this new tax applied only to the richest 2 percent of society, most legislators had little to fear from voters generally. In fact, taxing the rich was a popular thing to do among Democratic legislators, who had just been returned to power on a platform of curbing the rich and powerful.

From this point on, war became the engine behind the expansion of the income tax. Supporting our men in battle was a powerful justification for increasing tax burdens and served to protect legislators from electoral retribution. Congress passed most wartime increases quickly, enthusiastically, and without public protest. During World War I the income tax was broadened considerably. The proportion of the labor force paying taxes increased from 2 percent to 13 percent, and the maximum tax rate increased from 7 percent to 77 percent. The income tax became the leading source of federal revenue within five years of its inception.[4] World War II quickly transformed the income tax from an elite to a mass tax, raising to 64 percent the proportion of the labor force paying taxes. The top marginal rate increased to 94 percent.[5]

Every time America went to war, Congress expanded the tax base and increased tax rates. Congress enacted major tax increases in 1916, 1917, 1918, 1941, 1942, 1950, 1951, and 1968. Every time peace broke out, Congress worked to bring the rates down again. Tax reductions, however, never quite equalled the tax increases.[6] This series of decisions produced a ratchet effect and allowed the income tax to expand over time without legislators ever having to support explicitly a tax expansion. Legislators were asked to support national emergencies, not to increase permanently the revenue capacity of government. Over the entire period from 1913 to 1981, Congress raised income taxes only twice during peacetime. Both occasions came during the Depression and were in response to the widely held belief, among citizens and politicians, that balancing the budget would contribute to economic recovery.[7]

4. Ibid., pp. 75–87.
5. Ibid., pp. 110–130.
6. The only exception was the 1968 act, which was a temporary surcharge from the start.
7. Witte, *Politics and Development of the Federal Income Tax*, pp. 96–108, 249.

Inflation also produced handsome tax increases without legislators ever having to vote for them. Inflation reduced the real value of personal exemptions, the standard deduction, and various credits that were expressed in dollars. Inflation also increased taxpayers' nominal incomes and forced them into higher tax brackets, even though their real incomes often remained unchanged. These twin effects gave the income tax a very high inflation elasticity. Each 1.0 percent increase in inflation generated a 1.55 percent increase in governmental revenue.[8] The revenue effects were relatively mild in the 1950s and 1960s, when prices increased 23 and 31 percent respectively, but they were spectacular in the 1970s, when prices increased 112 percent.[9]

Although Congress regularly enacted bills to reduce tax liabilities (with major efforts in 1945, 1948, 1954, 1962, 1964, 1969, 1971, 1975, 1976, 1977, and 1978), tax revenues continued to grow. Figure 8.1 shows how income tax revenues as a percentage of GNP increased steadily throughout this period, from 7.0 percent of GNP in the late 1940s to 8.9 percent in the early 1980s. The time was a happy one for elected politicians. Legislators repeatedly had the pleasure of voting to cut nominal taxes while the system continued to produce modest tax increases. These new revenues were then used for other legislative pleasures, such as creating or expanding expenditure programs.

Legislators could hardly have done better in insulating themselves from electoral retribution for establishing and expanding the income tax if they had consciously designed a system to accomplish just that end. They escaped electoral retribution for establishing the income tax by limiting its incidence to the richest 2 percent of society. They escaped electoral retribution for expanding the income tax by doing so when the nation was at war and when most citizens were willing to make financial sacrifices at home in order to sustain those who were making even greater sacrifices abroad. They escaped electoral retribution for expanding the tax burden in the postwar period by allowing the hidden hand of inflation to increase real taxes while they repeatedly voted to cut nominal taxes. Citizens were unable to hold their representatives accountable for the increased taxes they were paying because there were no identifiable governmental actions on which to lay the blame and for

8. Edward M. Gramlich, "The Economic and Budgetary Effects of Indexing the Tax System," in Henry Aaron (ed.), *Inflation and the Income Tax* (Washington, D.C.: Brookings Institution, 1976), pp. 271–290.

9. U.S., Office of the President, *Economic Report of the President* (Washington, D.C.: Government Printing Office, 1987), p. 307.

Figure 8.1 Individual income taxes as percentage of GNP, *1940–1985*

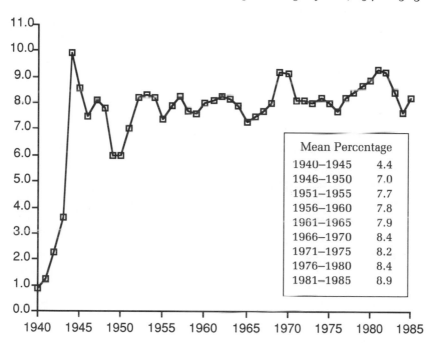

Mean Percentage	
1940–1945	4.4
1946–1950	7.0
1951–1955	7.7
1956–1960	7.8
1961–1965	7.9
1966–1970	8.4
1971–1975	8.2
1976–1980	8.4
1981–1985	8.9

Source: U.S., Office of Management and Budget, *Historical Tables: Budget of the United States Government, FY88* (Washington, D.C.: Government Printing Office, 1987), table 2.3.

which legislators had been forced to choose sides. Throughout this period most legislators had squeaky-clean records, having never voted to increase taxes and having frequently voted to cut them.

THE RISE OF TAX PREFERENCES

The basic structure of the income tax today looks remarkably similar to the structure that Congress created in 1913. From the very beginning the income tax law included more than a dozen exemptions, exclusions, and deductions. The original law contained a personal exemption of $3,000, allowed for the exclusion of interest on state and local bonds, permitted deductions for state and local taxes, business expenses, casualty losses, and interest paid on all forms of indebtedness, and included a graduated system of rates ranging from 1 to 7 percent.

The most dramatic change over the next seven decades was the altered balance among the various components of the tax law, including the near elimination of the personal exemption, the establishment of high marginal rates, and the creation and expansion of many new exclusions, deductions, and credits. Congress first reduced the personal exemption from $3,000 to $1,000 during World War I, then reduced it to $500 during World War II, and then held it virtually constant for the next three decades, while inflation eroded its value to a mere $137 (in 1939 dollars).[10] These reductions transformed a tax that once affected only 2 percent of the labor force into one that touched most full-time workers. Congress also increased tax rates and kept them relatively high. The initial top rate of 7 percent was increased to 77 percent during World War I, reduced gradually during the 1920s to 24 percent, increased again during the Depression to 79 percent, further increased during World War II to 94 percent, and kept above 90 percent until 1964, when Congress reduced it to 70 percent.[11] Meanwhile Congress created and expanded a host of new exclusions, exemptions, deductions, and credits (collectively known as tax preferences or tax expenditures), which, among other things, helped to protect citizens from the effects of higher rates and lower personal exemptions.

Why would Congress choose to create and expand tax preferences rather than increase the personal exemption or reduce tax rates? Although no definitive answer is possible for any series of decisions spread over seven decades, Congress did display remarkable consistency in its choices throughout this period, suggesting that there was nothing accidental about them. Congress chose to create or expand tax preferences in every major revenue act from 1916 to 1981. It did so during times of war and times of peace, when the budget was in surplus and when it was in deficit, and during periods of Republican control and Democratic control.

Although legislators can profit from their association with any form of tax relief, the rewards differ depending on the exact form of relief. Across-the-board rate reductions are probably the least rewarding, because it is so difficult to produce perceptible benefits at reasonable cost. No one believes that citizens will notice a one percent reduction in their taxes or, if they do happen to notice, that they will be inspired to reward

10. Joseph A. Pechman, *Federal Tax Policy*, 5th ed. (Washington, D.C.: Brookings Institution, 1987), pp. 81, 313.
11. Ibid., p. 313.

their representatives for their good fortune. Yet producing larger and more perceptible benefits is enormously costly. Reducing everyone's taxes by 10 percent requires the government either to reduce its expenditures by a similar amount or the nation to tolerate a vast increase in the deficit.

The rewards are considerably greater when legislators create or expand tax preferences because most tax preferences offer several forms of group and general benefits. Every tax preference promises group benefits to those taxpayers who will have their tax liabilities reduced. Most of them also promise group or general benefits to several broader publics that would gain indirectly when the direct beneficiaries adjust their behavior to take advantage of the new tax provisions. The establishment of a deduction for charitable contributions in 1917, for example, had more to do with the wishes of charitable organizations, who did not want their contributions to dry up when the top tax bracket was increased from 15 to 67 percent, than it did with the efforts of wealthy citizens to avoid taxes.[12]

The second advantage of tax preferences is that most of them do not cost much in the short term. A single new tax preference may promise substantial group benefits to a small group of taxpayers and substantial group benefits to several broader publics and yet still cost the treasury very little. A few hundred million dollars concentrated on some small segment of society is easily noticed by the beneficiaries, whereas the financial costs are mere noise in the vast federal budget. The political logic of creating new tax preferences is thus very similar to the political logic of creating new expenditure programs. To be sure, an individual tax preference may grow over time and eventually cost a substantial sum, and all tax preferences taken together already cost an enormous sum; but these facts need not affect legislators' calculations about whether to create a single tax preference.

A third attraction of tax preferences is that they allow legislators to accomplish ends that would be difficult to achieve by more direct means. Proposals to benefit either the very rich or the very poor offer good examples, for in each case some legislators are reluctant to be associated with direct subsidy programs. Legislators who are disinclined to support welfare programs are often much more comfortable voting to create or expand the earned income credit—a $4 billion provision that operates

12. C. Harry Kahn, *Personal Deductions in the Federal Income Tax* (Princeton, N.J.: Princeton University Press, 1960), p. 46.

like a negative income tax to increase the incomes of the working poor (including those who pay no income taxes).[13] Tax credits simply sound more appealing than welfare payments to the legislative ear. Tax preferences are also the preferred mechanism for delivering welfare payments to wealthy individuals or large corporations. Legislators who would never dream of supporting proposals to send direct subsidies to banks, the steel industry, owners of capital, or heirs to great fortunes achieve the same ends by enacting tax preferences. Such tax preferences have the dual advantage of being just as perceptible to the direct beneficiaries as subsidies would be and yet far less visible to citizens generally.

A final attraction of tax preferences is that they can be used to encourage the supply of general benefits with a minimum of fuss and without establishing an extensive administrative apparatus. Congress has created tax preferences to encourage economic investment, stimulate the construction of housing for low-income citizens, promote the rehabilitation of historic structures, encourage energy conservation, stimulate industrial research and development, and subsidize the construction of facilities for controlling pollution. Although alternative means for achieving these ends surely exist, few are less intrusive than tax preferences. In fact, the principal difference between regulatory programs and tax preferences is that the former achieve public purposes by imposing group costs while the latter work their magic by offering group benefits. It should come as no surprise that legislators prefer alternatives that deliver group benefits to those that impose group costs.[14]

The attractions of tax preferences have been evident from the day Congress first established the income tax. As Table 8.1 reveals, Congress included 14 tax preferences in the original law, created roughly one a year over the next six decades, and then added nearly two a year during the 1970s. Together these 91 provisions cost an estimated $248 billion in lost revenue in 1982—nearly three quarters of the $347 billion that the individual and corporate income taxes actually raised for governmental coffers in that year.

Table 8.1 might seem to imply that Congress has been creating smaller and smaller tax preferences over time, thus suggesting that the problem of tax preferences has been diminishing. In fact, most tax prefer-

13. Pechman, *Federal Tax Policy*, pp. 112–113.

14. See Charles L. Schultze, *The Public Use of Private Interest* (Washington, D.C.: Brookings Institution, 1977).

Table 8.1. Origin and value of tax preferences, 1913–1981

Period	Tax preferences created during each period		1982 revenue loss (millions of dollars)	
	Total	Per year	Total	Per provision
1913	14	14.00	79,765	5,698
1914–1945	30	.94	101,219	3,374
1946–1969	25	1.04	49,205	1,968
1970–1981	22	1.83	18,180	826
Total	91	1.32	248,369	2,729

Source: This table was constructed from a list of all tax preferences compiled by John Witte. The estimates of lost revenue were made by the Office of Management and Budget. See John F. Witte, *The Politics and Development of the Federal Income Tax* (Madison: University of Wisconsin Press, 1985), pp. 276–282.

ences begin as small items, which is why they are relatively easy to create. Over time Congress revises many of these provisions to make them even more attractive to taxpayers (and more costly to the treasury), and taxpayers become more adept at adjusting their behavior to take advantage of these provisions. The deduction for retirement savings illustrates both trends. In 1962 Congress allowed self-employed individuals to set up Keogh plans to shelter their retirement savings from taxation (much as employer contributions to pension funds had been tax free since 1926). Although Keogh plans quickly became popular among the self-employed, the small number of participants (650,000) kept the revenue losses modest ($1.7 billion in 1988). In 1975, 1976, and 1981 Congress broadened this tax preference so that employees who were already covered by employer-sponsored pension plans could set up their own tax-free individual retirement accounts. Suddenly banks and brokers were telling everyone how to reduce their taxes by moving their savings into these special accounts. By 1984 there were 15 million taxpayers with individual retirement accounts, and the annual revenue loss was over $11 billion (and growing rapidly).[15] In a few short years Congress had transformed a modest tax preference into the seventh largest revenue loser in the tax code.

Congress began tinkering with tax preferences soon after creating the first ones in 1913. Between 1913 and 1969 it approved some 154 modifications in the existing tax preferences. As one might expect, expansions in coverage and increases in benefits outnumbered contractions, although the margin was relatively small (81 to 66). During the 1970s the trend toward modifying existing provisions accelerated and the bias in favor of expansions increased. Between 1970 and 1981 Congress enacted 164 additional modifications, with expansions now outnumbering contractions by a large margin (105 to 43).[16]

Why did Congress suddenly accelerate the creation and expansion of tax preferences in the 1970s? If one assumes that legislators' motives for creating and expanding tax preferences were unchanged, then one must consider both means and opportunity. In both instances there were significant changes. The means for financing new and expanded tax preferences increased, as the rampant inflation of the 1970s pushed most taxpayers into higher and higher tax brackets and enlarged governmental revenues. Congress thus had the revenue to enact frequent tax "reduction" acts, and it passed them in 1971, 1975, 1976, 1977, 1978, and 1981. The opportunities for mischief increased as the power of the House Ways and Means Committee waned and as the Senate became more important in tax matters.[17] Whereas Ways and Means had long been the guardian of the treasury and had somehow managed to enact contractions as well as expansions in tax preferences, the Senate Finance Committee demonstrated a clear bias toward expansions (by a ratio of better than 4 to 1).[18] The Senate was also a more hospitable place for amending bills on the floor. Whereas tax bills were usually protected from amendment on the House floor by a closed rule, the Senate operated as an open shop where amendments were always welcome. Floor amendments were clearly biased toward expanding tax preferences (also by a ratio of better than 4 to 1).[19]

The switch from the quiet back-room deals of the Ways and Means Committee to the more open procedures of the Finance Committee and the Senate floor shows how tax preferences thrive in the sunshine. It is

15. Pechman, *Federal Tax Policy*, pp. 111–112.

16. There were also 7 neutral changes in the earlier period and 16 neutral changes in the later period. These data were compiled by John Witte and are summarized in *Politics and Development of the Federal Income Tax*, p. 315.

17. Catherine E. Rudder, "Tax Policy: Structure and Choice," in Allen Schick (ed.), *Making Economic Policy in Congress* (Washington, D.C.: American Enterprise Institute, 1983), pp. 196–220.

18. Witte, *Politics and Development of the Federal Income Tax*, pp. 321–324.

19. Ibid., p. 322.

relatively easy for legislators to turn down proposals for expanding tax preferences, or even to approve contractions, if their actions are hidden from public view. It is considerably more difficult to do so if legislators must vote publicly, either in committee or on the floor, to deny their constituents a share of group benefits. As Congress began in the 1970s to write tax bills more openly, legislators faced an increasing number of roll-call votes on tax preferences. In fact, during this one decade there were more than twice as many roll-call votes in favor of creating or modifying tax preferences as there had been in the six previous decades.[20] As legislators voted publicly on these matters, they quite naturally voted to approve expanded tax preferences.

Between 1970 and 1981 Congress went on something like a spending spree with tax preferences. It created tax preferences faster than ever before, modified them more frequently than ever before, and used these modifications to expand coverage more often than ever before. The growth in tax preferences was dramatic by any measure. Table 8.2 reveals that the revenue loss from all tax preferences more than doubled in constant dollars between 1967 and 1982, while revenue loss as a fraction of both GNP and total tax receipts nearly doubled. By 1982 the government lost almost as much revenue from tax preferences as it gained from the income tax system as a whole.

This growth in tax preferences made it even more difficult for Congress to readjust tax rates in response to inflation. Although Congress did adjust tax brackets periodically, the adjustments were never sufficient to keep citizens from drifting into higher tax brackets. Table 8.3 shows how Congress failed to protect the median taxpayer from markedly higher tax rates. Between 1950 and 1980 income tax receipts as a proportion of the gross national product increased by 54 percent (from 0.059 to 0.091), while the average tax rate for a typical family earning the median income *quadrupled* (from 0.031 to 0.119).[21] By 1980 this family was paying a marginal tax rate of 24 percent, up from 17 percent in 1950.[22]

---

20. There were 96 such votes between 1970 and 1981, compared with 45 from 1913 to 1969. Ibid., p. 327.

21. This quadrupling was slightly attenuated for those families who itemized deductions. Most families, however, used the standard deduction. Only 19 percent of all families in 1950 (and 31 percent in 1980) itemized their deductions, and the percentages were considerably smaller for those earning the median family income. See Pechman, *Federal Tax Policy*, p. 372.

22. If the Social Security tax is included, the marginal tax rates were 30 percent and 19 percent, respectively.

Table 8.2. Growth of tax preferences, 1967–1982

Year	Revenue loss from all tax preferences[a]	Revenue loss as percentage of GNP	Revenue loss as percentage of all income tax receipts
1967	101,811	4.4	38.0
1969	117,173	4.8	37.0
1971	116,464	4.6	42.1
1973	132,061	4.7	40.7
1975	156,585	6.3	56.6
1977	168,581	6.1	53.2
1979	190,604	6.4	54.7
1981	243,213	8.0	65.9
1982	253,515	8.2	73.5

a. Estimates of revenue loss are in millions of 1982 dollars. Revenue loss and income tax receipts include both the individual and corporate income taxes.

Sources: The original data were compiled by John Witte from estimates made by the Congressional Budget Office. The adjustments for inflation were added using the 1982 implicit price deflator for GNP. See John F. Witte, *The Politics and Development of the Federal Income Tax* (Madison: University of Wisconsin Press, 1985), p. 292.

THE POLITICS OF TAX REDUCTION

The time was certainly ripe for a tax cut in 1981. Despite the tax acts of 1975, 1976, 1977, and 1978, which together reduced tax liabilities by some $49 billion, the income tax continued to extract a larger fraction of national income in each successive year.[23] As Figure 8.1 shows, income tax revenues as a percentage of GNP increased steadily from 7.7 percent in 1976 to 9.6 percent in 1981. Rapid inflation pushed people into higher tax brackets faster than legislators could enact tax reductions. Just in the three years since the last tax act in 1978, prices had increased by an unprecedented 36 percent.[24] By 1981 the question was not whether Congress should enact tax relief, but how

23. For estimates of the net revenue changes associated with each tax bill, see Pechman, *Federal Tax Policy*, pp. 40–41.

24. *Economic Report of the President*, p. 307.

Table 8.3. Tax payments for a typical family of four, 1940–1980

	1940	1950	1960	1970	1980
1. Median family income	1,900	3,319	5,620	9,867	21,023
2. Personal exemptions	2,800	2,400	2,400	2,500	4,000
3. Standard deduction	—	332	562	987	3,400
4. Taxable income	0	587	2,658	6,380	13,623
5. Tax	0	102	532	1,098	2,511
6. Average tax rate	.000	.031	.095	.111	.119
7. Marginal tax rate	.000	.174	.200	.195	.240
8. Income tax receipts/GNP	.009	.059	.080	.091	.091

Note: Taxes are calculated for a married couple with two children, earning the median family income, and taking only the standard deduction.

Sources: Data compiled by the author. Line 1 for 1940 is estimated from distributional data in U.S., Bureau of the Census, *Historical Statistics of the United States* (Washington, D.C.: Government Printing Office, 1975), series G270 and G271; data from 1950 to 1980 are from U.S., Bureau of the Census, *Statistical Abstract of the United States, 1987* (Washington, D.C.: Government Printing Office, 1986), p. 436. Information to calculate lines 2, 3, 5, and 7 is contained in Joseph A. Pechman, *Federal Tax Policy*, 5th ed. (Washington, D.C.: Brookings Institution, 1987), pp. 65, 313–318. Line 4 equals line 1 minus lines 2 and 3. Line 6 equals line 5 divided by line 1. Line 8 is from U.S., Office of Management and Budget, *Historical Tables: Budget of the United States Government, FY88* (Washington, D.C.: Government Printing Office, 1987), table 2.3.

much relief the government could afford and what form that relief should take.

There were simultaneous pressures on Congress to reduce tax rates and to expand tax preferences. Both pressures were a consequence of the inequities that had entered the system in the previous decade. Most of the tax relief that Congress granted during the 1970s was in the form of new or expanded tax preferences. Although these preferences helped to shelter some taxpayers from the higher tax brackets into which inflation had pushed them, many taxpayers were ineligible for these preferences. While some groups petitioned Congress to expand existing tax preferences so that even more taxpayers would be sheltered, others demanded that the rates themselves be reduced. The case for the latter was strengthened by the fact that, while prices had increased by 125 percent between 1971 and 1981, Congress had adjusted the tax rates only once (in the Revenue Act of 1978).[25] Many taxpayers who thought of themselves as middle class found themselves paying rates designed for the rich.[26]

Despite the pressures for tax reduction, Congress actually had little revenue to spare. Although it was true that inflation had produced real tax increases for five consecutive years, it was also true that governmental expenditures were growing rapidly. The federal deficit remained stuck at about 10 percent of federal expenditures throughout most of the 1970s and served to constrain excessive tax cutting. Under the usual rules of tax politics the president would not have proposed and Congress would not have approved a large tax reduction.

In 1981 neither Congress nor the president played by the usual rules of tax politics.[27] A month after taking office President Reagan proposed cutting individual tax rates by 30 percent and creating new tax preferences that would reduce corporate tax revenues by more than 50 percent. Less than six months later Congress approved a tax cut that was even more generous than that which the president had proposed. The final bill reduced total revenues from the individual and corporate income taxes by over 30 percent.[28] The revenue loss of $162 billion annually was approximately equal to the annual deficit that plagued the federal government for the rest of the decade.

Why would Congress approve such a massive tax cut when the federal government was already running a large deficit? The simple answer is that the president demanded that Congress reduce taxes, offered a fig leaf to hide the fiscal irresponsibility of it all, and then structured the process so that tax cutting became irresistible. Ordinarily presidents propose prudent fiscal policies and help to restrain Congress from cutting rates indiscriminately or from creating excessive tax preferences.[29]

25. For changes in the consumer price index, see *Economic Report of the President*, p. 307. For changes in tax rates, see Pechman, *Federal Tax Policy*, pp. 317–318.

26. Witte, *Politics and Development of the Federal Income Tax*, pp. 236–239.

27. For accounts of the 1981 tax bill, see "Congress Enacts President Reagan's Tax Plan," *Congressional Quarterly Almanac, 1981* 37 (1982): 91–104; Rudder, "Tax Policy: Structure and Choice," pp. 196–220; and Witte, *Politics and Development of the Federal Income Tax*, pp. 220–243.

28. When the tax provisions were fully effective in 1984, the revenue loss equaled $162 billion. Total income tax revenues in that year equaled $355 billion. See Pechman, *Federal Tax Policy*, pp. 41, 369.

29. The historical evidence suggests that Congress generally approves the fiscal policies of presidents rather than crafting its own fiscal policy. See Paul Peterson, "The New Politics of Deficits," in John Chubb and Paul Peterson (eds.), *The New Direction in*

Legislators rely on presidents to deliver them from temptation, just as they rely on the Appropriations and Ways and Means Committees to restrain their appetites for more spending and less taxing. In this case the president proposed a fiscally irresponsible policy, all the while claiming that it was the height of fiscal responsibility.

The administration's tax bill, entitled the "Economic Recovery Tax Act," was promoted as the second element of the president's economic program (along with the spending cuts discussed in Chapter 7). The same logic of retrospective voting that made it risky to oppose the president's proposed expenditure cuts in May and June made it equally risky to oppose the tax cuts in July. Those who contemplated voting against the president's tax plan, and especially those from districts filled with Reagan supporters, could easily imagine citizens tracing future economic woes back to their votes thwarting the president's program. To be sure, calculations about explicit economic policy and retrospective voting had a lesser impact on the tax bill than they had on the bill to cut expenditures. The underlying forces were already favorable for tax cuts, and legislators' calculations about retrospective voting simply reinforced their basic proclivities.

Why weren't legislators worried about producing ever increasing deficits and about the electoral repercussions from doing so? The president offered two forms of political insulation. From the beginning, the administration argued that these were supply-side tax cuts, that they would quickly unleash a torrent of innovation, investment, and economic activity, and that the resulting surge in the economy would generate sufficient revenue to erase any short-term deficits. Few legislators believed this scenario would unfold as scripted, but at least it provided a rationale to show how everyone was intending to balance the budget, not to double the deficit.[30] Although legislators could easily be punished for failing to give the president's program a chance, once they approved it they transferred the responsibility for future economic calamities to the president. There was also safety in knowing that even the most conser-

---

American Politics (Washington, D.C.: Brookings Institution, 1985), pp. 365–397. See also Chapter 7.

30. For example, Senator Paul Laxalt (R., Nev.), the president's closest friend on Capitol Hill, said at a White House meeting a year later, "If there had been a secret ballot in the Senate last year, there wouldn't have been more than 12 votes for the tax cut." Steven R. Weisman, "Reaganomics and the President's Men," *New York Times Magazine* (October 24, 1982): 28.

vative president in two generations could not charge legislators with acting irresponsibly by voting to cut taxes. Allen Schick argues that the way citizens perceive a deficit depends largely on how the president defines it.[31] When presidents dig in their heels and declare that any deficit beyond a certain level is irresponsible, they increase the chances that those legislators voting to increase the deficit beyond that level will themselves appear irresponsible. In this case, President Reagan had already defined the tax cut as responsible fiscal policy. For many legislators this stance provided all the insurance they required even if, as many feared, the deficits multiplied.

The broad outlines of the president's bill thus survived legislators' scrutiny for electoral defects. Congressional leaders then proceeded to transform an acceptable bill into an irresistibly attractive one, employing the ordinary rules of tax politics. They scaled back the reductions in tax rates and multiplied the tax preferences. Essentially they used a modest contraction in general benefits to fund an explosion in group benefits. The president proposed a 30 percent across-the-board reduction in rates; Congress settled on 23 percent. The president proposed a faster system for depreciating capital assets. Congress accepted this proposal and then added a long list of tax preferences on its own.

The multiplication of tax preferences was contagious and occurred at every stage in the process.[32] The administration opened the bidding by proposing that businesses be allowed to depreciate capital assets more rapidly than ever before. The Ways and Means Committee accepted part of the president's proposal and added provisions for middle-income taxpayers, including a new deduction for married couples with two incomes and an expansion of individual retirement accounts to include all taxpayers. The administration redrafted its plan to include many of the committee's proposals and added new provisions designed to attract conservative Democrats (such as tax breaks for oil producers). The Senate Finance Committee built on this base by adding new provisions to aid savings banks, oil producers, and small businesses. The Ways and Means Committee then added even more benefits for oil producers and further reduced estate and gift taxes. The Senate responded with a series of floor amendments that covered everything from child care to credits for taxpayers in south Alabama who lost pecan trees to Hur-

31. Allen Schick, *Congress and Money* (Washington, D.C.: The Urban Institute, 1980), p. 351.

32. "Congress Enacts Tax Plan," *Congressional Quarterly Almanac, 1981*, pp. 91–104.

ricane Frederick. This time the conference committee, which usually eliminates most tax provisions passed by a single house, practiced the politics of inclusion and incorporated most of them into the conference report. The final bill literally contained something for everyone and was politically irresistible. The Senate approved it 67 to 8, and the House concurred, 282 to 95.

Why did a bill that once focused on reducing tax rates evolve into the largest explosion of tax preferences in history? First, the president's bill offered both the means and the opportunity for something that comes naturally to legislators. Everyone realized that this would be the last tax-reduction train leaving the station for a very long time and scrambled to add their favorite provisions. The total cost of the bill was already so high that no one expected to see another tax-reduction bill for a long time. Moreover, the huge cost of the original proposal helped to finance scores of special provisions. Scaling back the rate reductions from 30 to 23 percent financed at least $30 billion in new or expanded tax preferences. Second, the usual mechanisms for regulating the growth of tax preferences were absent in 1981. Although President Reagan threatened to veto any bill that offered too little tax reduction, he never objected to the creation of new tax preferences. In fact, the administration sparked the explosion of tax preferences and helped to legitimate their use when it first created preference items for the explicit purpose of attracting conservative Democrats.[33] The Ways and Means Committee was also in no position to control the legislative process as it usually did. When the committee reported a bill that was less generous than that which the administration had proposed, the administration first campaigned to overturn the committee's bill on the House floor and then successfully substituted its own version. With neither the president nor Ways and Means protecting the general interest, legislators competed with each other to create and expand group benefits.

Congress also accepted one amendment that altered fundamentally the politics of taxation. The amendment, first approved by the Senate and later incorporated into the House bill, required that the income tax system be indexed to offset the effects of inflation.[34] This provision eliminated the mechanism that for seventy years had allowed taxes to in-

33. William Greider, *Education of David Stockman and Other Americans* (New York: Dutton, 1982), p. 51.

34. On the effort to index the income tax, see R. Kent Weaver, *Automatic Government: The Politics of Indexation* (Washington, D.C.: Brookings Institution, 1988), pp. 191–210.

crease without legislators ever having to vote to increase them. The support for the provision was largely ideological. Conservatives wanted to lock in the low rates and the tax preferences that they were about to enact, while liberals wanted to preserve their flexibility to create or expand expenditure programs in the future. This single amendment made the subsequent politics of taxation vastly more contentious. Once it became clear that Congress had cut taxes excessively in 1981 and created the largest peacetime deficit in American history, legislators were forced to consider the possibility of raising taxes. Legislators could no longer wait for inflation to erase their errors; they now had to choose between tolerating massive deficits or voting to increase taxes.

Congress twice chose to increase taxes. It passed the Tax Equity and Fiscal Responsibility Act of 1982, raising $27 billion annually, and the Deficit Reduction Act of 1984, which yielded another $23 billion annually. Legislators managed to increase taxes by carefully hiding their tracks on the specific tax provisions and packaging everything together as explicit economic policy (see Chapter 7). Legislators struggled to avoid direct association with specific tax provisions by using the full array of procedural strategies for avoiding traceability. When the House found itself unable to write a tax bill in 1982, it not only renounced its constitutional prerogative to originate all revenue measures, it also agreed to go directly to conference without ever considering the Senate's bill.[35] House members thus escaped frequent votes on the bill and simply had to vote to accept the conference report. Both tax bills raised revenue by adjusting or eliminating scores of tax preferences. Legislators drafted these bills behind closed doors so that those who would suffer the loss of specific preferences could not trace their pain to legislators' individual actions. Legislators then voted on these two bills as complete packages, no doubt hoping that citizens would interpret their actions as fiscally necessary steps to reduce the deficit rather than as the direct cause of citizens' loss of group benefits.

THE POLITICS OF TAX REFORM

Tax reform was never politically popular on Capitol Hill. Legislators might admire the idea of a tax system with low rates and no tax

35. Pamela Fessler, "House Sends Tax Bill Directly to Conference," *Congressional Quarterly Weekly Report* 40 (July 31, 1982): 1808.

preferences, but few believed that it was politically advantageous to replace a tax code supplying benefits to virtually every group in society with one that explicitly rejected the notion of group benefits. While economists argued that a reformed system would be simultaneously more efficient and more equitable, most legislators remained convinced that it was politically reckless to vote in favor of dismantling the existing system.[36]

Most previous efforts to reform the tax system consisted of proposals to terminate a few specific tax preferences. Such proposals were politically unworkable. The problem was that eliminating a single provision could neither make the system noticeably more equitable nor could it generate much revenue. The costs of termination, however, were very noticeable. Legislators feared that those denied their usual group benefits would exact their revenge at the polls, while the beneficiaries of tax reform would be unlikely to notice whatever small gains they might derive from a better tax system. President Carter attempted to broaden the attack by proposing the elimination of a larger collection of tax preferences, including the infamous three-martini lunch. His effort was no more successful, for the general benefits were still imperceptible to most citizens. Congress not only rejected the president's proposal, it used the occasion to create several brand-new tax preferences.

In 1985 President Reagan proposed a bill that was far more ambitious than previous reform efforts.[37] It promised dramatically lower rates for individuals (15, 25, and 35 percent) in exchange for eliminating or restricting many of the most popular deductions, including those for state and local taxes and for interest expenses beyond those incurred for a primary residence. Some of the deductions offered for sacrifice had been part of the tax code since its inception in 1913. The plan also promised lower corporate tax rates in exchange for eliminating the investment tax credit and various other special tax provisions. Sixteen months later Congress surprised most observers and passed a bill that went *beyond* the president's proposal. The final bill reduced rates for individuals to 15 and 28 percent and eliminated many additional tax

36. On economists' arguments, see Joseph A. Pechman (ed.), *The Promise of Tax Reform* (Washington, D.C.: Brookings Institution, 1984); Albert Ando, Marshall E. Blume, and Irwin Friend, *The Structure and Reform of the U.S. Tax System* (Cambridge: MIT Press, 1985); and David F. Bradford, *Untangling the Income Tax* (Cambridge: Harvard University Press, 1986).

37. It resembled most closely the Bradley-Gephardt plan, introduced by Senator Bill Bradley (D., N.J.) and Representative Richard Gephardt (D., Mo.) in 1982.

preferences that were not even on the president's list.[38] Among other things, Congress repealed the special exclusion for capital gains, eliminated most miscellaneous deductions, and restricted tax-free contributions to individual retirement accounts.

Why would Congress enact comprehensive tax reform after years of rejecting less ambitious reforms? Why would legislators, who had long enjoyed creating group benefits, suddenly agree to terminate those group benefits? The puzzle is genuine, for experts on the politics of taxation were practically unanimous in arguing that fundamental reform was politically impossible.[39] How, then, did coalition leaders accomplish this impossible dream?

A complete explanation for tax reform would begin by explaining why Senator Bill Bradley (D., N.J.) first championed this lonely cause in 1982, why President Reagan adopted the cause as his own in 1985, why Representative Dan Rostenkowski (D., Ill.) and Senator Robert Packwood (R., Ore.) chose to become advocates of tax reform after many years of helping to create tax preferences, and why dozens of other legislators volunteered their time, energy, and strategic talents to the task.[40] My own explanation skips over the reasons these individuals chose to become coalition leaders, for their reasons are already well known.[41] My aim is to show how these leaders went about building a

38. There is also a marginal rate of 33 percent. Essentially this five-point surcharge is used to phase out first the 15 percent tax rate and then the personal exemption for upper-income taxpayers. Even including this surcharge, no one pays a rate higher than 28 percent on total taxable income.

39. Writing in 1985, just as the president's proposal was unveiled, John Witte foresaw little chance for genuine tax reform. Several years earlier Eismeier concluded that "tax reform remains a product with no market." See Witte, *Politics and Development of the Federal Income Tax*, pp. 385–386; and Theodore J. Eismeier, "The Political Economy of Tax Reform" (paper presented at the annual meeting of the American Political Science Association, September, 1979), p. 19. See also George F. Break and Joseph A. Pechman, *Federal Tax Reform: The Impossible Dream?* (Washington, D.C.: Brookings Institution, 1975), pp. 13–18.

40. The best account of tax reform is especially good on these individual decisions. See Jeffrey H. Birnbaum and Alan S. Murray, *Showdown at Gucci Gulch: Lawmakers, Lobbyists, and the Unlikely Triumph of Tax Reform* (New York: Vintage, 1987).

41. My own knowledge of tax reform comes largely from reading the daily accounts in the *New York Times, Washington Post*, and *Wall Street Journal* during 1985 and 1986, the weekly accounts in the *Congressional Quarterly Weekly Report*, and Birnbaum and Murray's book, which was itself based on their reporting for the *Wall Street Journal*. After writing the first draft of this chapter, I also profited from reading the manuscript for Timothy J. Conlan, Margaret T. Wrightson, and David R. Bean's *Taxing Choices: The Politics of Tax Reform* (Washington, D.C.: CQ Press, 1989).

winning coalition, how they drew on the standard repertoire of strategies outlined in Chapter 5, and how they shaped strategies to protect legislators from electoral repercussions.[42]

Coalition leaders employed virtually every strategy in the book to advance the cause of tax reform. Although my own emphasis is on leaders' procedural and modification strategies, it is also true that strategies of persuasion were essential to the effort. From the very beginning, coalition leaders worked to persuade citizens, legislators, and the press that the current tax system was both inequitable and inefficient and that everyone would profit from a system with lower rates and fewer tax preferences. Although their efforts were probably more effective in undermining support for the current tax system than they were in creating broad popular support for the president's or any other reform plan, they nevertheless made it riskier for legislators to champion the status quo and made change seem more attractive.

Coalition leaders quickly discovered that comprehensive tax reform was easier to achieve than incremental reform. Whereas a proposal to eliminate or reduce a few tax preferences could offer only imperceptible general benefits, such as a minor rate reduction or a modest revenue increase, comprehensive reform offered dramatically lower tax rates that everyone could appreciate. This fact helped transform the politics of the situation. Rather than pitting a few groups with a great deal at stake against an indifferent general public with virtually nothing at stake, the new plan forced people to consider whether they were better off with high rates and lots of loopholes or with lower rates and fewer loopholes. The new lower rates became the principal attraction of tax reform. At several stages in the process when it appeared that the will toward reform was faltering, coalition leaders managed to reignite the reformist flame by offering even lower rates in exchange for terminating additional tax preferences.[43]

The general approach of asking legislators to support comprehensive

42. Birnbaum and Murray's excellent journalistic account of tax reform also leaves plenty of work for political scientists. After discussing why the House passed tax reform, they conclude that "the House bill had shown that *under the right conditions*, members of Congress would cast a vote for a tax bill that was in the general interest, even though it went against the wishes of legions of powerful lobbyists. It showed that, *under the right circumstances*, the special interests could be defeated." Unfortunately, Birnbaum and Murray never specify what those conditions or circumstances might be. They describe the conditions of the moment, but they do not generalize about those conditions. *Showdown at Gucci Gulch*, p. 175 (emphasis mine).

43. This occurred most dramatically in the Senate Finance Committee when Senator Packwood brought tax reform back to life by proposing a top rate of 25 percent—half the

tax reform rather than chiseling away at tax preferences one at a time was identical to the approach that the Reagan administration used in 1981 to persuade legislators to eliminate $35 billion in expenditure programs as part of its economic recovery program (see Chapter 7). In both cases legislators began to feel pressure for terminating group benefits only after the general benefits were made visible. In both cases coalition leaders had to eliminate lots of group benefits in order to make the general benefits visible.

Coalition leaders were political realists. They made no attempt to reform the system completely, either by enacting a brand-new tax code or by eliminating all tax preferences. Instead they drafted a bill that was reformist in tone but one that also reflected the political realities of coalition building. They may have modeled their bill after a pure reform plan, but long before they asked elected politicians to support the bill they made hundreds of modifications. Their strategies of modification are evident in Bradley's original bill, in the two versions drafted by the administration, and in the various plans put forth by Rostenkowski and Packwood in their respective tax-writing committees.

Coalition leaders worked especially hard to guarantee that tax reform would not increase most people's taxes. In fact, the final bill offered 80 percent of all individual taxpayers a tax cut, averaging 6.1 percent each.[44] The aim was not so much to convince citizens that they would profit from tax reform and then hope that these citizens would pressure legislators to support the bill, for that is not how most legislators make decisions.[45] The intent was to protect legislators from electoral repercussions. Legislators could vote in favor of tax reform without fear that their votes would come back to haunt them when constituents filed their next returns. Most constituents would never bear any net costs from tax reform and, thus, would have no incentive to look for anyone to blame.

---

current rate—just after the committee had scuttled a less ambitious plan. Ibid., pp. 204–213.

44. "Highlights of the Tax Bill," *New York Times* (August 18, 1986): A1.

45. If that were how legislators made decisions, tax reform would never have passed. Just before Congress completed action on the bill, a New York Times/CBS News Poll revealed that only 11 percent of Americans expected to pay lower taxes under the new plan, while 36 percent expected to pay more. Even among the 13 percent who claimed to have heard or read a lot about the bill, only 17 percent believed the bill would reduce their taxes while 50 percent expected an increase. See Adam Clymer, "Doubt Found on Fairness and Cuts," *New York Times* (June 25, 1986): D7.

The reductions for 80 percent of taxpayers were financed by modest increases for the remaining 20 percent of individual taxpayers and a massive increase in corporate taxes. The increases for individual taxpayers had to be modest. If they had been large, they might have created an angry minority with strong incentives for electoral retribution.[46] In fact, most taxpayers faced increases of only a few percent. The very small minority who faced large increases consisted of those who enjoyed above-average tax preferences and who had used these provisions to shelter much of their income from taxation. Proponents also endeavored to avoid redistribution across income classes, lest legislators view the bill through ideological lenses. The redistribution in the bill was largely within income classes (from those who enjoyed above-average tax preferences to those who enjoyed few) and from corporate taxpayers to individual taxpayers.[47] The final bill reduced tax liabilities for individuals by $24 billion annually and increased corporate taxes by an identical amount.

Increasing corporate taxes by 40 percent would ordinarily be a difficult feat. It helped that the 1981 tax bill had been so generous to corporations that the entire corporate tax was in danger of extinction. Corporate income taxes as a percentage of GNP had declined from 4.2 percent in 1960, 3.3 percent in 1970, and 2.4 percent in 1980, to a minuscule 1.1 percent in 1983.[48] It also helped that a conservative Republican administration was proposing the corporate tax increase. No one could be accused of being antibusiness with President Reagan leading the parade. The cause gathered momentum when a labor-funded research

46. For a while it appeared that the bill would increase individual taxes by about $29 billion during the first year and that the tax cut would not take effect until the second year. Most taxpayers would have discovered this unpleasant news just as they filed their 1987 returns in April 1988. Although most senators were willing to tolerate this short-term problem, House members, who had to face the electorate just a few months later, were adamant that the problem had to be fixed. Senator Robert Dole, who expected to be competing in presidential primaries in April 1988, also worried that such a tax increase would create a backlash against the bill's authors. Despite the costs, the conferees found the funds to eliminate the first-year increase. See Birnbaum and Murray, *Showdown at Gucci Gulch*, pp. 270–271.

47. The provision removing six million low-income families from the tax rolls was redistributive but completely noncontroversial, for it merely restored a long-standing policy that inflation had gradually eroded.

48. U.S., Office of Management and Budget, *Historical Tables: Budget of the United States Government, FY88* (Washington, D.C.: Government Printing Office, 1987), table 2.3.

group published a report demonstrating that 128 major corporations, including General Electric, General Dynamics, Boeing, Lockheed, Dow Chemical, and W. R. Grace, paid no federal incomes taxes during at least one of the years between 1981 and 1983, despite $57 billion in profits.[49] The media covered the report extensively. Although real estate firms, basic manufacturing industries, and defense contractors—the principal beneficiaries of corporate tax preferences—lobbied heavily against the bill, their claims were undermined by stories that portrayed them as tax cheats who refused to bear their fair share of the burden. The cause accelerated when many retail, wholesale, high-tech, and service firms began lobbying for the bill. These corporations had few tax preferences to shield them from the current 46 percent rate, and they would profit handsomely if the rates were reduced. Finally, many proponents reminded legislators that citizens vote, corporations do not. Although eventually corporate taxes are passed on to citizens in their roles as consumers and shareholders, their "payment" is indirect and therefore untraceable to legislators' actions, whereas an increase in citizens' own taxes would be directly traceable.

The real danger on the corporate side was related to tax preferences, not tax rates. Most corporations were interested in retaining whatever tax preferences benefited their specific industries, and given how much their political action committees contributed to congressional campaigns, they had every reason to expect that legislators would defend their interests. Coalition leaders dealt with this problem by making several strategic modifications, but even more importantly by adopting procedural strategies that made it difficult for corporations to blame specific legislators for their loss of group benefits.

Coalition leaders tinkered repeatedly with the list of tax preferences to be sacrificed and the list to be saved.[50] These modifications were political, not principled, and were designed to maximize support for the entire package. Coalition leaders quickly learned that a reform bill needed to be geographically neutral in order to survive all the legislative hurdles. The president proposed eliminating the deduction for state and local taxes, but this provision affected disproportionately states with higher taxes (such as New York). Legislators from these states who sat

49. Dale Russakoff, "The Day the Tax Bill Was Born," *Washington Post National Weekly Edition* (July 14, 1986): 14–15.

50. For convenient tables listing the tax preferences included or excluded from various versions of the tax bill, see the *New York Times* (November 25, 1985): D10; (May 8, 1986): D23; and (August 18, 1986): B7.

on the tax-writing committees stood together and refused to support any package that did not retain this deduction.[51] Legislators from oil-producing states were equally stubborn in demanding the retention of tax preferences for the petroleum industry. Although coalition leaders failed to terminate any major tax preferences that were geographically concentrated, they were far more successful in eliminating those that were geographically dispersed. Legislators on the tax-writing committees could protect but a limited number of tax preferences without undermining the entire bill. They quite naturally chose to protect geographic benefits, lest they be accused of neglecting their constituents, while allowing coalition leaders to terminate dozens of group benefits that were geographically dispersed. Many legislators may have wished to help the real estate, financial, and restaurant industries, but none had a powerful reason to demand protection for these industries as their price for supporting the whole bill.

The reform proponents also insisted that the bill must be revenue neutral. This helped to keep the focus on tax reform and away from such ideologically charged and contentious issues as how large a deficit the economy could tolerate or how to reduce the already massive deficit. The bill was equally imperiled from both sides. One threat was that those who sought to reduce the deficit would transform a reform bill into a tax increase. This transformation would not only undermine legislators' ability to deliver tax cuts to 80 percent of their constituents, it would also drive away those legislators who refused to be associated with any tax increase. The second threat was that legislators would continually attach small amendments to save their favorite tax preferences. Many legislators might support the individual amendments, each of which would appear costless, and then refuse to be associated with the final bill because it would produce a large increase in the deficit. The pledge of revenue neutrality, vigorously enforced by the central coalition leaders, eliminated both threats.

Coalition leaders created a bill that was political feasible by minimizing the number of taxpayers who would pay more taxes and by keeping the whole bill revenue neutral, distributionally neutral, and geographically neutral. None of these three principles were firmly established on day one. Coalition leaders discovered their political necessity along the way, as they tested the waters with different versions of the bill. Democratic leaders in the House originally attempted to draft a bill that bene-

---

51. Birnbaum and Murray, *Showdown at Gucci Gulch*, pp. 128–132.

fited middle-income taxpayers at the expense of the rich, but they abandoned the effort when it became clear that redistribution diminished the support for tax reform. Several senators learned the same lesson when they attempted to use tax reform to reduce the deficit. Coalition leaders eventually established these principles to keep the choice facing legislators relatively simple—between a tax system with high rates and lots of preferences and one with low rates and fewer preference items.

Despite the fact that the reform bill eliminated scores of tax preferences, it was hardly squeaky clean. The final bill included nearly 700 transition rules with a five-year cost of $11 billion.[52] Transition rules are special clauses that exempt particular taxpayers from general provisions in a tax bill. One provision allowed the city of Memphis to build a parking garage with tax-exempt bonds, while another allowed Pan Am to continue claiming the investment tax credit for future purchases of aircraft. Transition rules were especially useful for keeping the tax-writing committees united. Senator Packwood, for example, achieved the unanimous support of the Finance Committee for reporting his bill to the floor only after he announced that there would be "no transition rules unless you vote for the bill."[53] Although these new tax preferences violated the spirit of tax reform, such favors were essential for holding the coalition together. In any event, the new tax preferences, most of which were one-time benefits rather than permanent entitlements, cost but a small fraction of what the old preference items cost (approximately $60 billion annually).[54]

This account shows how coalition leaders designed a bill that was politically feasible. It was politically attractive because it offered large rate reductions for all taxpayers and a genuine tax reduction for 80 percent of all individual taxpayers. The bill also had substantial liabilities. It increased corporate taxes by $24 billion, and many corporations worked either to defeat the bill or to alter its impact. It also terminated lots of group benefits for both individual and corporate taxpayers. Even taxpayers who would profit from lower rates and fewer tax preferences would profit even more if they could manage to save a few more of their favorite tax preferences.

52. "Congress Enacts Sweeping Overhaul of Tax Law," *Congressional Quarterly Almanac, 1986* 42 (1987): 524.

53. David Rosenbaum, "Tax Writers Discover Little Favors Mean a Lot," *New York Times* (May 9, 1986): D4. See also David Rosenbaum, "The Favors of Rostenkowski: Tax Revision's Quid Pro Quo," *New York Times* (November 27, 1985): A1.

54. Birnbaum and Murray, *Showdown at Gucci Gulch*, p. 288.

Enacting such a delicately balanced bill required the most careful procedural strategies. The fundamental problem was that most legislators wanted to be counted in favor of the general benefits associated with tax reform without being blamed for the group costs associated with terminating specific tax preferences. Legislators who were asked to vote publicly on terminating specific tax preferences had to consider the possibility that the beneficiaries of those preferences might trace their loss of group benefits to legislators' individual votes. To forestall this possibility, coalition leaders had to weaken the traceability chain for group costs either by eliminating the identifiable actions that produce costs or by making legislators' individual contributions as nearly invisible as possible.

Coalition leaders relied on the full array of procedural strategies in an effort to weaken the traceability chain, including drafting an omnibus bill, meeting in secret, delegating politically difficult decisions to those who would suffer the least, avoiding recorded votes, and adopting restrictive rules. The decision to push for a single omnibus bill rather than a long series of incremental reforms was essential to the effort, for it kept legislators' eyes focused on the general benefits. The strategic problem was to write an omnibus bill without asking either committee members or rank-and-file legislators to take public positions on the specific provisions. Masking individual responsibility proved to be more troublesome at the committee stage. In fact, both tax-writing committees became laboratories for demonstrating the importance of proper procedures when legislators are imposing group costs on their constituents. Each committee first attempted to write a reform bill in public but soon discovered that sunshine was incompatible with reform. Each committee then devised procedures for masking individual responsibility and eventually delegated substantial authority to its chairman or to special task forces. In the end, each committee managed to approve an omnibus bill that was a genuine reform.

After spending the summer of 1985 holding hearings on tax reform and taking testimony from hundreds of interest groups, the House Ways and Means Committee settled down in early October to draft a bill. Although the committee decided to meet in closed session to hide from these very same interest groups, closed doors proved to be insufficient protection. All that the proponents of a specific tax preference had to do to pressure committee members to retain a favorite tax preference was to demand a recorded vote. By creating an identifiable action for which committee members had to choose sides, proponents guaranteed that legislators could be held accountable for the loss of group benefits. Repeatedly committee members demanded roll-call votes on specific tax preferences, and just as regularly their colleagues voted to retain them.[55] Less than two weeks after starting, it became clear that the committee could not draft a reform bill in any sort of public arena. The final showdown occurred on October 15, when the committee voted both to restore the charitable deduction for taxpayers who do not itemize deductions and to *expand* the deduction that banks take for reserves to cover future losses. The latter amendment would have reduced revenues over five years by $5 billion more than current law allowed and nearly $8 billion more than the reform proposal would allow.[56]

Chairman Rostenkowski eventually decided to draft a bill outside the committee room. He personally negotiated deals with some committee members, offering to retain a few of their favorite tax preferences (such as the deduction for state and local taxes) in exchange for their unwavering support of tax reform. He also delegated many of the most contentious issues to twelve task forces that met in secret, assigning each one a revenue target but leaving the details to the task force members. The full committee then received the reports of the task forces behind closed doors and decided to accept most of their decisions without any recorded votes. By masking individual responsibility, the committee was able to report out a reform bill. The committee's bill reduced tax rates a bit less than the president's bill had and eliminated a different combination of tax preferences, but it was a genuine reform.

The House offered very agreeable floor procedures for approving an omnibus bill that imposed costs on dozens of groups in society, for the long tradition in the House had been to consider a complicated tax bill under a closed rule prohibiting amendments. In this case the House Rules Committee proposed a restrictive rule that allowed only two technical amendments plus a Republican-sponsored substitute. Initially, the House rejected the restrictive rule, 223 to 202, as Republicans vented their frustration at being excluded from most of the drafting sessions. After a week of intense lobbying by the administration, the House approved a new rule that was virtually identical to the first and then approved the entire reform bill by a voice vote.[57]

55. Ibid., pp. 121–125.

56. Pamela Fessler, "Panel Votes Breaks for Banks, Charitable Gifts," *Congressional Quarterly Weekly Report* (October 19, 1985): 2102–2103.

57. The lack of a recorded vote on final passage was a genuine accident and not part of an attempt to hide behind the anonymity of a voice vote. The opponents simply failed to

The Senate Finance Committee then proceeded to replicate the experience of the Ways and Means Committee. The committee first directed its chairman to draft a new bill that the committee could use as the basis for action. Unfortunately, after Senator Packwood introduced his draft, the committee conducted its markup session in public and allowed recorded votes on most amendments. Once again the defenders of specific tax preferences demanded recorded votes on individual items marked for extinction, and once again committee members voted to restore most of them.[58] The committee approved amendments costing $10 billion during the first week of deliberations and $19 billion during the second week—and all this before members reached some of the larger and more controversial issues. With the committee voting to retain most of the current law and with the revenue loss mounting, Senator Packwood suspended the markup session.

Senator Packwood then met privately with six reform-minded senators and drafted a new plan that eliminated more tax preferences than the president's proposal had and pushed rates even lower. The entire committee then reviewed the plan behind closed doors while Packwood kept revising it to meet their objections. Only after committee members were comfortable with the plan did the committee hold any public sessions. In its very first decision the committee agreed that all amendments to the bill must be revenue neutral. This agreement prevented senators from restoring tax preferences one at a time, with each amendment appearing relatively costless. Instead it required that anyone proposing to restore one tax preference must simultaneously propose to eliminate another in order to finance it. By pitting group interests against group interests, rather than group interests against the general interest, this procedure made it difficult to devise acceptable amendments. After approving several minor amendments, the committee approved the entire plan 20 to 0.

Unlike the House, the Senate does not ordinarily consider tax bills under restrictive rules that limit amendments. Senators take pride in their right to talk forever and amend forever. Once again the greatest danger to reform was that senators would demand roll-call votes on amendments that would restore specific tax preferences. To counter this threat, Senator Packwood first obtained agreement from senators

demand a roll-call vote in the short interval between the voice vote and the final gavel. See Birnbaum and Murray, *Showdown at Gucci Gulch*, pp. 174–175.

58. Ibid., pp. 199–203.

that each floor amendment must be revenue neutral.[59] Although the Senate still considered eighty-seven amendments and conducted twenty-four roll-call votes, the stipulation of revenue neutrality kept the bill from unraveling. None of the adopted amendments violated the bill's emphasis on reform nor affected the tax rates. After three weeks of debate, the Senate passed the committee's bill virtually intact, 97 to 3.

Four months later, after long and difficult negotiations between House and Senate conferees, Congress approved a plan that grafted portions of the House bill onto the framework of the Senate bill. Once again legislators were reluctant to become associated with specific provisions, so the entire conference was held behind closed doors. Senator Packwood explained why secrecy was so essential to the conference in an observation that suggests full appreciation for the notion of traceability:

> When we're in the sunshine, as soon as we vote, every trade association in the country gets out their mailgrams and their phone calls in twelve hours, and complains about the members' votes. But when we're in the back room, the senators can vote their conscience. They vote for what they think is good for the country. Then they can go out to the lobbyists and say: "God, I fought for you. I did everything I could. But Packwood just wouldn't give in, you know. It's so damn horrible."[60]

In fact, the conference delegated some of the most difficult issues to Chairmen Rostenkowski and Packwood, who together worked out a grand compromise. Individual conferees could therefore claim with greater than usual force that *they* weren't responsible for the loss of specific group benefits. The House approved the conference report 292 to 136, and the Senate concurred 74 to 23.

These procedural strategies *allowed* legislators to reform the tax sys-

---

59. The basic agreement on revenue neutrality was buttressed by the Budget and Impoundment Control Act of 1974, which allowed any senator to raise a point of order against the consideration of a measure that would decrease revenues if Congress had not yet adopted its annual budget resolution. Although this prohibition could be overturned by a majority vote waiving the point of order, it was much easier to defend a procedural vote of this kind than it was to defend the subsequent amendment restoring group benefits. Only one senator challenged the agreement by proposing an unbalanced amendment, but the Senate refused, 54 to 39, to allow its consideration. See "Congress Enacts Sweeping Overhaul of Tax Law," *Congressional Quarterly Almanac, 1986* 42 (1987): 515–516.

60. Birnbaum and Murray, *Showdown at Gucci Gulch*, p. 260.

tem, but they did not *force* legislators to do so. At each stage legislators had to agree to tie their own hands, and most of their decisions to limit the range of choice were unaffected by electoral calculations. When legislators decided to meet in secrecy, to delegate difficult decisions to the chairmen, to prohibit amendments, or to require that amendments be revenue neutral, they were declaring that they were personally in favor of tax reform. If legislators had been personally opposed to tax reform, all they had to do was insist that the sun must shine on any tax bill, knowing that sunshine would have destroyed tax reform. It is hardly surprising that many legislators were disgusted with the current tax system, but it is a healthy reminder about the limits of electoral explanations to recall that legislators' own personal policy preferences were necessary conditions for tax reform. If legislators had not chosen to accept these extraordinary procedures in order to weaken the traceability chain for group effects, the electoral connection would have prevented many of them from ever supporting tax reform.

There can also be little doubt that these procedures were essential for tax reform. Both the House and Senate tax-writing committees attempted to write a reform bill first without such restrictions and then with them. In each case, the initial lack of any restrictive procedures helped to generate an increase in tax preferences; only with the introduction of such procedures were legislators able to approve tax reform. Seldom do politicians run identical experiments in both House and Senate for the sole benefit of social scientists. When they do, our debt to them is enormous.

9

Energy Policy

Energy policy was a major item on the congressional agenda throughout the 1970s. Energy supplies, which had once seemed cheap and plentiful, were suddenly expensive and hard to obtain. Petroleum shortages first emerged after the Arab oil embargo in 1973 and again during the Iranian revolution in 1979; each resulted in long lines at gasoline stations across America. Natural gas shortages appeared in 1970 and grew more slowly; eventually they became so severe that schools and industries were forced to close in eleven northern states during 1976 and 1977. Energy prices increased more rapidly during this decade than ever before. The Organization of Petroleum Exporting Counties quadrupled the world price of oil in 1973, and then tripled it again in 1979 and 1980. Energy prices as a whole increased twice as fast as other consumer prices.

These events created social and economic problems that became political problems when people looked to Washington for solutions. If government did not "solve" any of these problems, it was not for lack of trying. Congress and the president probably devoted more time to energy problems during the decade than to any other domestic issue. Congress enacted dozens of bills that addressed the energy crisis directly and inserted energy provisions in bills in many other areas, ranging from transportation, housing, and the environment to taxes, antitrust, and foreign policy.

Only a robust theory can explain congressional actions on energy during the 1970s, for Congress enacted contradictory policies and switched course many times. It enacted oil price controls early in the decade, rejected various plans for decontrolling oil in the middle of the decade, and finally decontrolled prices at the decade's close. Natural gas went through a similar cycle as Congress first strengthened existing regulations, then resisted attempts at decontrol, and finally deregulated natural gas prices. Legislators rejected and then ultimately embraced a tax on the windfall profits derived from domestically produced petroleum. Explaining these disparate actions with the standard interest group or ideological models is not very rewarding. Neither the constellations of interests nor the ideological makeup of Congress changed significantly during this period. What changed was the way citizens, experts, and politicians saw the problems, and the way coalition leaders structured the legislative situation so that legislators could eventually discard existing approaches and replace them with fundamentally new schemes.

Energy politics was highly contentious throughout the 1970s in part because the stakes were so high. Energy was a large part of the national economy even before OPEC raised the stakes. In 1970 energy expenditures constituted 8.1 percent of the gross national product.[1] OPEC's unilateral actions in raising world petroleum prices had the immediate effect of transferring an additional 2 percent of American GNP to oil exporting countries.[2] As the prices of other domestic fuels then increased to match world petroleum prices, energy became a far larger component of the American economy. By 1980 energy expenditures constituted 13.6 percent of GNP—up a whopping 5.5 percentage points and $100 billion in a single decade.[3] Much of the conflict of the 1970s concerned how the gains and losses associated with this massive sectoral shift would be apportioned within American society. Reallocating $100 billion in costs and benefits would be a difficult feat in any political system. It was especially difficult for the United States government because Congress had to approve any plan. Congress hates to impose large and direct costs on anyone; imposing $100 billion in costs on most of American society was practically unthinkable.

A completely free domestic market in energy could have reallocated these costs almost immediately. Markets are wonderfully speedy devices for solving even the most painful allocation problems. In a completely free market the prices of domestically produced fuels would have

1. U.S., Bureau of the Census, *Statistical Abstract of the United States, 1987* (Washington, D.C.: Government Printing Office, 1986), pp. 416, 545.

2. The value of American petroleum imports increased from 0.3 percent of GNP in 1973 to 2.3 percent in 1980, with little change in the volume of those imports. Ibid., pp. 416, 683.

3. Ibid., pp. 416, 545.

risen in step with the world price of oil. Energy consumers would have immediately paid much higher prices for all forms of energy, while energy producers, both foreign and domestic, would have collected huge profits. Foreign producers did, of course, reap huge profits; military action aside, there was little the United States government could do to thwart them. Domestic producers were not so fortunate, because most domestic energy markets were already tightly regulated by the federal government when the energy crisis struck.

This chapter focuses on the politics of oil and natural gas during the decade of the 1970s. To gain some perspective on these issues I first show how the United States found itself in the predicament of having simultaneous shortages of its two major fuels. The background details are crucial, for these twin shortages had as much to do with failures in American policy as they did with the actions of OPEC. Past actions not only contributed to the problems, they also limited the range of politically feasible solutions.

THE POLITICS OF OIL

The federal government has a long history of regulating the petroleum industry. Initially, regulation tended to serve the interests of the industry. In 1935 Congress created a domestic oil cartel to restrict production and then allowed it to persist for more than three decades. Twenty years later it approved a quota system that severely restricted oil imports and then allowed these quotas to persist until 1973. Both sets of actions served producer interests at the expense of consumer interests. Then the tide shifted. Throughout the 1970s Congress favored consumers over producers. The government established an elaborate system of price controls for petroleum and petroleum products that sacrificed the industry's profits for consumers' short-term interests in lower prices. At the end of the decade Congress enacted yet another new policy—one with a relatively neutral impact on the various group interests.

This section attempts to show why Congress was so slavish to producers' interests for so long and why it suddenly switched sides and favored consumers. My intent is to show how the incidence of costs and benefits at various times affects both how ordinary legislators calculate political consequences and how coalition leaders manage the legislative process in anticipation of these calculations. I also attempt to show how modest changes in policy outcomes can affect the relative power of organized interest groups and inattentive publics.

Prior to 1970, federal regulation of the petroleum industry not only served the interests of that industry directly and exclusively; most regulations were enacted at the industry's specific request.[4] During World War I and again during the 1930s the federal government allowed a committee of producers to regulate both the production and pricing of all petroleum. After the Supreme Court invalidated this approach in 1935, Congress passed the Connally Hot Oil Act and created an Interstate Oil Compact Commission to "coordinate" the production controls that oil-producing states had adopted. All of these controls were designed to limit the amount of oil produced, lest newly discovered oil reduce the market price of oil and limit the profit margins of established producers. Although advocates usually defended these controls as necessary for conserving a precious natural resource, their intent was to conserve something even more precious—their own profit margins. At this they were quite effective.

Although this regulatory system was an effective means for maintaining oil prices (and industry profits), it could succeed only as long as the United States imported very little oil. In 1949 the United States first became a net importer of oil, and by 1953 imports accounted for 14 percent of consumption.[5] To maintain domestic prices, state regulatory commissions ordered further cuts in domestic production. The cost of production was so much lower in Venezuela and the Middle East that imports seemed likely to capture an ever increasing share of the American market. Oil producers were severely divided over what, if anything, the federal government should do. The major oil companies were happy to watch imports grow, for they were the ones importing the oil and profiting from the lower overseas production costs. On the other hand, the so-called independent producers sought to restrict imports, which were nibbling away at their market shares and profits. Coal producers also favored import restrictions, because cheap residual oil from Venezu-

---

4. For background on American policy toward the petroleum industry, see Gerald D. Nash, *United States Oil Policy, 1890–1964* (Pittsburgh: University of Pittsburgh Press, 1968); David Howard Davis, *Energy Politics*, 3d ed. (New York: St. Martin's Press, 1982), pp. 59–129; and Richard H. K. Vietor, *Energy Policy in America since 1945* (Cambridge: Cambridge University Press, 1984), pp. 91–145.

5. All data are from the U.S. Department of Energy, as published in Congressional Quarterly, *Energy Policy*, 2d ed. (Washington, D.C.: Congressional Quarterly, 1981), p. 5.

ela had begun to penetrate industrial markets that had long relied on coal.

In 1953 and again in 1955 Congress considered amendments to trade bills that would have limited oil imports to 10 percent of domestic production. Congress defeated both amendments. In 1955 it considered an innocuous-sounding amendment that authorized the president to impose quotas on any article that was "being imported into the United States in such quantities as to threaten to impair the national security." Advocates made it clear (at least to legislators from oil and coal states) that "any article" meant crude oil and residual oil.[6] This amendment sailed through Congress and quickly became Section 7 of the Trade Agreements Extension Act of 1955. From 1956 to 1959 the Eisenhower Administration experimented with various voluntary quotas to restrict oil imports, and then in 1959 it imposed mandatory quotas. These quotas remained the cornerstone of American oil policy until President Nixon removed them in 1973. The quotas not only protected domestic production, they allowed it to increase. Between 1959 and 1972, during a time when the world price of oil was but a fraction of the domestic price, United States production of oil increased by 50 percent.

Why would Congress create and then tolerate a regulatory system that restricted domestic production and kept petroleum prices artificially high? Why would Congress create and then tolerate import quotas that had the same effect? Two standard explanations are unsatisfactory. Those who argue that these events simply prove the power of big business in American politics must face the uncomfortable fact that most large businesses have *not* been able to acquire protection from both domestic and foreign competitors. Moreover, the largest oil companies were opposed to import quotas, so if anything, import quotas demonstrate the power of smaller businesses over bigger businesses. Others argue that these actions simply follow from the immense power of the petroleum industry in American politics, which itself follows from the industry's regional concentration, campaign contributions, and the like. But these arguments also don't explain much. If the industry was so powerful in the 1950s and 1960s, why did it suffer so many defeats in the 1970s? A satisfactory explanation needs to account for the less happy events as well as the steps taken in the 1930s and 1950s that profited the industry so well.

My own explanation begins with the incidence of costs and benefits

6. See "Senators Battle Trade Bill Curbs," *New York Times* (April 30, 1955): 1.

under current and proposed policies and shows how legislators' calculations about the political risks associated with various policies depended on their estimates of who would profit and who would pay. The discovery of vast new oil reserves in Texas during the 1930s and the discovery of vast reserves in the Middle East during the 1950s threatened bankruptcy for many domestic producers. Once challenged, producers were compelled to agitate for governmental relief. Legislators from oil-producing regions had little choice but to support whatever remedies were put before them. Those who opposed production controls or import quotas and who contributed to the eventual bankruptcy of many businesses in their districts would have created a powerful campaign issue that could be used against them—an issue with all the elements required for traceability and retrospective voting: large and perceptible costs, an identifiable governmental action, and visible individual contributions.

Legislators from nonproducing regions heard little from consumers, and most had nothing to fear from retrospective voting. To be sure, consumers did have something at stake, for retail prices would surely have plummeted if Congress had not approved restrictions on production in the 1930s and imports in the 1950s. But consumers seldom expect that the price of anything will plummet, and it is hard to imagine how any challenger could convince them that prices would have dropped dramatically if only their representative had worked to block these interventions in the petroleum market. The causal logic was too complicated to make a good campaign issue. The prospects for retrospective voting were somewhat higher in New England during the 1950s. New England imported more oil than any other region, and thus import quotas had the potential to increase oil prices there. As most politicians know, higher prices that are directly traceable to a legislator's vote make a wonderful campaign issue.

In the 1930s Congress easily sided with petroleum producers, who were facing major losses and who lobbied heavily for governmental relief, rather than with consumers, who were merely forfeiting an opportunity to gain lower energy prices (and who were unlikely to learn about their forgone opportunity anyway). Regulating petroleum production was especially easy in the 1930s, given the range of price and entry regulations that Congress was enacting to protect other industries from the ravages of the Depression. It was far more difficult for Congress to side with petroleum producers in the 1950s. Part of the reason was that import quotas would have imposed particularly large costs on New England, where industrial and commercial firms had been converting from Appalachian coal to Venezuelan residual oil. Lobbyists for the marketers and users of residual oil were quite effective in showing legislators from the Northeast what was at stake.[7] Import quotas also went against the postwar American fascination with free trade. Legislators from non-producing regions had no reason to violate free-trade principles when all of the benefits from quotas would flow to a few producing states. As long as the issue was framed as import quotas versus free trade, quotas were at a severe disadvantage. Congress twice rejected such quotas, in 1953 and 1955.

The breakthrough in establishing oil import quotas was the transformation of the question from one of restricting free trade into one of promoting national security. Few legislators in 1955 could oppose giving the president authority to restrict imports if they "threatened the nation's security."[8] The amendment was sufficiently general (not even mentioning oil, to say nothing of the more controversial residual oil) that it also broke resistance in the Northeast.[9] Legislators from the Northeast had little to fear anyway, for the amendment merely granted the president authority to impose quotas. Delegating politically difficult decisions to the president was a time-honored way of breaking the traceability chain. In this case it ensured that, even if fuel prices were to rise, the price increases could not be traced to a congressional action.

Once established, import quotas were relatively easy to maintain. The status quo has a decided advantage in American politics, and the advantage is even greater for policies that do not require annual congressional review. Federal officials who managed the program adjusted the quotas periodically to maintain supplies and keep prices from increasing. With steady prices, there was little to rouse consumers into action or to stimu-

7. Vietor, *Energy Policy in America*, p. 101.

8. Oil imports did, of course, have implications for national security. No one with an appreciation for the history of World War II can doubt that access to petroleum supplies can be crucial in wartime. Unfortunately, import barriers could guarantee supply only as long as American reserves held out. Import quotas, which amounted to a policy of "drain America first," may have contributed to American security in the 1950s and 1960s, but they surely diminished security in the 1970s and beyond. If security were really the concern, establishing a strategic petroleum reserve would have been more sensible. It would have been far cheaper too.

9. There were no floor votes on the amendment, which is one measure of how non-controversial it had become. In the only roll-call vote on the matter, the Senate Finance Committee approved it 13 to 2.

late legislators to challenge the petroleum industry's privileged position. As domestic reserves became increasingly scarce in the early 1970s, and shortages of heating oil became particularly acute, the Nixon Administration first suspended quotas on crude oil destined for home heating and then abandoned all import quotas in April 1973.

If there was an energy problem between the early 1930s and the late 1960s, it was a problem of excessive oil supplies. Of course, this excess was only a problem for domestic oil producers, who saw their businesses at risk. For consumers it was an enormous opportunity. Oil producers were very effective in demanding protection from foreign competition, while consumers were largely unaware of what opportunities they were missing. By 1970 the tide was turning. Petroleum shortages and rising prices forced legislators to be more attentive to consumer interests and less concerned with the interests of oil producers.

THE REGULATION OF OIL PRICES

The federal government regulated petroleum prices for nearly a decade, from August 1971 to January 1981. Throughout this period the regulatory regime served the interests of consumers quite directly, while domestic oil producers suffered its effects. Why did the federal government switch sides and begin to favor the interests of consumers over producers? Why did this new regulatory regime eventually give way to one that favored neither side explicitly?

The origin of oil price regulation had nothing at all to do with the politics of energy. Price controls were born in an election-year squabble between President Nixon and the Democratic Congress over who should be blamed for the accelerating inflation of 1970. Democratic legislators attempted to insulate themselves from any blame for spiraling inflation by passing a law that gave the president discretionary authority to freeze wages and prices (and then attaching it to a veto-proof defense bill). The president claimed that he would never use such authority, but that hardly mattered. Democratic legislators simply needed to show before the 1970 election that *they* had passed a law outlawing inflation which *he* was unwilling to implement. A year later, however, the tables were turned. President Nixon was preparing to run for reelection, and many people in the administration feared that voters would blame him for inflation. In August 1971, Nixon used his discretionary authority and imposed an economy-wide freeze on all wages and prices.

This ninety-day freeze was then followed by an elaborate federal scheme for administering most wages and prices. After the political crisis had passed and the president was safely reelected, Nixon abandoned the entire regulatory apparatus for setting wages and prices and substituted a new program of voluntary guidelines.

In 1971, when price controls were first established, oil was just another commodity; by 1973 it was a problem commodity. Within weeks of the president's termination of price controls, the price of heating oil jumped 8 to 10 percent.[10] Congress quickly held hearings and pressured the administration to do something. In March 1973 the president singled out oil for special treatment and reimposed mandatory controls. Price controls inevitably create shortages. There were already shortages of heating oil during the winter of 1973; gasoline shortages emerged the following summer. When the Arabs then imposed an oil embargo on the United States in October 1973, Congress responded to what everyone thought was a short-term problem by passing the Emergency Petroleum Allocation Act.[11] This act required that the president establish and administer a mandatory system for allocating all petroleum and petroleum products among regions, refiners, and retailers so that no one would suffer disproportionately.[12]

Thus, the nation acquired strict controls on petroleum prices and allocation almost by accident. No one set out to establish a broad regulatory regime. No interest group lobbied for it. No legislator championed it. Elected politicians were attempting to solve several small problems, not to erect a vast regulatory apparatus. In 1970 the problem was that Democratic legislators wanted to transfer to the president any blame for inflation. In 1972 the problem was that the president needed to make inflation disappear until after the election. In 1973 the problem was the oil embargo, and legislators sought to ensure that no segment of society would suffer unduly.

By 1974 the problem was the regulatory system itself. Although the government was regulating the pricing and allocation of all petroleum in the United States, it had little control over the world price of oil, the domestic production of oil, or the consumption of petroleum products. In effect, it controlled the pipeline, but not how much was pumped in or out. This regulatory system quickly produced an imbalance between

10. Vietor, *Energy Policy in America*, p. 240.

11. "Mandatory Fuel Allocation Program Approved," *Congressional Quarterly Almanac, 1973* 29 (1974): 623–631.

12. It also extended the president's authority for controlling oil prices until 1975.

supply and demand and created recurrent shortages. The government's options were three: (1) decontrol oil prices and allow higher prices to elicit greater supply and dampen demand, (2) administer prices in a way that would mimic market prices, or (3) regulate both the production and consumption of all petroleum and petroleum products. Initially, the government experimented with various combinations of the second and third options. It finally chose complete decontrol in 1979, but only after rejecting that option several times before. Why did Congress choose such a rocky road?

President Ford first proposed removing all controls on the domestic price of oil in 1975 in order to stimulate production and reduce consumption. Under the plan the government would phase out controls over a thirty-month period so that prices would rise gradually. The law allowed the president to decontrol prices unless either the House or Senate vetoed his plan within five days. The House did, in fact, veto Ford's initial plan (262 to 167), and, when Ford then submitted an even more gradual plan for decontrol, the House vetoed it too (228 to 189).[13] Either plan would have produced large increases in the price of both gasoline and heating oil by the time of the 1976 election, and legislators were clearly very uncomfortable with voting for any plan whose costs could be traced so directly to their votes. As it happened, President Ford was also reluctant to be too closely connected with decontrol. For a few days in December he had the complete authority to decontrol all oil instantly, and Congress would have had to pass a brand-new law over *his* veto to reestablish controls.[14] The president declined the opportunity. He much preferred sharing the blame with Congress, for he, too, was up for reelection in 1976.

Congress not only insisted that price controls be retained for another forty months, it extended those controls to "new" oil and forced a rollback of domestic oil prices by more than 12 percent.[15] It was easy to

13. "Extending Oil Price Controls," *Congressional Quarterly Almanac, 1975* 31 (1976): 221.

14. The window of opportunity opened because the law authorizing price controls had expired before Congress and the president had agreed on a temporary extension. In the interim Ford's only option was complete and instantaneous decontrol, however, not the gradual decontrol that he wanted. See Congressional Quarterly, *Energy Policy*, p. 38; and Pietro Nivola, *The Politics of Energy Conservation* (Washington, D.C.: Brookings Institution, 1986), p. 40.

15. "Ford Ends Stalemate, Signs Energy Bill," *Congressional Quarterly Almanac, 1975* 31 (1976): 220–245.

continue controls on old oil—that which was already under production in 1972—because doing so did not alter the incentives to search for new reserves.[16] The Senate voted to continue these controls by an overwhelming 62 to 23. But extending price controls to new oil, which the administration had deliberately left uncontrolled, would have undeniable effects on the willingness of oil companies to explore for new reserves. Even so, the Senate voted to control new oil by a still substantial 54 to 31. In 1975 the United States truly was marching to a different drummer. While the world price of oil was soaring, Congress was voting to *reduce* oil prices in the United States. Most legislators found it politically irresistible to vote for expanding the scope of price controls because they did not want higher energy prices traced to their actions. Policy experts might differentiate between old oil and new oil, but legislators knew that voters would notice only the difference between stable prices and higher prices.

President Carter proposed a different solution in 1977 as part of his National Energy Plan. His Crude Oil Equalization Tax would have gradually lifted controls on new oil, retained all controls on old oil, and imposed a tax on all domestic oil equal to the difference between these controlled prices and the world price of oil.[17] Consumers would pay dearly for all petroleum products and thus would have a powerful incentive to conserve. The only problem was that no one wanted to be associated with imposing such a tax on consumers. Legislators were as reluctant to raise prices with a tax as they were to decontrol prices. Under either scheme, higher prices would be directly traceable to legislators' actions. Moreover, the oil companies were intensely opposed to an equalization tax, since the revenues from such a tax would flow to the government, whereas the revenues from complete decontrol would benefit them. The equalization tax seemed to serve no one's immediate interests, however much it might have served the nation's long-term interest.

Congress was equally unwilling to pass a gasoline tax to encourage conservation. Although it considered several proposals in 1975, 1977, and 1980, ranging from a stiff fifty-cents-per-gallon levy to a modest three-cents-per-gallon tax, it rejected them all. In the five roll-call votes on gasoline taxes, an average of 79 percent of all House members op-

16. Although controls on the price of old oil had no effects on the supply side, they did hinder attempts to reduce the demand for oil by encouraging conservation.

17. "Carter Energy Bill Fails to Clear," *Congressional Quarterly Almanac,* 1977 33 (1978): 708–745; and "Energy Bill: The End of an Odyssey," *Congressional Quarterly Almanac, 1978* 34 (1979): 639–667.

posed any tax increases, no matter how small.[18] Such taxes would have
imposed immediate and direct costs on all motorists, with all costs traceable to legislators' actions, while offering only modest and distant general benefits, as decreased consumption reduced the nation's demand for
foreign oil. Proposals that contain immediate group and geographic
costs and only distant general benefits are inherently unattractive to
legislators who face the electorate biennially.[19]

Congress found itself unable to approve any scheme that would raise
energy prices directly. Removing price controls and imposing energy
taxes were equally unpopular because legislators did not want to be
associated with any mechanism that increased energy prices. Throughout the 1970s legislators did approve many proposals to deal with the
energy crisis. They adopted research programs for every imaginable
alternative fuel, including solar, geothermal, wind, nuclear, and synthetic sources of energy. They created grants and tax credits to encourage individuals, businesses, and institutions to conserve energy. They
forced utilities to switch to coal and automakers to produce more efficient cars. They extended daylight savings time and reduced highway
speeds. They readily approved dozens of programs to encourage energy
production or to discourage its consumption. But legislators refused to
approve any plan that would directly increase energy prices, for such
increases would then be directly traceable to their own actions.

In April 1979 President Carter announced that he intended to use his
administrative discretion to decontrol the price of oil, with price controls
to be lifted gradually between June 1979 and October 1981.[20] The
president took advantage of the fact that the Energy Policy and Conservation Act of 1975 required mandatory controls for forty months (until
June 1979), after which they were discretionary. In exchange for decontrol, he asked Congress to approve a windfall profits tax that would
capture roughly half of the increased profits that oil companies would
earn from decontrolled oil.[21]

18. Nivola, *Politics of Energy Conservation*, p. 217.

19. Congress did pass a five-cents-per-gallon increase in the gasoline tax in 1982, but
this bill was essentially the financing scheme for a major public works bill that involved
the reconstruction and repair of highways and transit facilities across the nation. As such it
promised large and immediate group and geographic benefits and was relatively popular
among voters, interest groups, and legislators. See Nivola, *Politics of Energy Conservation*, pp. 236–241.

20. When President Reagan took office he accelerated the schedule, achieving total
decontrol by February 1981.

21. "Carter and Congress on Energy," *Congressional Quarterly Almanac*, 1979 35
(1980): 605–632.

President Carter succeeded where others had failed in part because he was willing to assume all the blame for increasing petroleum prices. He neither consulted legislators for their views, nor did he ask Congress to endorse his decision. Legislators could, of course, move to reestablish mandatory controls, but against a determined president that would require a two-thirds majority in both House and Senate.[22] House Democrats quickly went on record against the president's decision. At a meeting of the Democratic caucus they voted 138 to 69 to continue controls. Even so, there was little chance of actually reversing the decision. Speaker O'Neill (D., Mass.), who supported continued controls, stated: "We are going through a bit of a charade here because I don't see how it [legislation extending controls] can ever get by a filibuster in the Senate."[23] In a political world that favors the status quo, President Carter gave decontrolled prices the same advantage that controlled prices had enjoyed since 1971. Advocates of mandatory controls, who once profited because their favorite policy was established policy, were suddenly the outsiders. They now had to pass new legislation, and to do so they had to overcome all of the devices that give the status quo such a powerful advantage, ranging from the senatorial filibuster to the presidential veto.

Decontrol was also helped by the events of 1979 and by the growing sense that the United States had done little since the 1973 embargo to insulate itself from foreign actions (oil imports continued to increase throughout the 1970s). The year opened with the Iranian revolution and the temporary shutdown of all Iranian oil production. Within a few months OPEC had doubled the price of oil. By summer long lines had reappeared at gasoline stations across the country. Many legislators began to have doubts about the efficacy of continued controls. Perhaps none was more important than John Dingell (D., Mich.), chairman of the House Commerce Committee's Subcommittee on Energy and Power and a longtime defender of price controls. A year later he said in an interview:

> It was my view that we ought to hold prices down. Then all of a sudden I realized that a lot of the conservation was coming from

22. At first Carter said he would not veto a congressional effort to extend controls, but a few days later he insisted that he would withhold a veto only if Congress passed an equally effective plan to restrain consumption, encourage domestic production, and reduce the nation's reliance on imported oil—something Congress had been unable to do for nearly a decade. See Ann Pelham, "House Democrats Back Oil Price Controls," *Congressional Quarterly Weekly Report* 37 (May 26, 1979): 997–998.

23. Ibid., p. 997.

cost increases. Now I don't like that, but it has provided a far stronger stimulus than anything I have been able to do through the passage of legislation. [Asked if anything in particular had changed his mind, Dingell admitted that personal experience had been a factor.] I moved into a little town-house and it costs me $70 a month to heat it. Then I insulated and caulked to beat hell and double glazed the windows, and all of a sudden it's costing me $40.[24]

Not all legislators underwent a conversion in faith and became strong advocates of decontrol, for many still believed that too direct a connection with increased prices was politically risky; but those who were convinced did chip away at the number of legislators willing to work actively to reestablish controls. Democratic leaders, for example, managed to keep proposals for restoring price controls off the House floor for more than six months.[25] During this time citizens had ample opportunity to blame everyone from Iranian revolutionaries and OPEC to President Carter and the oil companies for rapidly rising oil prices. With blame finally deflected away from Congress, House members voted overwhelmingly in October to leave well enough alone and allow market forces to prevail.

Essential to the strategy of achieving decontrol was its coupling with the windfall profits tax.[26] The latter was a levy on the large profits that oil producers would earn as domestic prices rose to the level of world prices. The president himself needed such a tax lest he be seen as too friendly toward a very unpopular industry, and it was also helpful in persuading several legislators to allow decontrol to take effect. They might have preferred to reestablish controls, but if they couldn't easily accomplish that, then at least they could take credit for imposing a $230 billion tax on the oil industry.[27] Persuading more conservative legislators, and particularly those from producing states, to support the tax required a bit more strategic magic. For once President Carter seemed to have the magic touch. He convinced Russell Long (D., La.), chairman of the

24. Congressional Quarterly, *Energy Policy*, p. 26.

25. James Everett Katz, *Congress and National Energy Policy* (New Brunswick, N.J.: Transaction Books, 1984).

26. See Vietor, *Energy Policy in America*, pp. 258–270; and Christopher Ohman, "The Journey of the Windfall Profits Tax through Congress" (unpublished seminar paper, Princeton University, January 1982).

27. This was the administration's estimate of what the tax would yield over the next decade. The actual revenues were much lower as a consequence of the large drop in world oil prices in the early 1980s.

Senate Finance Committee and longtime champion of the petroleum industry, that a windfall profits tax was the key to continued decontrol. Long told the Finance Committee: "I have no doubt if we don't pass a tax, the president is going to withdraw his decontrol plan. . . . It's like getting old. When you think about the alternative, you don't feel so bad about it."[28]

Many of the major oil companies also accepted some sort of a windfall profits tax as the price they had to pay for decontrol.[29] The House and Senate wrestled with the distributional issues for nearly a year, deciding exactly how the tax would be assessed on various types of oil (Alaskan oil, offshore oil, deep wells, stripper wells, old oil, upper-tier oil, heavy oil, oil owned by Indians, oil owned by state and local governments, production by tertiary recovery, and so on). These were all debates about the group and geographic costs and benefits. Once they were resolved both the House and Senate approved the tax in March 1980.

It would be difficult to argue that the United States pursued a sound oil policy from 1935 to 1981. Beginning in 1935 it created and then tolerated a domestic oil cartel (administered by the states) that restricted the production of oil. This scheme maintained the profits of domestic oil producers while denying consumers any of the benefits of newly discovered oil. Beginning in 1959 it created and then tolerated import quotas that protected domestic producers from foreign competition. Once again the government denied consumers the benefits of lower-priced oil in order to protect producers' profits.[30] For thirty-five years American oil policy delivered enormous benefits to domestic oil producers while imposing equally large costs on American consumers. Then in 1971 the tables were turned. For the next ten years the flow of benefits was reversed and consumers were the beneficiaries. Price controls deprived domestic producers of the profits they would have earned if they could have sold their petroleum at market prices. Consumers saved billions of dollars by buying petroleum products at regulated prices.[31] In 1981 the group benefits were again redirected. Decontrol forced consumers to pay higher prices, while a tax on windfall profits

---

28. Congressional Quarterly, *Energy Policy*, p. 42.

29. Vietor, *Energy Policy in America*, p. 266.

30. Estimates of the annual transfer from consumers to producers range from $4 to $7 billion. See Vietor, *Energy Policy in America*, p. 142.

31. Estimates of the annual transfer from producers to consumers range from $14 to $50 billion. See Joseph P. Kalt, *The Economics and Politics of Oil Price Regulation* (Cambridge: MIT Press, 1981), p. 286.

channeled many of the benefits into governmental rather than corporate coffers.

United States oil policy appears particularly short-sighted if one focuses on the general costs associated with each of these phases. Import quotas amounted to a policy of "drain America first." The United States refused to import oil when it was cheap, preferring to consume its own limited and higher priced reserves. As its own reserves dwindled, it was forced to import oil from what were now very expensive and unstable foreign supplies. Price controls on domestic petroleum also produced enormous general costs. Throughout the 1970s American consumers burned a precious natural resource at a price far below what it cost to replace it (the replacement cost being the price of imported oil). The United States postponed for nearly a decade the transformation to a more energy efficient economy, while it depleted its own reserves and became increasingly dependent on foreign suppliers. All three regulatory schemes also introduced large inefficiencies in the allocation of petroleum by protecting less efficient producers and creating other deadweight losses.[32] Only after 1981 was American policy relatively neutral toward group interests and free of its bias against more general and long-term benefits.

Why would the government adopt policies with such different distributions of group benefits—first serving producer interests, then consumer interests, and then favoring neither? Why would it first design a succession of regulatory schemes that served various group interests at the expense of longer-term general interests, and then replace all three regulatory schemes with a system that intentionally sacrificed group interests for more general interests? Those who believe that regulation always serves the interests of organized producers would have a tough time explaining these shifts. Although they may be able to explain the rise of a domestic cartel in the 1930s and perhaps import quotas in the 1950s, they cannot explain why price controls persisted for a decade or why decontrol was accompanied by a windfall profits tax.

Interest groups are surely a part of the explanation. When legislators hear mostly from interest groups, when those groups speak in unison, and when legislators have no reason to fear the arousal of inattentive publics once a policy is in place, they frequently choose to serve these attentive and organized interests. Interest groups explain exactly one of

32. Kalt estimates the deadweight losses from price controls alone as $1 to $6 billion annually. Ibid., p. 289.

these decisions—the regulation of production in the 1930s. Legislators were pressured by oil producers to do something to save their businesses. Meanwhile they heard nothing from consumers and had no reason to believe that stable (rather than falling) prices would rouse inattentive consumers into action at a subsequent election. Not surprisingly, legislators sided with producers. The situation became more complicated when producers demanded import quotas in the 1950s. Legislators from the Northeast were especially reluctant to support quotas, which would have imposed on their constituents large costs that might have been traceable to their actions. Congress twice rejected import quotas before proponents designed a clever package that broke the traceability chain (by redefining the vote as one on national security and by delegating vague authority to the president). Even though producers eventually acquired quotas, this episode still demonstrates how inattentive publics can shape both the legislative process and its outcomes.

What is more, inattentive publics can *dominate* legislative outcomes, overpowering even the strongest interest groups. Legislators kept extending and renewing price controls, not because ordinary citizens were pressuring them to do so and not because oil producers were inarticulate, but because legislators feared the effects of retrospective voting. Although most citizens were probably unaware of the debates in Congress, their ignorance really didn't matter. Most legislators were very much aware of what citizens could do to them if they voted to eliminate price controls, thereby doubling the price of gasoline and heating oil. Arguments that decontrol would be in the nation's long-term interest carried little weight in the electoral arena. Politicians are seldom rewarded for delivering general benefits in the distant future— especially when they must first impose large and traceable costs in the immediate future.

Arguments that decontrol would serve the nation's long-run interests gradually penetrated the policy-making community. Policy experts, executive officials, and many legislators came to believe that market prices were the best stimulus for both conservation and exploration. For elected politicians, believing in decontrol was the easy part. Working to achieve it required either a reckless form of courage or some careful procedural safeguards that ensured that no one had to make the ultimate political sacrifice. Presidents were not immune to these political calculations. President Ford failed to exploit a small window of opportunity when he could have decontrolled oil with the stroke of a pen. And

President Carter spent several years looking for a more indirect approach before finally biting the bullet in 1979. Legislators then struggled to show how much they were against decontrol without actually blocking what many of them privately favored.

GASOLINE RATIONING

The Arab oil embargo of 1973 convinced many people that the nation needed a system for allocating oil supplies in times of shortage. President Nixon first asked Congress for the authority to allocate oil and ration gasoline in November 1973, three weeks after the embargo was imposed. Despite popular support for gasoline rationing, and despite repeated votes in Congress in favor of the *concept* of gasoline rationing, it required nearly seven years before Congress and the president could agree on exactly how gasoline would be allocated during an emergency. The story of rationing shows just how difficult it is for legislators to impose direct costs on their constituents. It also shows what must be done strategically if they are to do so.

Public opinion polls reported strong support for a standby system of gasoline rationing. Support for rationing was evident both in 1973, 1974, and 1979, when there were long lines at gasoline stations, and in the intervening years when there was merely talk about how vulnerable the United States had become to the whims of exporting nations. Citizens interviewed in 1978 and 1979, for example, strongly preferred gasoline rationing to waiting in line, to higher prices, and to higher gasoline taxes.[33] Exactly why citizens preferred rationing by such overwhelming margins is not certain, but most observers suggest that people viewed rationing as the most equitable solution, requiring everyone to tighten their belts by the same amount.[34]

As long as the public was strongly in favor of rationing, legislators had little to fear by authorizing it. Within two months of President Nixon's 1973 request, both House and Senate had approved provisions that

33. The first two comparisons favored rationing by a ratio of 2 to 1, the last by a ratio of 3 to 1. The first two findings are from a CBS News/New York Times Poll, June 1979; the third is from a Gallup Poll, April 1978. See *The Gallup Poll: Public Opinion, 1978* (Wilmington, Del.: Scholarly Resources, 1979), pp. 137–138. For other relevant results, see the *Harris Survey*, September 1973; and the CBS/New York Times Poll, July and August 1977.

34. Carolyn Shaw Bell, "Rationing: Some Ins and Outs," *New York Times* (August 2, 1979): A17; Nivola, *Politics of Energy Conservation*, pp. 220–221.

required the president to draft a standby rationing plan. Although the president eventually vetoed the omnibus energy bill to which these provisions were attached, his objections had nothing to do with rationing.[35] In 1975 Congress again approved a bill requiring standby rationing. This time President Ford signed it. The bill required the president to draft and submit to Congress a contingency plan for rationing gasoline in times of great shortage. Both houses had to approve the plan within sixty days for it to be available for actual use.[36]

Once the question turned to approving a specific rationing plan, legislators had second thoughts. Presidents Ford and Carter drafted several rationing plans, but Congress never approved them.[37] In May 1979 the Senate finally accepted Carter's third plan, but the House rejected it overwhelmingly (159 to 246). Part of the problem was that no one could agree on an equitable way to allocate gasoline. The Carter administration began with a proposal that would distribute rationing coupons equally among all car owners. The Senate, which overrepresents rural areas, insisted that any plan must take into account rural citizens' special needs. Then others wanted special provisions for farmers, suburban dwellers, oil drillers, and so on. If differing conceptions of equity were the only problem, Congress could probably have resolved the matter on its own. Compromise, logrolling, and splitting the difference usually allow legislators to resolve distributional conflicts in due time. The more serious problem was that legislators were reluctant to support any plan. The fear was that if the government ever had to implement a rationing plan—*any* rationing plan—many citizens would be seriously dissatisfied with their own allocations.[38] Those who were most dissatisfied would have a powerful incentive to punish at the polls those leg-

35. "Emergency Energy Act," *Congressional Quarterly Almanac, 1973* 29 (1974): 682–697; and "First Emergency Energy Bill Vetoed," *Congressional Quarterly Almanac, 1974* 30 (1975): 727–732.

36. "Ford Ends Stalemate," *Congressional Quarterly Almanac, 1975.*

37. "New Standby Gas Rationing Powers Voted," *Congressional Quarterly Almanac, 1979* 35 (1980): 649–655.

38. Dissatisfaction was inherent in any plan that failed to take into account *all* the factors that affect gasoline consumption. Consider, for example, a plan that required an average drop in consumption of 25 percent. A traveling salesman who usually consumed three times as much gasoline as an average motorist could hardly be happy with a plan that treated him just like everyone else. Coupons that allowed him 25 percent less than average would actually require him to reduce his consumption by 75 percent. Yet no plan could ever include all of the relevant factors from occupation and length of commute to the ratio of necessary driving to recreational driving.

islators who had been careless enough to support the plan in the first place. Once again, legislators anticipated the consequences of retrospective voting and rejected any plans for imposing direct costs on their constituents.

The strategic route around this predicament was to break the traceability chain so that if a rationing plan were ever implemented, citizens would not be able to trace any of the costs to legislators' roll-call votes. To accomplish this feat, congressional leaders drafted a new bill that again required the president to design a standby allocation plan and submit it to Congress. This time, however, the plan would be considered approved unless both houses adopted a joint resolution of disapproval within thirty days.[39] Since the president can veto a joint resolution, it would actually require a two-thirds majority of both houses to disapprove the president's plan. Congress intentionally designed a procedure that made it virtually impossible to reject a president's plan.[40] Representative Clarence Brown (R., Ohio) put it best: "Congress is telling the president, 'Here's the authority to ration—you go ahead and do it. But we are not going to be implicated by voting for or against a specific plan.'"[41]

Weakening the traceability chain was precisely what was needed to enact a standby gasoline rationing plan. The Senate approved the bill that delegated rationing authority to the president, 77 to 13. The House approved its version, 263 to 159. President Carter then submitted to Congress a variant of one of the rationing plans that legislators had rejected a year earlier. Neither the House Commerce Committee nor the Senate Energy Committee chose to report out a resolution disapproving the plan, so opponents had to offer discharge motions on the floor.[42] On the last day provided by law, the Senate rejected (31 to 60) a motion "to discharge the Energy Committee from further consideration of the resolution to disapprove the president's standby gasoline rationing plan." On the same day the House rejected (205 to 209) a similarly

39. "Gasoline Rationing," *Congressional Quarterly Almanac, 1979* 35 (1980): 655–661.

40. The House version of the bill failed to include any mechanism for blocking the president's plan. House members much preferred giving the president a blank check to ever having to deal with the issue again themselves. The Senate, where the six-year term helps to insulate members from immediate electoral retribution, preferred some mechanism for legislative review, even if it was too difficult to use in practice.

41. "Gasoline Rationing," *Congressional Quarterly Almanac, 1979*, p. 658.

42. "House Subcommittee Backs Standby Gas Rationing Plan," *Congressional Quarterly Weekly Report* 38 (July 5, 1980): 1890; and "Rationing Plan in Place," *Congressional Quarterly Weekly Report* 38 (August 2, 1980): 2165, 2239, 2242.

worded discharge motion. Thus, legislators allowed the standby plan to be approved by hiding behind two procedural motions. These procedural motions had the added advantage of being indecipherable to citizens who might want to blame their legislators if gasoline rationing were ever implemented.

On July 30, 1980—nearly seven years after President Nixon requested it—the United States had in place a standby plan for rationing gasoline in an emergency. No one knew whether the president would ever choose to implement it. If he did, legislators had nothing to fear. None of them had voted in favor of the plan, and none could ever be blamed for its disagreeable effects.

Whether the United States should have a standby plan for rationing gasoline is open to debate. Some prefer a market approach for allocating supplies under all imaginable circumstances, while others argue that rationing is a more equitable and less disruptive way to handle severe supply shortages. Both sides would agree that if rationing is ever justified, it is during a period when the government already controls prices. When the normal price system is disengaged, rationing is the only real alternative to Soviet-style queuing for the allocation of scarce supplies. Elected politicians seemed to agree. Shortly after establishing price controls they also authorized the president to design a rationing scheme. Unfortunately, it took longer to agree on a rationing plan than it did to decontrol oil. By the time a standby system was in place, the nation was within a few months of complete decontrol.

THE REGULATION OF NATURAL GAS

The first federal effort to regulate the natural gas industry was by common consent. Congress passed the Natural Gas Act of 1938 without any controversy and with the full support of producers, pipeline companies, state public service commissioners, and representatives of northern cities. Over the next forty years natural gas evolved into one of the most contentious issues in American politics.[43] Producer and consumer groups came to see their interests as diametrically opposed. The geographical concentration of producers in the southwest and con-

43. For an excellent account of the politics of natural gas, see M. Elizabeth Sanders, *The Regulation of Natural Gas: Policy and Politics, 1938–1978* (Philadelphia: Temple University Press, 1981).

sumers in the north transformed this group conflict into a regional conflict. The two political parties also took opposite positions on whether the natural gas industry should be regulated—Republicans aligning with producers and Democrats with consumers.

Congress switched sides several times over this forty-year period. From the late 1940s to the mid–1950s Congress sided with producers and approved two bills that would have deregulated portions of the industry (both died after presidential vetoes). In the 1960s and early 1970s it sided with consumers and supported efforts to maintain and expand federal regulation. Finally, after two full years of debate, Congress approved the Natural Gas Policy Act of 1978 and deregulated a large portion of the industry. Why did Congress have such trouble resolving these conflicting demands? Why did it switch sides several times? Once again my argument shows how the incidence of group and geographic costs and benefits affects congressional decision making. As the incidence of those costs and benefits changes, so, too, do congressional decisions. These examples also demonstrate how difficult it is for legislators to impose costs on their constituents and what strategies are required if they are to do so.

The Natural Gas Act of 1938 was very popular. It promised something for everyone and seemed to impose costs on no one.[44] The bill proposed to regulate as public utilities all pipelines involved in the interstate transportation of natural gas. The bill was designed to stimulate the construction of a national system for distributing natural gas and to keep pipeline companies from exploiting either producers or consumers. The bill did nothing to interfere either with the rights of producer states to regulate production or with the rights of consumer states to regulate distribution.

Public service commissioners and representatives from urban areas with gas service favored the bill because federal regulation would keep pipeline companies from charging monopoly prices in localities served by a single interstate pipeline (as most were). Representatives from urban areas without gas service favored the bill because it promised to stimulate the construction of new pipelines. Producers were in favor because new pipelines would expand their markets. Even the pipeline companies were in favor. Although they had to give up the right to charge monopolistic prices when they served an area exclusively, the bill promised to regulate (in other words, restrict) the construction of

44. Ibid., pp. 17–71.

competing pipelines. Thus, they traded the opportunity to make extraordinary profits when they were lucky enough to have no competitors (which was balanced by the possibility of losing a great deal of money if a competitor constructed a nearby pipeline) for the right to earn a regulated rate of return with absolutely no risk. No real opposition to the bill existed in any direction. The House Commerce Committee reported the bill unanimously, and the House and Senate approved it by voice votes.

Over the next two decades the natural gas industry expanded rapidly. By 1955 the industry served 26.1 million residential customers, up from 7.4 million in 1935 and 11.0 million in 1945.[45] During this time the Supreme Court began to reinterpret the Natural Gas Act of 1938 in a way that threatened producers' interests. In 1947 the Court suggested, though it did not rule explicitly, that the Federal Power Commission could regulate sales by independent producers to interstate pipeline companies. Although the Federal Power Commission declined to assert such authority, the State of Wisconsin challenged the FPC in court. In 1954 the Supreme Court ruled explicitly that the commission had the authority to regulate the sale of all gas to interstate pipelines. Under pressure from state public service commissions, the FPC began to do so immediately.

At the very first hint of trouble, producers began to lobby Congress for relief.[46] In 1947 the House passed by voice vote a bill that would have forestalled any efforts to regulate natural gas producers. (The Senate did not act.) In 1949 the House approved, 183 to 131, a bill that exempted independent producers (those not owned by pipeline companies) from FPC regulation. This time the Senate agreed to the bill, 44 to 38, but President Truman vetoed it. In 1955 the House again passed a deregulation bill, 209 to 203, and the Senate concurred, 53 to 38. Although President Eisenhower supported the bill, he eventually vetoed it after a scandal erupted. Senator Francis Case (R., S.D.) had announced just prior to the Senate's vote that a corporate lobbyist had offered him a $2,500 cash "contribution." President Eisenhower did not want to be associated with the then tainted bill. In 1958 prospects again looked good for passage of a deregulation bill. This time, however, the effort was derailed after the *Washington Post* published a letter from a Texas producer that suggested that a huge fund-raising dinner he was hosting in

45. U.S., Bureau of the Census, *Historical Statistics of the United States* (Washington, D.C.: Government Printing Office, 1975), series S188.

46. Sanders, *Regulation of Natural Gas*, pp. 72–124; Vietor, *Energy Policy in America*, pp. 64–90.

Houston to honor the House Minority Leader, Joseph Martin (R., Mass.), was actually an occasion to allow producers to "show their appreciation" for all Martin's efforts in their behalf. (Their appreciation totaled over $100,000.) Again, the issue of corruption was enough to sink the effort to eliminate federal controls. Over the next decade, legislators from producer areas introduced several bills to accomplish the same task. By then the tide had turned; none ever emerged from committee.

Why did Congress first support producers' interests overwhelmingly, then become more evenly divided, and finally become so sympathetic to consumers' short-term interests that no committee was able to report out a deregulation bill for the next two decades? Why did producers once wield such power in Congress, and then a few years later find their interests virtually ignored? When the House first passed bills in 1947 and 1949, gas production was still unregulated. Producers were fighting off future regulation, which they estimated (correctly) would cost them a great deal of money. But because the bills would merely perpetuate the status quo, they did not seem to impose any direct or traceable costs on consumers. Legislators could hardly be accused of voting against consumers' interests when consumers were already enjoying relatively cheap and plentiful gas and these bills would merely continue the present system. With producers organized and caring intensely about the issue, with consumers unorganized and relatively indifferent, and with an issue that had none of the elements required for retrospective voting, legislators easily sided with producers.

Over the next decade the situation changed dramatically. First, as new pipelines spread across the nation, more citizens in more congressional districts became natural gas consumers.[47] Just between 1947 and 1954 the number of residential customers more than doubled.[48] As a result more legislators had to consider how their votes on natural gas might look to consumers. Second, once the Federal Power Commission began to regulate (and restrict) the sale price of natural gas, voting to deregulate these prices would have imposed costs on consumers that were directly traceable to legislators' actions. After all, the purpose of regulation was to hold down the price of natural gas. Removing those regulations was almost certain to produce an immediate increase in prices.

47. Sanders, *Regulation of Natural Gas*, pp. 89, 97–106.
48. *Historical Statistics of the United States*, series S188.

By the 1960s, deregulation was an impossible dream.[49] New Democratic appointees to the Federal Power Commission, with the enthusiastic support of both the administration and the oversight committees in Congress, started to *reduce* prices paid to natural gas producers.[50] For the first time, regulated gas sold in interstate markets cost less than unregulated gas sold in intrastate markets. The growing difference between these prices was the best measure of how much consumers in regulated markets would have to pay if the government deregulated producer prices. By 1974, for example, average prices in the unregulated markets of Texas and Louisiana were twice the regulated interstate prices, and new contracts were selling for four times the regulated price.[51] As long as regulation kept the price of natural gas below the market price, legislators from consuming states had to be careful about supporting any plans to deregulate production. Deregulation would impose large and immediate costs on consumers—costs directly traceable to legislators' actions.

THE DEREGULATION OF NATURAL GAS

The FPC's pricing policy contained the seeds of its own destruction. The FPC could (and did) compel producers to sell at below-market prices gas that had already been committed to the interstate market. But it could not force producers to search for new gas, nor could it compel them to commit new reserves to the interstate market. Producers responded to these perverse incentives by reducing their exploration for new reserves and by committing most of what they discovered to the intrastate markets (which were beyond the FPC's jurisdiction). From 1966 to 1975 the proportion of reserves committed to intrastate markets increased from 32 percent of new discoveries to 87 percent.[52] The amount of newly discovered gas that producers allocated to the interstate market decreased by a factor of eight.[53] Throughout this period gas production continued to expand to meet consumers' practically insatiable demand for this clean, convenient, and relatively inex-

---

49. Vietor, *Energy Policy in America*, pp. 146–162.
50. Sanders, *Regulation of Natural Gas*, pp. 111–114.
51. Vietor, *Energy Policy in America*, pp. 287–288.
52. Ibid., p. 289.
53. Producers committed only 1.3 trillion cubic feet to interstate markets in 1975, down from 10 trillion cubic feet in 1966. Ibid., p. 289.

pensive fuel. Unfortunately, this expansion was achieved more by depleting existing reserves than by discovering new gas. Proven reserves declined from a sixteen-year supply in 1967 (the last year in which new discoveries exceeded annual consumption) to an eight-year supply a dozen years later.[54]

Declining reserves eventually created severe gas shortages in interstate markets. In the late 1960s most pipeline companies stopped serving new communities and most distribution companies refused to serve new neighborhoods. In 1970 pipeline companies began to curtail gas service for industrial customers whose contracts allowed temporary interruptions in exchange for lower rates. By 1973 they were forced to interrupt service for other firms that had no such clauses in their contracts. The Federal Power Commission eventually devised an elaborate system for allocating limited supplies among eight categories of users, ranging from industrial customers who faced immediate curtailments to residential customers who were the last to suffer. During the height of the crisis (the winter of 1977) gas curtailments forced 8,900 industrial plants in the East and Midwest to shut down, suspending employment for more than a half million workers. Many schools were also forced to close.[55] Meanwhile, gas consumption continued to expand in the major producer states, where gas was sold in unregulated markets. Although gas was increasingly expensive in these intrastate markets, it was readily available. Moreover, it was increasingly devoted to "inferior" uses, such as generating electricity and fueling industrial boilers. By 1975 nearly one-quarter of all gas produced in the United States was consumed by electrical utilities and industrial customers in three producer states: Texas, Oklahoma, and Louisiana.[56]

Natural gas shortages became apparent even before the Arab oil embargo raised everyone's energy consciousness. The Senate first held hearings on the subject in late 1969, and these hearings were repeated in both House and Senate over the next several years. In April 1973—six months before the embargo—President Nixon proposed deregulating all newly discovered gas. What the embargo did was to put even greater pressure on natural gas markets. With oil imports restricted and with oil prices escalating rapidly, natural gas became even more attractive to those industrial, commercial, and residential customers who

54. Ibid., p. 197; Sanders, *Regulation of Natural Gas*, p. 126.
55. Vietor, *Energy Policy in America*, pp. 275–277; Sanders, *Regulation of Natural Gas*, pp. 125–127; Nivola, *Politics of Energy Conservation*, p. 87.
56. Sanders, *Regulation of Natural Gas*, p. 127.

could switch fuels. Gas was especially attractive in interstate markets, where prices were fixed, and yet these were the markets least able to provide adequate supplies.

Virtually everyone agreed that the United States needed a new policy toward natural gas. The disagreement was over what that new policy should be. One side looked admiringly at the intrastate markets, where gas was readily available, and argued that the United States should deregulate all its natural gas. This side included most legislators from the major producer states, for these states would profit handsomely if one of their largest exports could be priced competitively. It also included legislators of conservative persuasion who believed that free markets were always superior to governmental regulation for allocating scarce resources. They argued that higher prices would encourage both exploration and conservation and thereby solve the problem of shortages. The other side believed that federal regulation should be expanded to include the intrastate markets, so that the plentiful supplies committed to those markets could be shared nationally and so that the lower prices in interstate markets could be maintained. This side included most legislators from areas that imported large volumes of gas from producer states. Many of these legislators argued that natural gas producers had contrived the entire gas shortage to force the government to deregulate gas prices.[57] If producers were forced to export gas to consumer states and if producer areas were prohibited from using their own gas for inferior uses, there would be plenty of gas for everyone and price controls could be maintained.

These arguments dominated the debate from 1970 until 1978, when Congress finally passed the immensely complicated Natural Gas Policy Act. Why did it take so long to resolve the conflict when everyone agreed that the current policy was unworkable? Part of the problem was that the stakes were so high. Immediate and total deregulation would have transferred immense sums from consumers to producers. Some consumers might see their home heating bills—already a major item in their household budgets—double or triple overnight. Most producers anticipated their profits increasing by even larger margins. These are not the sort of stakes that encourage one side or the other to retire

57. The House and Senate held hearings, and the Federal Trade Commission launched several investigations, on whether the gas industry was monopolistic and anticompetitive and whether it was manipulating data on reserves. Vietor, *Energy Policy in America*, pp. 202–224; Aaron Wildavsky and Ellen Tenenbaum, *The Politics of Mistrust* (Beverly Hills, Calif.: Sage Publications, 1981).

gracefully. Compromise between the two sides was also difficult to achieve because, although the two sides were closely matched in Congress, one side had the edge in the Senate while the other controlled the House. Each could imagine how the other house might switch sides, and thus each could envision total victory just around the corner. Visions of victory on both sides provide little encouragement for forging a compromise.

The forces in favor of deregulating natural gas were considerably stronger in the Senate. This conclusion follows from the basic distribution of group costs and benefits among the states. The Senate overrepresents producer areas because producer states (with the exception of Texas) tend to be sparsely populated.[58] The Senate underrepresents consumer areas because gas consumption is concentrated in the populous states of the Northeast and Midwest.[59] The Senate also overrepresents the so-called spectator states—those that neither consume nor produce much gas—for these are largely rural and sparsely populated states.[60] Senators from spectator states held the balance of power in the Senate throughout the fight for a new natural gas policy. Since they had no direct constituency interests at stake, they were free to vote as they pleased. Many of them ended up supporting deregulation—some because of their own conservative beliefs, others because their states contained other extractive industries and they sympathized with the plight of gas producers, and still others because deregulation seemed the more compelling solution to the problem at hand.

The Senate first considered natural gas deregulation in December 1973 when Senator James Buckley (Cons., N.Y.) offered an amendment on the floor to an unrelated energy bill. The amendment was a far-reaching proposal that would have deregulated the price of all new gas sold in interstate commerce and all old gas after existing contracts expired. The Senate eventually tabled the proposal, 45 to 43, after various committee leaders complained that the floor amendment was an attempt to "short circuit the orderly legislative process." This procedural issue aside, the vote suggested that the Senate was probably ready to

58. Legislators from the six largest producers after Texas (Louisiana, Oklahoma, New Mexico, Kansas, Wyoming, and Alaska) constitute 12 percent of the Senate but only 5 percent of the House.

59. Actually the producer states are also the largest consumers. Here I refer only to the consumption of federally regulated gas in interstate markets, not to the unregulated gas in intrastate markets.

60. On spectator states, see Sanders, *Regulation of Natural Gas*, pp. 12, 104–105, 138.

approve complete deregulation. This near victory for the proponents of deregulation came at a time when the difference between interstate and intrastate prices was still modest.[61] Two years later the Senate approved its first deregulation plan, 50 to 41, but by then the gap between interstate and intrastate prices was widening quickly, and the Senate adopted several amendments to soften the political impact of deregulation. One amendment required that natural gas distributors channel lower-priced old gas to residential customers (voters) and divert higher-priced new gas to industrial users. A second amendment postponed deregulation until just after the next heating season, lest large increases occur in an election year.[62]

Consumer areas were much better represented in the House. In fact, they dominated the proceedings. In 40 percent of all House districts more than half of the households used natural gas drawn from the interstate markets. In another 28 percent of the districts, between one-quarter and one-half of the households used interstate gas.[63] Thus, over two-thirds of all House members represented areas where imported natural gas was a major fuel. Producing areas—even by the most generous definition—constituted only one-tenth of the House. As long as representatives of consuming areas remained relatively united, no change in natural gas policy was possible.

Legislators from consuming areas had every right to fear the effects of voting to deregulate natural gas. They need only check the price of natural gas in intrastate markets to see what would happen to prices in interstate markets if controls were suddenly lifted. Rarely is there such a convenient measure of the likely costs of legislative action. Immediate and total deregulation would have been relatively painless in 1970, when interstate prices lagged about 15 percent behind intrastate prices. But as Congress dawdled and the disparity in prices grew, the economic and political pain of deregulation became evident. Immediate deregulation in 1974 could have doubled prices in interstate markets. By 1975 it could have tripled them.[64] For legislators the painful step was *voting* to

61. "Natural Gas Deregulation," *Congressional Quarterly Almanac, 1973* 29 (1974): 641–643, 700–701.

62. "Gas Deregulation Issue Considered," *Congressional Quarterly Almanac, 1975* 31 (1976): 252–259.

63. Sanders, *Regulation of Natural Gas,* p. 160.

64. These three estimates are based on the average wellhead prices for natural gas from the Permian Basin sold in interstate and intrastate markets in 1970, 1974, and 1975 (as reported in Vietor, *Energy Policy in America,* pp. 159, 288).

impose such costs on their constituents, for that simple act provided the final element required for retrospective voting. Whatever their differences, most legislators could agree that citizens were ready, willing, and able to punish those who doubled or tripled their home energy bills.

In February 1976 the House approved its version of deregulation, 205 to 201. It hardly deserved the name. The House version deregulated the price of only a tiny fraction of all gas—newly discovered gas that was sold by small, independent producers. It continued price controls for the thirty or so major gas companies that together produced more than 60 percent of the nation's natural gas.[65] Meanwhile, the bill actually enlarged federal controls over the gas industry by extending federal regulations to the intrastate markets for gas sold by the major producers. The aim was to force these producers to move gas from intrastate to interstate markets, all under a single controlled price. The Senate was so opposed to the House version that it refused to go to conference. Both bills died quietly when Congress adjourned eight months later.[66]

Congress finally enacted a natural gas bill in 1978, but only after one of the most tortuous legislative journeys in memory, highlighted by a House-Senate conference committee that deliberated for ten months. The odyssey began in April 1977, when President Carter proposed his National Energy Plan, a complex package of tax and regulatory measures designed to encourage energy conservation, penalize those who wasted fuel, and change the way oil, natural gas, coal, and electricity were priced.[67] The natural gas bill was the most controversial part of the entire package.

The president's proposal on natural gas was intended to be a compromise position, but it managed to offend both sides. The president proposed to keep federal controls on interstate gas and to extend those controls to include intrastate gas—and thus angered the proponents of complete deregulation. He also proposed pegging the price of new gas sold in either market to the price of domestic crude oil, guaranteeing that the price of gas would increase significantly—and thus enraged those who believed that controls should be used to restrain, not increase prices. Whatever its merits, the bill did occupy a middle position be-

65. Vietor, *Energy Policy in America*, p. 211.

66. "Gas Deregulation," *Congressional Quarterly Almanac, 1976* 32 (1977): 171–174.

67. For a simple summary of the complicated details of this odyssey, see "Carter Energy Bill Fails to Clear," *Congressional Quarterly Almanac, 1977* 33 (1978): 708–745; and "Energy Bill: The End of an Odyssey," *Congressional Quarterly Almanac, 1978* 34 (1979): 639–667.

tween the divergent approaches that the House and Senate had been taking. It thus provided a vehicle for compromise, even though the final bill differed significantly from the president's proposal.

How can one account for Congress passing any natural gas bill after so many years of stalemate? How can one account for the shape of the specific bill that legislators did approve? Part of the explanation is that many legislators from consuming areas had come to accept the notion that price increases were necessary to encourage production and elicit greater supplies. The persistent shortages in regulated markets and the growing surpluses in intrastate markets were facts that did, after a while, speak for themselves. What these legislators could not accept were large and immediate price increases directly traceable to their own actions. It was one thing to be persuaded intellectually of the need for higher prices. It was quite another to be seen as the *cause* of those higher prices.

As the bill wended its way through Congress, coalition leaders proposed a series of modifications that took much of the political sting out of the price increases. First, leaders revised the bill so that price controls on new natural gas would be removed gradually over a seven-year period. Consumers would never face any large and sudden price changes that might stimulate the search for political villains. The price increases would creep up on them slowly, partially disguised by the economy-wide inflation. Second, the revised bill established a system of incremental pricing under which gas distributors had to sell higher-priced gas to industrial facilities while reserving lower-priced gas for residential consumers. This provision also helped to protect individual consumers from large and sudden price increases. Of course, industrial firms were free to pass their increased costs on to those who bought their products, but this indirect approach had the political advantage of deflecting any blame for higher prices away from legislators and toward business. It effectively destroyed the traceability chain by making the connection between legislative action and price increases too difficult to follow.

Coalition leaders also modified the bill to make it more appealing to the proponents of deregulation. Specifically, they proposed to eliminate price controls on new gas, intrastate gas, and old gas from deep wells, all effective January 1, 1985. As of that date price controls would remain only for old gas already under production, and those prices would be adjusted annually for inflation. The proponents of deregulation had been agitating for relief since 1947. The revised bill promised them some relief immediately and gave them most of what they wanted within seven years. Eventually, as old gas fields became exhausted, they would achieve the total deregulation they sought.

Coalition leaders were able to satisfy both the proponents and the opponents of deregulation by recognizing that they had fundamentally different time perspectives. The opponents were primarily worried about what would happen to gas prices before the next couple of elections. What happened seven years later might be personally troubling, but it was not politically troubling. No one believed that voters would punish legislators in 1986 for actions they took in 1977 and 1978. The proponents had a longer view. They were primarily concerned with dismantling a system of price controls that had thwarted the gas industry for three decades. To be sure, they would have preferred immediate deregulation and including old gas too. Waiting seven more years to achieve deregulation, however, was a small price to pay for something they had been seeking for thirty years.

Persuading House members to support the compromise bill required some fancy footwork. Speaker O'Neill invented and adapted several procedural rules that helped the reform coalition to stick together and that provided further political insulation for legislators who represented high-consumption areas. From the very beginning he insisted that the House act on the National Energy Plan as a single package. For six weeks the package was split into pieces, while the five regular standing committees held hearings and marked up the individual provisions. These committees then reported their bills to a brand-new committee—the Ad Hoc Energy Committee—that the Speaker created to manage the entire package. To this committee he appointed several loyal lieutenants and a working majority of members who had previously opposed complete deregulation.[68]

The Speaker then persuaded the House Rules Committee to send the entire energy package to the floor under a modified closed rule.[69] The rule prohibited motions to strike any portion of the 580-page package and allowed only a few specific amendments. For the sixty-page natural gas bill, the rule permitted only two amendments: one to expand the definition of new gas, the other to deregulate all gas. These amendments aside, legislators were given no other opportunities to vote on

68. Vietor, *Energy Policy in America,* p. 308.

69. Bob Rankin, "Gas Deregulation Vote Set in Energy Debate," *Congressional Quarterly Weekly Report* 35 (July 30, 1977): 1563–1564.

what to do about natural gas. The rule was designed to protect House members who represented consuming areas from ever having to vote in favor of increasing natural gas prices.[70] They could show how much they abhorred complete deregulation by voting against the deregulation amendment. (They did, and it lost.) They could say anything they wanted about how much they detested the natural gas bill, but as long as a majority voted in favor of the omnibus package of five energy bills, the natural gas bill would become law.

Twice House members had to agree to tie their own hands, lest they be tempted to tinker with or reject the natural gas bill. The first time the energy package came before the House in August 1977, they did so with ease. House members adopted the modified closed rule, 238 to 148, and then approved the energy package as a whole, 244 to 177. Fourteen months later, after the Senate and the conference committee had made the natural gas bill far less reflective of House interests, the House barely approved the closed rule for the umbrella bill, 207 to 206.[71] This procedural vote was actually the most important vote on the entire energy package. Opponents of the natural gas compromise were convinced they could defeat the natural gas bill if only they could force a separate vote.[72] Lacking a separate vote, the House approved both the National Energy Act and all its component bills by a wide margin (231 to 168). After thirty years the House finally approved a new natural gas policy without legislators ever having to vote either on the details of the policy or on the policy as a whole. All legislators' records would show was that they had voted to approve President Carter's vast National Energy Plan.

70. I am grateful to William T. Murphy, then a lobbyist for a large gas company, for this insight, which he shared during a visit to Princeton University in November 1978. It was this observation that first launched my own thinking about how leaders can use procedural rules either to strengthen or to weaken the traceability chain.

71. Technically the motion was "to order the previous question (thus ending debate) on adoption of the resolution to waive all points of order" so that the House could then adopt the closed rule. The opponents first had to defeat this motion so that they could then propose a more open rule allowing a separate vote on the natural gas bill. The situation may seem complicated from afar, but everyone on the floor of the House knew that this obscure procedural vote was actually an attempt to split off the natural gas bill and defeat it. Everyone also knew that constituents would never connect this procedural vote with what happened subsequently to natural gas prices, whereas they could easily connect a vote on a separate gas bill with whatever disagreeable consequences followed. See David Rosenbaum, "Energy Bill," *Congressional Quarterly Weekly Report* 36 (October 14, 1978): 2920; and "H Res 1434," *Congressional Quarterly Weekly Report* 36 (October 21, 1978): 3092.

72. Ann Pelham, "Energy Bill," *Congressional Quarterly Weekly Report* 36 (October 21, 1978): 3039–3043.

It would be difficult to defend United States policy toward natural gas, especially the policy followed from the late 1960s to the early 1980s. The initial federal involvement was largely successful. The Natural Gas Act of 1938 stimulated the construction of a national system for distributing gas, transforming a small regional industry into the supplier of one-quarter of the nation's energy needs. The problems began in 1954, when the federal government started to regulate the price of gas. Although at first the inefficiencies were relatively minor, once the Federal Power Commission began to reduce regulated prices while market prices were rising, the problems quickly multiplied. The natural gas shortage of the 1970s, for example, was a direct consequence of federal decisions to hold natural gas prices below market prices. These decisions also promoted distortions in the use of fuels. While industry and electric utilities consumed vast amounts of natural gas (rather than domestically produced coal), the owners of new homes were unable to join the gas network and instead became dependent on imported oil. Those who enjoyed access to gas did not have to burn it efficiently because they were not paying its true (replacement) cost.[73]

Why would the government adopt such policies in the first place? Why did it retain those policies for so long, especially when the costs became apparent to everyone? Once again the argument that governmental regulation is designed to serve the interests of organized producers explains very little of this saga. Organized producers were opposed to price regulation when the Supreme Court first suggested it in 1947. For seven years they worked actively to block it, and for the next twenty-four they endeavored to rescind it. Even when success came in 1978, it was in the form of partial and gradual deregulation, under which some gas fields could remain regulated well into the next century.

To be sure, gas producers were influential in Washington, especially in the late 1940s and early 1950s. Under their watchful eyes Congress passed one bill to forestall regulation (1949) and another to rescind it (1955). If Presidents Truman and Eisenhower had not vetoed these bills, gas producers would have remained free from governmental regulation. Once regulation began, however, the balance of power shifted. For the next two decades Congress failed to approve any measures to deregulate the gas industry. Moreover, when Congress finally did pass a plan for gradual deregulation in 1978, it did so more because consumers

73. On any of these issues, see Paul MacAvoy and Robert Pindyck, *Price Controls and the Natural Gas Shortage* (Washington, D.C.: American Enterprise Institute, 1975).

were seriously dissatisfied with regulatory outcomes than because the gas industry finally won a great victory on its own.

The regulation of natural gas prices was a political accident. Neither Congress nor the president willed it. The Supreme Court created a loophole, state public service commissions helped to enlarge it, and then the courts forced the Federal Power Commission into the business of regulating producer prices. No one has ever argued that Congress would have ordered such regulation itself. In fact, the evidence is incontrovertible that Congress was opposed to regulating gas prices from at least 1947 until 1958. Once regulation began, however, it created a new class of beneficiaries with a strong interest in its continuance. These beneficiaries were not the gas producers, as "capture theory" would predict. They were the consumers of gas in interstate markets. In the beginning their numbers were small; but as the gas pipelines expanded, they soon constituted a majority of voters in a majority of congressional districts.

These consumers were not organized in any way. They had no lobbyists; they offered no campaign contributions; they did not flood the capital with postcards and telegrams whenever Congress considered natural gas regulation.[74] Most of them were not even aware that the federal government regulated the price of natural gas. They were the classic inattentive public. They were also a sleeping giant. Legislators were free to vote as they pleased on lots of issues before Congress, but natural gas was not one of them. Abolishing the regulatory system was sure to increase prices, and increased prices might awaken the sleeping giant. Voting in favor of deregulation was like leaving a trail for the giant to follow in case he awoke with vengeance on his mind.

Congress could have deregulated natural gas at any time if legislators had strongly favored that course. All they had to do was cover their tracks with a closed rule, a voice vote, an omnibus bill, or some other device that would break the traceability chain and forestall citizens from punishing legislators at the polls. They did not choose this course because many legislators strongly supported federal regulation on the merits (rather than on the politics) of the issue. They believed it was good public policy.[75] As coalition leaders, they stood ready to demand roll-call

74. In the 1970s Ralph Nader and other consumer lobbyists became active in opposing the deregulation of natural gas. Their involvement did not change the political equation very much, for by then Congress had been protecting consumers' unarticulated interests in regulated gas prices for two decades.

75. See, for example, the arguments of Senator Paul Douglas (D., Ill.), *In the Fullness of Time* (New York: Harcourt Brace Jovanovich, 1971), pp. 462–467.

votes, to propose embarrassing amendments, to oppose closed rules, and to split up omnibus bills. By doing so they would force other legislators from consuming areas to calculate electoral consequences, and they could thereby defeat any attempts to dismantle the regulatory apparatus.

Two changes allowed Congress to pass a gradual deregulation plan in 1978. First, the natural gas system was no longer able to satisfy consumers' twin desires for plentiful supplies and low prices. Citizens were suddenly pressuring legislators to do something about the supply shortages, and some of them were clearly willing to accept higher prices for assured supplies.[76] Second, many legislators had come to believe that higher prices were now a necessary condition for eliciting greater supplies. Coalition leaders who once stood ready to use their procedural talents to block reforms were now manipulating procedural rules to promote them. Speaker O'Neill is a superb example. For many years he firmly believed in New Deal–type regulation and worked actively to block any attempts to deregulate natural gas. By 1977 he was the master legislative strategist who devised the rules that made deregulation possible. Over time legislators changed their minds. These procedural rules then made it possible for them to change natural gas policy without giving future challengers good campaign issues to use against them.

THE POLITICS OF ENERGY

The recent histories of federal policy toward oil and natural gas are remarkably similar. For each the initial regulation of prices was a political accident, not a congressional choice. The Supreme Court, over the repeated opposition of Congress, decreed that gas prices should be regulated. The regulation of oil prices was but a small part of an economy-wide fixing of wages and prices. Once established, however, both regulatory schemes were difficult to dismantle. A majority of legislators refused to vote to deregulate either oil or gas, for they were unwilling to impose large, visible, and traceable costs on their constituents. Eventually, after nearly a decade of struggle, Congress did allow deregulation to occur. In the case of oil, legislators simply let the president

76. Shifts in mass opinion are always difficult to discern on complex issues, but there were dramatic shifts in elite opinion. By 1978 the *New York Times*, the *Washington Post*, the National Governors Conference, and the NAACP—all previously committed to regulation—were counted in favor of some form of deregulation. See Nivola, *Politics of Energy Conservation*, p. 98.

take the heat. In the case of gas, they used procedural devices to approve deregulation without appearing to have done so.

The politics of energy is a good deal more than the politics of oil and natural gas. Over the years Congress has passed legislation relating to each of the major energy sources, including coal, nuclear energy, electricity, hydropower, solar energy, and synthetic fuels. Moreover, pricing is merely one of the issues that legislators regularly address. Others include research, conservation, subsidies, taxation, and environmental trade-offs. Even so, the regulation of oil and natural gas has occupied center stage for the past several decades. Part of the reason is that these two fuels account for three-quarters of all energy consumed in the United States.

The politics surrounding the remaining fuels and energy issues has not been nearly so contentious as that surrounding oil and natural gas. Perhaps the best measure of this difference is how Congress handled the various parts of President Carter's National Energy Plan in 1977 and 1978. The president's plan contained proposals relating to the regulation, pricing, and taxation of virtually all fuels. Congress devoted most of its time to resolving matters related to oil and natural gas. The conference committee, for example, met for nearly a year before forging a compromise on natural gas and rejecting the crude oil equalization tax. By comparison, it reached agreement on all other issues—coal, utility rates, conservation, subsidies, and tax credits—in the first few weeks of conference meetings.[77]

Most other energy issues have been easier to resolve because Congress has found ways to deliver group and geographic benefits while imposing only the most general costs. The new approaches are particularly attractive for the task of encouraging energy conservation. Legislators readily approved President Carter's proposal to offer tax credits for citizens who installed insulation, storm windows, or solar equipment in their homes. Tax credits for businesses were equally popular. For those who paid little in taxes, Congress created several subsidy programs to spur energy conservation: low-income grants for the poor, subsidized loans for those below the median income, and a new grant program for schools and hospitals. Over the years Congress also approved programs to subsidize research and development for every imaginable source of energy, from coal and nuclear to geothermal, wind, and biomass. Gasohol has been a particular favorite in Congress because it also offers an

77. "Conference Action," *Congressional Quarterly Almanac, 1977* 33 (1978): 712.

alternative outlet for farm surpluses. Legislators have approved tax exemptions, loans, direct subsidies, and price guarantees to spur the development of this politically attractive fuel.[78]

Legislators appreciate research and conservation programs because they impose only general costs on society while delivering plentiful group and geographic benefits. Their enthusiasm for conservation does not extend to proposals that would impose more direct and immediate costs on their constituents. In 1977 President Carter proposed that industries and utilities should pay a stiff tax on any oil or gas they used as a boiler fuel (a proposal that was designed to encourage them to switch to coal). Among other things it would have increased electric rates. Congress rejected the notion of imposing any penalties in the near term. Instead, legislators decided that existing plants should stop using oil or gas as a boiler fuel by 1990 thirteen years later—and then inserted a long list of exemptions that guaranteed that many plants would never be required to switch fuels. Conservation is a fine thing, but, as usual, legislators preferred the carrot to the stick.

78. In 1979 ninety House members even organized a "Congressional Alcohol Fuels Caucus," which met biweekly to plot strategy on gasohol. See Bob Livernash, "Gasohol Bandwagon Rolling in Congress," *Congressional Quarterly Weekly Report* 37 (October 20, 1979): 2321–2326.

Part Three

Assessing Congressional Action

10

Citizens' Control
of Government

To what extent are citizens able to control their government in a representative system? This is—or should be—one of the central questions in political science, one that should occupy the combined talents of democratic theorists and institutional specialists. All too often scholars avoid addressing the issue directly, hoping that their results speak for themselves (they rarely do). The question is especially difficult to answer for the American system. In the United States, the sharing of power among legislators and an elected executive, coupled with the lack of strong parties to unite the two branches, makes the links among citizens, elected officials, and policy outcomes more complicated than in, say, a parliamentary system.

THE ROLE OF PARTIES

It is easy to see how citizens could achieve control in a representative system where most citizens choose among legislative candidates according to the party performance rule. This rule posits that a citizen first evaluates current conditions in society, decides how well he or she likes those conditions, and then either rewards or punishes the governing party by supporting or opposing its legislative candidates. If all voters employed the party performance rule, legislators from the governing party would have a powerful incentive to anticipate citizens' needs, to devise and enact effective programs for fulfilling those needs, and to produce pleasing outcomes by election day. Of the four decision rules discussed in Chapter 3, the party performance rule requires the least information and analysis on the part of citizens and demands the most in performance on the part of legislators.

Even though the evidence is strong that at least some citizens use something like the party performance rule in congressional elections, this rule does not provide a firm basis for citizens' control unless it is the predominant decision rule in congressional elections. Legislators work together to produce pleasing effects only if they believe citizens will reward them for their team successes and punish them for their team failings. If citizens use the party performance rule in conjunction with the various candidate-centered rules, or if many citizens reject the rule completely, then legislators have every incentive to emphasize their personal attributes and positions and no incentive to behave as loyal team members. Whenever legislators see a conflict between making themselves look good and making their party look good they naturally choose the former, for as individuals calculating at the margin, they can always do more to affect their own images than they can to affect their party's performance in office.

For similar reasons the party position rule offers an inadequate foundation for citizens' control of government. Although it appears that some citizens choose their legislators according to where the parties stand on the issues, this method of choosing provides only a weak link between citizens' preferences and legislators' actions. If many citizens shift their allegiance from one party to the other, whether in response to the issues of the day or as part of a longer-term realignment, then the new cohort of legislators may have different policy preferences from those of the legislators they replace. The defect in the party position rule as a mechanism for citizens' control is that nothing impels new legislators to enact their parties' promises. Citizens' evaluations are prospective judgments about what the parties promise rather than retrospective appraisals of their performance. Once in office, legislators can distance themselves from their parties' positions and concentrate on their own individual positions and accomplishments.

Under current conditions in American politics, then, it is difficult to see how either the party performance rule or the party position rule provides an adequate mechanism for citizens' control of government. In order to work properly, these mechanisms require the subordination of candidates to parties; yet citizens have proven themselves increasingly independent of party. Meanwhile legislators do everything in their power to insure that citizens focus on the legislators rather than on their party teams.

INDIVIDUAL LEGISLATORS

If party no longer provides a mechanism for citizens' control of American government (and perhaps it never did), does this leave citizens powerless to affect governmental decisions? It does not. Both the incumbent performance rule and the candidate position rule permit a certain degree of control. In a system with weak parties, however, citizens' control is necessarily a multistep process in which influence may be exerted over legislators' individual decisions, over the setting of the agenda, and over policy outcomes. These three matters of individual responsiveness, agenda control, and policy responsiveness require separate investigation.

Individual responsiveness refers to the degree to which legislators' individual actions reflect their constituents' policy preferences. Here the incentives are strong for individual legislators to keep their public positions and actions within the bounds of what their constituents find acceptable. There need not be a one-to-one correspondence between a legislator's positions and those of his or her constituents on every issue that comes before Congress, or even a strong correlation between constituency opinion and roll-call voting. What *is* required is that legislators work hard to identify issues that could be used against them and to discover the safest position on each issue. At times these calculations impel legislators to follow the intense preferences of a small minority, at times they encourage legislators to anticipate the potential preferences of a larger group, at times they make legislators attentive to the special needs of their core supporters, and at times they encourage legislators to reach out to their regular opponents.

The central question is not really whether legislators are responsive to citizens, but rather *which* citizens legislators respond to and under what conditions responsiveness varies. As we have seen in previous chapters, legislators are responsive to narrow and organized interests when they are asked to decide about issues for which the group costs and benefits are both visible and directly traceable to their actions while the general costs and benefits are less visible. The power of the National Rifle Association, the dairy lobby, and the banking industry over legislation affecting gun control, dairy price supports, and financial regulation illustrates the point. Yet legislators can also feel bound by the potential preferences of broader and inattentive publics. They are especially responsive to inattentive publics when they are asked to decide about an issue for which the group costs could become visible and traceable if

Congress enacted the wrong policy. The degree to which legislators followed the potential preferences of sugar consumers in 1974 or natural gas consumers throughout the 1970s supports this point.

Although it is easy to demonstrate that under the proper conditions legislators respond to citizens' preferences and potential preferences, responsiveness by itself does not guarantee citizens' control over policy outcomes. If the agenda is controlled by other forces, then citizens' influence over the final stage in decision making may offer them little real influence over the important decisions in society. This was the essential insight of Peter Bachrach and Morton Baratz, who argued that the power to keep something off the governmental agenda is at least as important as the power to choose among the few policy options that do make the agenda.[1] Their insight is usually used to support the assertion that corporations or other powerful elites control governmental decision making by keeping all the interesting and important issues off the agenda. In this view, elites are powerful not because they affect the final choices in government but because they guarantee that these choices are between Tweedledum and Tweedledee.

Even if one accepts the basic argument that the ability to keep items off the governmental agenda is an important source of power, it should be noted that the argument also applies to ordinary citizens. Congress frequently avoids acting on problems or considering specific policy options because legislators fear retribution by ordinary citizens. A few examples make the point. Throughout the 1970s Congress refused to consider imposing a massive gasoline tax, despite the evidence that, if coupled with an income tax rebate to avoid either redistribution among income groups or growth in tax revenues, it would be the least intrusive method for curbing demand for imported oil. Throughout the 1980s Congress refused to consider any reductions in Social Security payments for current beneficiaries, despite the massive budget deficit and despite the fact that Social Security expenditures accounted for nearly a quarter of federal expenditures. When Congress considered tax reform in 1986, no one proposed eliminating the deduction for mortgage interest, despite the fact that eliminating this very expensive tax preference would have allowed Congress to reduce tax rates by a few extra points. None of these proposals made it on the congressional agenda because

1. See Peter Bachrach and Morton S. Baratz, "Two Faces of Power," *American Political Science Review* 56 (1962): 947–952; and Bachrach and Baratz, "Decisions and Nondecisions: An Analytical Framework," *American Political Science Review* 57 (1963): 641–651.

legislators believed that ordinary citizens would not tolerate the imposition of such large, visible, and traceable costs.

The power of the electoral connection may actually be greater at earlier stages of decision making, when legislators are deciding which problems to pursue or which alternatives to consider, rather than at the final stages, when legislators are voting on particular amendments or on a bill's final passage. After sifting through all the roll-call votes taken in Congress over several years, I am struck by how inconsequential many of these decisions really are. Legislators often vote on the trivia in political life—whether to increase or decrease slightly the funding for some program or whether to move the cost of the savings and loan bailout "off budget" rather than counting it as part of the federal deficit. Yet scores of political scientists occupy themselves analyzing these roll-call votes and attempting to determine (among other things) how much constituency opinion affects legislators' decisions. Not surprisingly, they often find that the correlations are weak or nonexistent. Their findings do not, however, prove that legislators are unresponsive to constituency opinion.

Consider the case of the nuclear freeze resolution, which the House debated in 1982 and 1983. Marvin Overby demonstrates that constituency opinion, as measured by the results of ten statewide referenda, had only a modest impact on the first roll-call vote in 1982 and no impact at all on two votes taken in 1983.[2] Initially this seems very puzzling, because the nuclear freeze movement was one of the great grass-roots movements of recent decades. How is it possible that a movement that forced ten states to hold referenda, and achieved strong majorities in nine of them, could not then influence legislators' decisions? The answer is that the movement won most of its points at earlier stages in the legislative process. Its first victory was in forcing the nuclear freeze on the agenda over the determined opposition of the Reagan administration. Its second victory was in forcing opponents of the measure to thwart the proponents by drafting a substitute resolution that was actually a variant of the original freeze proposal. By the time House members were asked to vote on the nuclear freeze, they were essentially choosing between the very strong original proposal and a somewhat weaker proposal backed by the Reagan administration.[3] Legislators could vote as they pleased because most citizens could not tell the difference between

2. L. Marvin Overby, "Assessing Constituency Influence: A Loglinear Model of Congressional Voting on the Nuclear Freeze, 1982–1983" (paper presented at the annual meeting of the Southwestern Political Science Association, March, 1989).

3. Ibid.

the two resolutions. Moreover, the movement actually won the major battle, even though in the end it failed to enact its most-preferred version.

The story of tax reform also supports the argument that constituency opinion can have powerful effects on congressional policy making without ever revealing itself in voting decisions. Those who search for constituency influence by studying roll-call votes would be hard pressed to find it by analyzing all the recorded votes on tax reform. In the House there were only two votes on procedural matters, no recorded votes on amendments, no recorded votes on final passage, and only a single roll call on the conference report. Although the Senate conducted roll-call votes on twenty-four amendments, most of these amendments were on relatively minor matters. Despite the lack of significant divisions that might be related to constituency pressures, and despite the overwhelming majorities that eventually approved the bill, the complete story of tax reform demonstrates that legislators were constantly calculating electoral effects and that most of their initial calculations suggested that the whole enterprise was politically dangerous. One cannot begin to understand how coalition leaders managed to produce a winning coalition in this environment, nor why they incorporated into the bill the specific provisions that they did, without first understanding how legislators balanced various constituency pressures. Unfortunately for those who assess constituency influence by analyzing roll-call votes, virtually all of the relevant decisions were made early in the legislative process, behind closed doors, and without recorded votes (see Chapter 8).

Although both attentive and inattentive publics can affect the governmental agenda, attentive publics have the clear advantage. Inattentive publics manage to keep some items off the agenda because legislators believe that adopting particular proposals would impose costs on these groups and thereby rouse them to political action. These inattentive publics are unable to force legislators to place items on the governmental agenda, however, because legislators know that inactivity leaves no evidence that can be used to rouse inattentive publics against them. Attentive publics have advantages on both fronts because they do not have to rely on the rule of anticipated reactions. They can monitor exactly who is doing what on Capitol Hill and attempt to nudge policy makers toward including (or excluding) specific items on the agenda. They can also monitor inactivity on Capitol Hill and pressure the appropriate legislators to initiate action. The constant surveillance by attentive publics is a more precise form of control than the possibility of detection by inattentive publics, and it is symmetric with respect to promoting or preventing action.

Does influence over the agenda and influence over legislators' individual decisions translate into influence over policy outcomes? Are these mechanisms sufficient for citizens to obtain the policy outcomes they really want? Under the proper conditions these mechanisms do help to provide such control, but their success depends in part on the length and complexity of the causal chain connecting a policy instrument with its policy effects. When a causal chain is short and simple, citizens are more likely to know which policy instrument will produce the appropriate effects and are better able to monitor the performance of their representatives. When a causal chain is long and complex, or when a problem in society stems from multiple causes, citizens may be incapable of doing the appropriate policy analysis and political analysis.

Consider the ease with which citizens can hold their representatives accountable on an issue like flag burning. Once the Supreme Court ruled that flag burning was constitutionally protected, it became only a matter of time before Congress would pass a bill attempting to prohibit flag desecration, for both the bill and the procedures required to enact it were simple and easy for citizens to understand. With public opinion strongly in favor, with veterans' groups and the president pushing for action, and with the news media covering the story closely, legislators had little choice but to grant citizens' demands.[4]

Contrast this with the difficulty of holding representatives accountable on complex issues, such as energy or the economy. Most problems in these areas stem from multiple causes, and most of the standard solutions involve long and complicated causal chains. It is difficult for citizens to know what the best solution would be to a problem like inflation, and it is equally difficult for them to monitor legislators' actions

4. The House approved the bill on flag desecration 380 to 38, and the Senate followed, 91 to 9. Once Congress passed this bill, it became much easier to block a constitutional amendment on the same subject—especially in the Senate, where the electoral clock ticks more slowly—because most senators had used the previous vote to establish their position against flag burning. The Senate rejected the proposed constitutional amendment 51 to 48 (15 votes short of the two-thirds required). For the complete story, see Martha Angle, "Flag-Desecration Legislation Passed by House," *Congressional Quarterly Weekly Report* 47 (September 16, 1989): 2400; Joan Biskupic, "Senate Amends, Then Passes Bill on Flag Desecration," *Congressional Quarterly Weekly Report* 47 (October 7, 1989): 2646; and Joan Biskupic, "Anti–Flag Burning Amendment Falls Far Short in Senate," *Congressional Quarterly Weekly Report* 47 (October 21, 1989): 2803–2804.

on these matters. To the extent that citizens are poor policy analysts, they may obtain the policy instruments they favor but fail to get the policy outcomes they really want because their chosen instruments are incapable of producing the desired effect. Some would argue that this was the case for natural gas in the 1970s. Consumers obtained the regulations they seemed to prefer, but these regulations inhibited rather than promoted the supply of affordable natural gas.

The degree of citizens' control also depends on what procedures Congress employs. As previous chapters have shown repeatedly, legislators' responsiveness to both attentive and inattentive publics varies depending on the procedures that govern how legislators record their positions. When legislators are asked to vote on narrow matters for which the group effects are large and the general effects negligible, they quite naturally pay greater attention to the group effects. When many narrow issues are combined into an omnibus bill that helps to camouflage the group effects and accentuate the general effects, legislators pay greater attention to the general effects. Despite the importance of procedures, citizens seldom have much influence over procedural strategies. Coalition leaders usually select the terms for debate and action. Even when legislators must ratify the chosen procedures with a recorded vote, legislators are generally free of scrutiny. Few citizens have acquired a proper appreciation for the importance of closed or restrictive rules.[5]

The model of citizens' control that I have been discussing is essentially an auditing model. Citizens do not instruct legislators on how to vote, nor do they necessarily have well-defined policy preferences in advance of congressional action. Legislators nevertheless have strong incentives to consider citizens' potential preferences when they are deciding how to vote for fear that making the wrong choice might trigger an unfavorable audit. The fear is not simply that citizens will notice on their own when a legislator errs, but that challengers will investigate

5. Presidents and journalists could easily raise citizens' consciousness on the importance of some procedural votes. President Reagan did so in 1981 and thereby pressured House members to support the closed rule on his budget proposal (see Chapter 7). The *Wall Street Journal* did so in 1989 by including in an editorial the names of more than a hundred Democrats in the House who claimed to support the repeal of a tax provision that was particularly burdensome for small businesses but who had actually opposed the procedural device that was required to include the repeal amendment in the pending bill. Several weeks after the editorial appeared, House members passed the repeal amendment, 390 to 36. See Paul Starobin, "Section 89 Repeal Drive: Taking No Prisoners," *Congressional Quarterly Weekly Report* 47 (September 30, 1989): 2543–2547.

fully a legislator's voting record and then share with citizens their interpretations of how he or she has gone wrong.[6]

Those who doubt the power of infrequent audits to affect politicians' behavior should first consider their own behavior when filling out their federal tax returns. Most taxpayers know that the probability of being audited is quite small; yet they nevertheless report most of their income and keep their deductions within the bounds of what they believe future IRS auditors will allow. The probability of audit may be small, but the potential sanctions for failing to anticipate what auditors will allow is very large—ranging from penalties and interest to fines and imprisonment. Although legislators do not face fines and imprisonment (at least for their roll-call decisions), they do face the severe sanction of electoral defeat if they repeatedly fail to anticipate what actions their constituents will allow. Moreover, citizens, like IRS agents, have help in monitoring compliance. Tax auditors receive reports from employers, banks, and brokers about taxpayers' financial transactions, from which they can make inferences about how faithful taxpayers are in reporting their income and deductions. Citizens receive reports from challengers, interest groups, and the media about legislators' positions and actions, and they too can make inferences about how faithful legislators are in representing their policy preferences.

The incumbent performance rule clearly requires more information and analysis than the party performance rule in order for citizens to control their government. Under the party performance rule, citizens can achieve control simply by knowing which party is in power and deciding whether or not they like current conditions in society. In contrast, the incumbent performance rule requires that citizens be both policy analysts and political analysts. They need to know something about the causes of society's problems and something about how various proposals would affect their interests. They also need to know some-

6. For a contrary view of citizens' control of government—one that asserts that it is practically nonexistent—see Robert A. Bernstein, *Elections, Representation, and Congressional Voting Behavior: The Myth of Constituency Control* (Englewood Cliffs, N.J.: Prentice Hall, 1989). My own views diverge from Bernstein's in several important respects. First, I do not require that citizens have policy preferences in advance of congressional action but rather argue that legislators anticipate how citizens might react if legislators failed to anticipate citizens' potential preferences. Second, I do not accept as evidence that legislators have failed to heed constituents' preferences on an issue the fact that there is no relationship between constituency opinion and reelection results, for such findings are equally consistent with the notion that legislators anticipate the likelihood of electoral retribution and adjust their decisions accordingly.

thing about what their legislators are doing to advance or retard those interests.

REFORMS

The complexity of the incumbent performance rule and the inequitable distribution of information required for its proper use make this a far less effective mechanism for controlling government than the party performance rule. This fact usually impels political scientists to close with a call for strengthening the parties. If only we had strong parties (they argue), then government would be more responsive, responsible, and accountable. Unfortunately, the tide has been moving in the opposite direction for several decades. Political parties today are weak, and no one has set forth a politically feasible plan for reversing the tide.

If parties are weak and the prospects for strengthening them are slim, then the alternative route for those who seek to increase citizens' control of government is to reform congressional procedures so that the incumbent performance rule functions more effectively and so that legislators are responsive to general interests as well as group interests. Although this was the intent of those who reformed procedures in the 1970s, many of the reforms have had the opposite effect. Reformers demanded that all committee meetings must be open, but all this openness has actually allowed narrowly based interest groups to monitor legislators more closely and has thereby made legislators more responsive to group interests. Reformers demanded an end to the closed rule because it was antidemocratic, but most of the amendments proposed without benefit of the rule have been particularistic proposals that serve group interests. Reformers demanded an end to secret, unrecorded votes, but the increased reliance on recorded votes has actually made it easier for narrow groups to hold legislators accountable because most of these votes are on particularistic amendments.

Several reforms have been more effective in promoting citizens' control and reducing the dominance of particularistic interests. The creation of budget committees and a congressional budget process has forced legislators to consider and act on the larger questions of economic policy rather than just on the narrower questions of how much to spend on specific programs. Changes in the selection process for the House Rules Committee have made this committee an ally of the party leadership and have thereby forced it to write rules that accommodate more general interests. Ad hoc committees have allowed Congress to handle questions that span many committees (such as energy), and special governmental commissions have helped legislators to act on issues that are too hot for existing committees to handle (such as Social Security). All of these changes and innovations allow both legislators and citizens to focus on the larger policy issues.

Most important, perhaps, is that legislators have been willing to ignore some of the reforms that have not worked. Committees now regularly close their doors when they are writing difficult bills, such as tax increases, that impose substantial costs on citizens. Even when they do meet in public, they sometimes work out the difficult issues in a huddle at the front of the room and then announce their decisions to the assembled reporters and lobbyists at the rear. The House Rules Committee has also refined the art of writing restrictive rules so that complicated bills do not unravel in a flurry of particularistic amendments, while still preserving both legislators' ability to make choices about the larger issues and citizens' ability to monitor legislators' choices.

Legislators have discovered the strengths and weaknesses of specific procedures by trial and error. Open meetings, open rules, and unlimited recorded votes seemed like good ideas when they were proposed, and they were backed by Common Cause and others who sought to reduce the power of special interests. Unfortunately, these reforms were based on a faulty understanding of the mechanisms that allow for citizens' control. We now know that open meetings filled with lobbyists, and recorded votes on scores of particularistic amendments, serve to increase the powers of special interests, not to diminish them.

A proper understanding of the incumbent performance rule suggests how procedures can be designed to reduce the power of special interests. The key is to ask legislators to stand up and be counted on the broader policy issues, issues for which the general effects overshadow the group and geographic effects, and to curtail the ability of legislators to propose endless particularistic amendments. Restrictive procedures of this kind need not be antidemocratic. Senator Packwood's proposal that all amendments to the tax reform bill must be revenue neutral had to be approved by his colleagues before it became effective. Once approved, it prevented senators from proposing a series of attractive amendments that would have gradually undermined the entire bill. Similarly, legislators must approve closed and restrictive rules before they are bound by their provisions. Presumably they approve such restrictions on their own autonomy only if they believe that the resulting bills are politically acceptable.

I am convinced that it is possible to increase the potential for citizens' control of government without first transforming weak parties into strong parties. In order to do so, however, one needs to understand the links among citizens, legislators, and policy outcomes. The more one understands how those links operate, the more likely it is that reform efforts will actually contribute to democratic control of government.

Index

277